THE LINE BETWEEN
FAITH &
STUPIDITY

THE LINE BETWEEN
FAITH &
STUPIDITY

**One couple's journey to 24 countries…
with no money.**

CHRIS GUNN
with JESSICA GUNN

To my beautiful wife, Jessica;
Without your intercession, words would have never touched
paper. I love you dearly.

Also to the ecclesia;
As we continue to help each other and move in faith, stories like
ours can become the new norm.

Most importantly to Jesus;
Without you, I can't do anything.

"I am the true vine, and my Father is the gardener. He cuts off every branch in me that bears no fruit, while every branch that does bear fruit he prunes so that it will be even more fruitful. You are already clean because of the word I have spoken to you. Remain in me, as I also remain in you. No branch can bear fruit by itself; it must remain in the vine. Neither can you bear fruit unless you remain in me.

I am the vine; you are the branches. If you remain in me and I in you, you will bear much fruit; apart from me you can do nothing. If you do not remain in me, you are like a branch that is thrown away and withers; such branches are picked up, thrown into the fire and burned. If you remain in me and my words remain in you, ask whatever you wish, and it will be done for you. This is to my Father's glory, that you bear much fruit, showing yourselves to be my disciples.

As the Father has loved me, so have I loved you. Now remain in my love. If you keep my commands, you will remain in my love, just as I have kept my Father's commands and remain in his love. I have told you this so that my joy may be in you and that your joy may be complete. My command is this: Love each other as I have loved you. Greater love has no one than this: to lay down one's life for one's friends. You are my friends if you do what I command. I no longer call you servants, because a servant does not know his master's business. Instead, I have called you friends, for everything that I learned from my Father I have made known to you. You did not choose me, but I chose you and appointed you so that *you might go and bear fruit—fruit that will last—and so that whatever you ask in my name the Father will give you. This is my command: Love each other.*

If the world hates you, keep in mind that it hated me first. If you belonged to the world, it would love you as its own. As it is, you do not belong to the world, but I have chosen you out of the world. That is why the world hates you. Remember what I told you: 'A servant is not greater than his master.' If they persecuted me, they will persecute you also. If they obeyed my teaching, they will obey yours also. They will treat you this way because of my name, for they do not know the one who sent me. If I had not come and spoken to them, they would not be guilty of sin; but now they have no excuse for their sin. Whoever hates me hates my Father as well. If I had not done among them the works no one else did, they would not be guilty of sin. As it is, they have seen, and yet they have hated both me and my Father. But this is to fulfill what is written in their Law: "They hated me without reason."

When the Advocate comes, whom I will send to you from the Father—the Spirit of truth who goes out from the Father—he will testify about me. And you also must testify, for you have been with me from the beginning.'"

John 15

Table of Contents

FOREWORD

Perhaps the title *"The Line Between Faith and Stupidity"* captured your attention or at least your curiosity. It certainly did mine.

There is likely no other topic more preached, taught and written about than that of 'faith.' As believers, we know its importance in our life, its prominence in the scriptures and, most importantly, its ability to please our Father. But what does faith really look like when you are depending upon God's intervention every moment of every day? Chris and Jessica Gunn's year-long worldwide journey gives us a rare and enlightening glimpse into this lifestyle.

I've known Chris and Jessica for a number of years and so appreciate their candor, boldness and willingness to take calculated risks. Having read this book, I now see with greater clarity how these attributes nurture strong faith. As they travel from sunny, safe Florida to Thailand, Myanmar, Vietnam, Singapore, Malaysia, The United Kingdom, France, Denmark, Germany, Switzerland and other exotic places on the simple notion that God will direct their path and provide their needs, we get a modern day example of what it must have been like for Paul when he journeyed through Asia Minor asking his friends "to pray for us, too, that God may open a door for our message, so that we may proclaim the mystery of Christ." (Col 4:3)

Not only will their story encourage and challenge you to look at life from a different perspective, their transparency will invite you to journey with them as they face the fears, doubts, regrets and challenges that oftentimes come when you decide to 'walk by faith.' By the third chapter of this unusually honest and engaging account I found myself not only reading the book, but in it...feeling the same emotions they did, rooting them on, and anticipating how God was going to show up.

This book is especially needed now as so many of us rely on our careers, bank accounts, supermarkets, hospitals and all of the other modern day benefits to live a safe life. It was a wake-up call for me, and I believe it will be for you. The "greater things than these shall you do" promise isn't for the sedentary, predictable, couch potato Christian lifestyle, but for the courageous, the searcher and the bold. I'm eternally grateful that Chris and Jessica took one year out of their lives to model how to live all the years that are in front of us.

As Chris pens in his final chapter: "We hope that our story encourages you to do that very thing that is inside if you. Take the leap of faith! Don't rush it, but don't prolong it either. Have faith. Don't be stupid." I couldn't have said it better.

Vincent Cannatello
Pastor, Word of Christ International Church

PREFACE

Think about some of your craziest dreams. Perhaps you have quite a few. I happen to believe in a God that allows us to use our creativity to develop ideas and dreams for our lives, but I also wonder to what extent He inserts them into us as well. It's easy for Christians to go through life never beginning to break the surface of the dreams they have inside of them because there is a fundamental belief that God doesn't want us to fulfill them or be happy. Sure, there are some things for us to pursue and some for another person to, but I happen to believe the majority of us often shove great ideas and dreams under the rug because they seem logistically disorganized or just flat-out crazy.

This book does not discuss the dogmatic reasoning behind a dream my wife Jessica and I had and were able to explore, but rather, it examines the conflict we had of wanting to do something great with our lives and wondering if God would actually take care of us. Our goal is to simply use our story to get you out of your boat, whatever that looks like. *We are not in any way encouraging any reader to quit their job and travel the world.* With a credit card, a little risk and a notice to your boss, you can do that on your own. What we are interested in seeing is you accomplishing the dreams of the Father that are brewing inside of you and trusting Him to bring to fruition the things that you know you are not capable of doing in your own power.

 For non-believers: give this book a chance. I know I tend to speak to a semi-developed, Christian audience, and I apologize, but try to read our story with the question in your heart, "Do coincidences exist?" My goal is to answer that question, "no." If you conclude any hard answer to this question, hopefully you'll begin to find the truth that you are looking for.

You'll realize quickly that I'm a very real person. *Gasp!* I am passionate. I am blunt, and I like to ask the hard questions in order to get to the root of why we do things. I hate elevator talk and superficial discussion. The pendulum between free will vs. predestination swings for me constantly, and my understanding of things at the beginning of our journey shifted around by the end. Since the end of our journey, my maturity in the Lord has grown in ways this book does not reflect. I hope that this book helps you question the depths of God's interest in you, and I hope you question your beliefs. Mine are still sharpened daily.

Above all, I hope that you take a step toward the areas of your destiny you wouldn't have without reading this book. Even if it's one small step that changes who you are in 60 years, it was one step that you wouldn't have taken without this seed planted in your life, and that's the main reason it is here for you.

You won't walk away from this book knowing all the details and ins and outs of everything that happened. We don't talk about the $20 someone would randomly hand to us or the hundreds of people we were introduced to along the way. This isn't a European road trip travel guide or an insight into Asian cookery. It is not a debate, either. It's our story; the raw and real facts of it. We are not perfect, nor did we have abundant amounts of faith in every instance. In fact, there were a few moments we were in the "stupid" category. Hindsight is 20/20.

Just know that if the Lord ever calls you to do something radical, and that something just doesn't go away over time, pray for the Lord to give you breadcrumbs. Pray for Him to show you scripture, books, things in the news and on television and to connect you to people through meaningful conversations that direct your path in a way that leads to you taking the steps of faith you know are brewing in your heart.

Here I am! I stand at the door and knock. If anyone hears my voice and opens the door, I will come in and eat with that person, and they with me. (Revelation 3:20)

CHAPTER ONE

HAPPY NEW YEAR, YOU FAILURE

I really can't fathom living through that specific meltdown ever again. I'll always remember it through the trauma I felt burning inside, but to literally be in that position again is something I couldn't imagine happening. Something had to change. Something had to give, because on that day and in that very moment, I had nothing left to give except the very body I had.

The staircase in this one house seemed particularly harder to climb than on other days. The dark, stained hardwood steps required more of a grip from my worn-down Nikes, and the push-off for each step was followed by a moment of required rest. Each stair reminded me of how exhausted I truly was. I was reminded of my wasted college degree. I thought of my childhood home; how I once lived a life of wealth and now was consistently in faith for the next bill to be paid.

The Dyson vacuum I was once so honored to have at this one particular house because it vacuumed the floor so lightly felt like 300 pounds in my forearms. "How am I going to get through this job, let alone the next two jobs today?" Seconds seemed like minutes, and this house just wouldn't get done.

I wrapped up the vacuuming and mopping on the second floor and began to walk towards the top of the stairs that descended three steps to a landing that overlooked the glamorous living room. As I turned to the remainder of the picturesque, slightly-curved, entryway staircase, I started to lose my balance. I planted both of my feet on each step, took a deep breath and used everything within my core to push through to the next one. Jess walked my direction on the bottom floor with concern on her face, and as we met each other's eyes, I nearly dropped my bucket of dirty water all over the stairs because I didn't have the strength to grip the handle anymore.

What happened to me? I used to have so much spunk! I'm only 25, and I can't imagine going another day. How in the world am I going to make it to old age? Thoughts of frustration invaded my mind during this physically detrimental moment to my body. I began to mop the formal dining room, living room and foyer, and I couldn't even grip the mop. Panting and pushing, huffing and puffing, I started to black out. Jess fetched my water, and I laid down on the cool tile as she mopped the area around me. It was as if she took white chalk out and drew an outline of my body right there. I was good as dead anyways.

After twenty minutes or so of me laying on our clients' floor, praying it wouldn't dry so I could rest longer, I pushed myself to load our supplies into the car. As we drove away, I looked around at the enormous houses in the neighborhood thinking about how we couldn't get approved for a loan on a small house if we tried to on our faith-based income. Yet, these homes were mostly vacant vacation homes.

I remember that despite my physical exhaustion, I was more aggravated than I had ever been, shouting toward the car in front of us about how ridiculous our situation was; that we were still cleaning toilets for a living. I yelled about how much of a pee-on I felt from our clients and that I was worth more than what was reflected. How we ended up where we were didn't make sense unless you believe in the assumption that the sum of all the experiences and choices of your life add up to the moment you are currently living. I wanted out, and there was nothing I could do about it at that moment.

Poor Jessica. She, better than anyone in my world, could understand and relate to my frustration. I think it was that very fact that helped us get through the years that we cleaned. Not sure whether to be scared in that moment or just sit there and let me air out the stress within my veins, she turned her head to that adorable 2:00 position where a simple tear dripped down her cheek. It's the position where she's looking out her window and turning her head away from me but keeping it there just enough for me to still see the sides of her expressions. Happy New Year. It was January 2nd, 2013.

*   *   *   *   *

Each day, I would wake up to our radio alarm clock, and I would get mad at the announcers for waking me up. I bounced between Christian radio to NPR just to give myself something different to wake up to. So many mornings went by where we would lay in bed for a moment asking each other how it was possible we could work 12-18 hours of physical labor after the day before with all of the pain we were in and get up and do it again the next day. Although we never got the answer to that question, we somehow always pulled it off. We simply pushed ourselves to do it. There were bills to pay.

Jess and I had to rely on each other. Most times we would encourage ourselves by the amount each job would bring in by flashing the golden carrot in front of each other's eyes and saying our favorite *Finding Nemo* quote Ellen DeGeneres so famously said of, "Just keep swimming...Just keep swimming...."

This day, all the winds turned and developed into the perfect storm. My guard was down after making an 18-hour road trip the day before. Road trips are rarely fun for the driver especially when the first eight hours are spent driving through pouring snow and sleet. I had a headache from having to stay alert through the night. We left Ohio right after the clock struck midnight on New Year's, and the jobs in Florida on January 2nd were calling our names, so we had to get back quickly. There was no room in the budget not to. Our business fluctuated constantly, so we had to take every job we could to cover the

19

Quote.

potential days of drought.

The gusts of short-term physical exhaustion were blowing. The winds of long-term physical exhaustion were raging. The drafts of hopelessness were propelling into the storms of our dreams, and frustration was falling on us like never-ending hail. A depression had formed and hovered over us through the duration of each sustained element. Helplessness settled, yet we chose to live the life we were living on our own. We had a choice, but we chose cleaning.

*   *   *   *   *

Just a month and a half before that episode, Jess and I had a voucher to stay in a hotel room for free, and it was about to expire. We stayed on the seventh floor of a beautiful hotel in Tampa with a view of the skyscrapers. Twice a year we'd try to get away and stay in a hotel for a night, and our time would consist of holding a husband vs. wife *House Hunters* contest, as cable was a luxury that we chose to omit from our lives. We always made sure to get an early check-in and a late check-out. Rest came at a high price for us, and we made sure to "milk the squeeze," as I like to say. It's based on the idea that you squeeze "fresh juice" and then "milk it" for all it has.

This particular stay was unlike any other. We checked in with a different motive, and that was to find a way to bring change in our lives. Lying in a cool, dark room in a comfortable bed watching *HGTV* probably would have felt like lying in the dusty Lao dirt in a hot, stuffy room full of rats. There was more for us, and we needed to figure out how to get it. We wanted to see God move in our lives, and we were sick of living out a gospel that often focused on the day of our deaths rather than the life we had to live until that day came. There was one way we both knew how to begin seeing God intervene in our lives, and it was through making prayerful declarations.

Our experience with declarations has been very favorable throughout the duration of our marriage. It's a simple process: Jess and I make a list of the things we are believing God to come through for. These are the things that cannot happen without His intervention; the things we believe He has spoken into our hearts through prayer, dreams, and the prophetic, along with anything we believe that should come to fruition in our lives. We write them down, pray into each one with confident faith and even declare certain things to be done by certain dates. We are specific; even down to the amount, the color or the place. The more detailed we are with each item, the greater the amount of faith in our hearts we require. God loves it when believers *use* unwavering faith and trust in Him.

Jess and I believe that God takes our spoken word very seriously and that he takes our declarations even more seriously when we legalize them. Not only do we speak out our declarations through prayer and write them down, but we hang them somewhere to remind us of them regularly. We also sign our declaration sheet, date it and treat it like a contract between us and God. There are many note cards, journal pages and printed documents that we have nearly every line crossed off. Even with the declarations that never produced or have yet to come to fruition, we know God delights in our desire to see Him move in our lives for the things that are important to us.

Two of the very declarations I took seriously surrounded my employment. One of them was regarding an indoor rock climbing gym that we partnered with two other couples to get funding for and build. There was a market for it in our area, and if the economy would have sustained it, it would have been very profitable, but we just weren't willing to take on the high level of debt to start it up. The gym would have not only owned us, but it would have come at the cost of our freedom, because we

21

would have been required to work it to keep our costs down.

Some things had shifted through the development process, and we began to feel uneasy about moving forward. We received up to a $10 million offer to build, not just a climbing gym, but an entire athletic center located in the heart of the hottest, most-prime real estate of Sarasota, Florida at the time. As a result, I formed two declarations – one, that by Valentine's Day we would know what to do about the gym, and two, that I would have white-collar work. That was only a few weeks away.

White-collar work is something I know very well from my childhood and have always desired to do. My father is the epitome of the white collar industry. When I smelled the scent of the traditional green Polo by Ralph Lauren on him, it was a sign of his signature "today will be a successful day" internal pep talk – probably an indicator of the "just keep swimming" attitude he most likely had in 1978 when pioneering the company he still runs today. My brother followed right in his footsteps, minus the Polo.

That's not where I ended up in life, however. After high school and through college, I owned a car-detailing company and have always been good at working with my hands. A psychology degree didn't catapult me into business the way my dad and brother's focuses in accounting and finance did, so I focused on what I could already do well and entered the cleaning industry (which had some general crossover).

I also started cleaning because it was an option for work when I moved to Sarasota after marrying Jessica, and it was *flexible*. Our clients could be scheduled around the short-term mission trips we would take, so we never had to worry about PTO limitations, sick days or if we would be able to get the days off we needed. It was guaranteed to us at the cost of chronic pain, nonstop hours one month and no work the next month. Like I mentioned earlier, we believed in faith for our bills to be paid and calls for work to show up during slow times, which for a person like me (the product of a household specializing in financial services), was extremely difficult.

*   *   *   *   *

I am confident the root of my meltdown on the emotional end came at the result of one thing and one thing only: detachment from the Spirit of God. Somewhere along the way, cleaning went from a temporary solution to becoming "the answer." Jess and I slowly moved away from the various areas in ministry we conducted because of our lack of regular time spent in the Word and interaction with the Lord. We became engulfed in our own systems, and *we* made it impossible for God to intervene because we only cared about our finances being fulfilled, not *His destiny* for our lives to penetrate our own desires. What our body and souls wanted at the time was what we cared more about, and we ignored the importance of what the Spirit of God wanted from us. Mission trips were a once-in-a-while, "nice" work to do, and we killed ourselves month after month in order to make sure we had the time off to do them.

God's access to our lives had been limited to meeting our monthly budget, and He met us every time. Every bill was paid on time. One month when expenses were high, we would meet every cent. Another month when expenses were lower, we would only meet every cent. We were capped to the standard that our budget justified the extent to which we needed God, even though we were the ones laboring and toiling. I recall many Sunday nights when we would go to bed without one job set up for the upcoming week and would pray, "God, we've got to pay the bills. Please send work." Monday morning by 10:00, we would have to turn down work, because we were physically incapable of fitting it into that weeks' schedule. We'd blink, and the week had passed. Sometimes that's just the way blue-collar work functions because people often call on Monday mornings, but we believe our prayers launched us forward when necessary. Because we believed in God to provide our financial opportunities, looking at our budget with a $2,600 deficit midway through the month didn't scare us as much in month sixteen of our marriage as it did in month six. Either way, the deficit was always paid (along with really hard days of work).

*　　　*　　　*　　　*　　　*

As I was having my New Year's breakdown, I needed a pick-me-up. What does any blue-collar worker do for a pick-me-up? They buy a Big Gulp. A 64-ounce Cherry Coke was one of the few things I looked forward to in my day, next to the occasional Snickers bar. As we got back into the car at the gas station, not seeing what God was doing at that very moment, I asked Jess, "What are we doing?"

It seemed somewhat late to ask Jess what we were doing at that point. We had asked that question nearly every day. Cleaning does not require the use of your mind. In fact, it prohibits your mind from expansion through the overdevelopment of routine. Spray the mirror. Then spray the counter. Spray the inside of the toilet. Let sit. "What am I doing with my life?" Dust the picture. Clean the shower. Wipe the toilet. Empty the trash. Sweep the floor. Mop. "What the heck am I doing with my life?" Repeat.

This time, the question was asked differently. It had a tone of passion prowling in the distance waiting to gain momentum through the power of intentional goal-setting. It not only had the fuel of a puffed up New Year's resolution, but it had the anger of a tyrant unwilling to settle. Jess heard the unquestionably austere tone behind the question. There was meaning and sheer determination of follow-through. The level of her emotions were parallel with mine based on the lack of hesitation from the muscles in her tongue.

"I want to travel the world."

There was no simple response that I could give to my wife at that moment. All I knew is that I wanted the same thing, but had no clue how to make it happen. We settled it: we're going to go into our next job and come up with one thing we could do that day to start making that dream surface to reality. Cleaning no longer brought any level of contentment as a source of income. It didn't fit into our plans, and we couldn't make room for it anymore. We had to come up with an escape plan.

Being reminded of the 26 months that we had lived in financial faith at that point of our marriage, we created the death date of our cleaning company: the end of May/beginning of June. This allowed us to finish high season with our company and phase out our clients honorably based on their own schedules since many of them were "snowbirds" or those who live in South Florida for the winter.

We hated every second of persevering through the following months, but we felt it was important to take care of clients, all whom had in some way become special to us, blessed us in countless ways and taught us many things. It's an interesting relationship: you're the cleaner, and at the end of the day society tells you that is what you are worth, but the relationships were still important to us. In fact, *every* regular client we worked for had been used by God at some point to build our faith, support our missions or network us to important connections in our lives. They couldn't just be thrown to the curb. After all, how you exit one season is how you enter the next.

Now that we had plans to travel the world, the climbing gym was definitely not happening. By the time we had worked out everything in our hearts and decided that we would resign from our partnership, we "just so happened" to have the meeting to withdraw on February 13th: the day before Valentine's Day.

Early February rolled around, and I had designed a business that catered to a growing demand in the US: firearms accessories. This was following the events that took place in Newtown, Connecticut and the government's attempt to reform American gun laws. I wanted to capitalize on the increasing demand for accessories. After all, my last name is Gunn, so how fitting would it be to start Gunnsmoked Guns? It doesn't matter how you feel about guns, it's still a cool name. I secured my LLC and had my website and logo designed, believing a drop ship internet business would be the key to earn a self-sustaining income. It was portable, white-collar, and would be easy to market. "I'm Chris Gunn of Gunnsmoked Guns...." I could convince to any wholesaler to sell on my site as long as I had a confident attitude, personal touch or a bold handshake.

I didn't have a grasp on the basics of internet marketing or, so I called a friend of mine who had been very successful in the realm of System Engine Optimization (SEO). That phone call changed the entire spectrum of my year. He offered me a proposition to lay the foundation for a business he wanted to start but didn't have the time outside of his daily work. If I developed that business well, he suggested I would have no problem building Gunnsmoked Guns. He'd teach me to start a niche internet marketing company that he saw fitting for the times, and it would allow me to work from home earning great money at the cost of many free hours up front. We met to discuss the logistics, and I officially became "an entrepreneur."

The concept had finally formed: I would run an internet marketing company, and we'd have enough money to travel the world. We planned on visiting 12 regions of the world and rent a different place each month in 2014. It would be perfect. Goal: achieved. Was it really that easy?

CHAPTER TWO

LAUNCHED LIKE ARROWS

"There are people in this room tonight who have met at this very specific time, because God is going to launch you out like arrows into the nations."

I'll never forget the above word that would be specific to Jess and me. It was our first date. Jess and I had an unorthodox, 17-hour date of nearly non-stop talking. When Applebee's closed at 2am, we moved the conversation to the 24-hour Starbucks. We were both very serious from the beginning, and we had a lot of ground to cover (our entire lives'-worth). After dinner and midway through our date, Jess took me to a young-adult church meeting to "see how I worshipped." According to her, my ability to worship freely was a bolded box that had to be checked before pursuing me further. It was that night during the meeting that we heard the very word stated above.

Although it easily seemed to be something I connected to, Jess quickly recalled those exact words from a word of knowledge she had received when she was 14. During service as a teenage girl, Jess' pastor walked up to her and told her to get her parents saying he, "had a word from the Lord regarding her husband." After grabbing her mom and dad, Jess' pastor said that she would meet her husband in the mission field and they would be married quickly, but there was a purpose behind the speed. It was because they would be launched out like arrows into the nations. Jess, having forgotten this very word through her life and dating different boys (one to the point of an engagement), recalled the word she received when she was just a teenager and "almost fell out of her chair" knowing that I was undoubtedly her husband. We had met on a mission trip in Mexico just a few weeks prior over Christmas break in 2009.

*   *   *   *   *

Now that a plan about how we could pursue this life change had been outlined, planning for our world travels began. As many people do in the months of February and March in South Florida, we went to the hot tub at nighttime. It was there under the palm trees, looking up at the stars, that Jess and I spent many nights dreaming about what we would be doing that very hour the next year. It was freeing to detach ourselves from the next day's cleaning schedule and allow our dreams to absorb us.

With all the dreaming, however, there came an obstacle. How could we possibly do everything and go everywhere we wanted to? Hours were spent browsing the internet, sifting through blogs and resources to try and establish how much time would be required to enjoy each place, what we should be sure to see, what we should pack, etc. Occasionally skepticism would enter our minds to the point that the only question was, "Can this even happen?" Eventually, our doubts began to trump the desire to travel. Planning became overwhelming to us, and a lack of desire for traveling started to take root.

The benefits of hibernating in Sarasota for the remainder of our existence and living an average life started to shift our focus from the pros of leaving home to the pros of staying home. Distaste for travel settled so much that, when I would see a picture or statue of the Eiffel Tower, I would shake my head with disgust regarding the idea of leaving for an entire year. *"I can just Google the pictures of all the different places we'd go,"* I'd suggest. *"They probably look better than in person anyways."* I had forgotten the very reason we wanted to get out of cleaning in the first place - freedom. Through the company I was working tirelessly to grow, I was developing the means to which I could gain freedom. The need to attach the retrieval of that freedom to some far, out in the distance dream of traveling the world was no longer necessary.

The end of March rolled around, and we couldn't have longed to stay in Sarasota and start a family more. The thought of living an average life became more enticing as we focused our thoughts on settling into our comfort zones. By the beginning of May, our dreams were restricted to the pages of our journals and the corners of our hearts even though they were still at the forefronts of our minds. Traveling the world for a year seemed to become the product of an emotional New Year's resolution.

As with any idea that takes over my thoughts, I usually take it to the Lord for input. Regarding traveling, however, I had never asked God what He thought. Frankly, I thought He'd say "no," and then guilt would have eliminated our plans. We were so focused on simply "getting out" of cleaning that we didn't even consider God's contribution to the decision. I finally sought Him out, to which I received a quick, yet simple response in my heart. *"Chris - you are going, but it's not going to look like what you think it is going to."*

*　　　*　　　*　　　*　　　*

When we develop an unwavering trust for the fruition of the things we believe the Lord has spoken to us, it allows Him the opportunity to amaze us. By anchoring ourselves to a certain word and prohibiting anyone or any circumstance from inhibiting the production of that word into life, God can accomplish the destined situation fully, and I believe in some cases more quickly, because our doubt is not blocking the ability for Him to move powerfully. Our focus on the promises of God for our lives should never make room for the skepticism of even those whose opinions we hold of highest value. Our declarations, although sometimes said with little faith, hold merit because of the words we are actively professing.

Forgive me if you have never experienced or been required to have a similar level of trust in the Lord, but this is where the prophetic, in its very design, makes room for us through faith to permit God to produce something natural from a supernatural means. If we do not believe in the supernatural, skepticism closes the door for God to move. If we actually believe that God can do the impossible like we suggest when we remark "With God, *all* things are possible," the faith (the evidence of things unseen) we actively profess produces responses through the power of the Holy Spirit that are meant to breathe life into the things around us which are dead.

There was no doubt that we were going to take the plunge now that we had a word to hold onto regarding the following year. Through different series of prayer times with the Lord, Jess and I concluded we would begin in Bangkok, Thailand and that we were *not to plan anything in advance.* My new business was behind on its launch, however, and I hadn't made any money. The idea of quitting our cleaning jobs in just short of a month at that point was overwhelming, and our bodies had just enough oomph in them to finish out the spring cleaning season.

It was time to make our decision official: we were going to tell Jess' parents. The most difficult person to think about telling was her mom. I began to learn to stop worrying about the tiny variables when the Lord tells us to do something radical, because He usually has already worked many of the kinks out. For quite a while, Jess was stressed about telling her mom that we would be leaving for a year, or perhaps, even longer. It was hard enough that we were going to miss out on many of our friends' weddings or babies' births, but the thought of telling her mom put a huge weight on Jess' shoulders. Finally, the week before we were going to come out with the news, Jess' mom casually mentioned to her, *"I feel like you and Chris are going to be gone next year."*

I've also established through my personal experiences that when I am seeking direction, I'll get a specific scripture or word from the Lord or an idea during prayer time, and it will often be backed up with a word of knowledge. This was the very case at the end of May during another visit to Jess' hometown in Ohio. When we shared our plans with Jess' grandmother, she received a word to give us from the Lord through a book she owned.

By this time, the concept had evolved from a traveling adventure funded by my online work to being a journey the Lord would have His hand on. We would be "backpackers who did mission work wherever we went," but Jess' grandmother showed us it was a lot bigger than we had originally thought.

She had a difficult time finding the book. Jess' grandparents have an entire bedroom with bookshelves and boxes of books, so she tore up the bedroom for over ten minutes trying to find it. Once she located the book, she then had trouble finding the page. After quite some time flipping back and forth through the pages, she came to the page and knew she had found the word the Lord had for us. "Launch Out" was the title of the page in the book *Come Away My Beloved* by Frances J. Roberts. It said:

"My people, you have touched only the fringes. Yes, you have lingered on the shorelines. Launch out on the vast sea of My love and mercy, yes, My mighty power and limitless resources.

For if you would enter into all that I have for you, you must walk by faith upon the waters. You must forever relinquish your doubts; and your thoughts of self-preservation you must forever cast aside. For I will carry you, and I will sustain you by My power in the ways that I have chosen and prepared for you. You shall not take even the first step in your own strength.

For you are not able in yourself-even as flesh is always unable to walk the way of the Spirit. But my arm shall uphold you, and the power of My Spirit shall bear you up.

Yes, you will walk upon the waves, and the storm will only drive you more quickly to the desired port. Chart and compass you shall not need, for My Spirit will direct your goings, and are not the winds held in My fists? Be not fearful but believing."

What do you do with a word like this? How do you handle it properly when everything in it hits home and applies to your life; when it's crystal-clear direction that you need in a time of uncertainty? There's only one way, and that is through responding with a confident *"yes."*

Immediately following that word, Jess' grandmother envisioned a 3-pronged report folder sitting on the kitchen table. It had our story already written and bound, and all Jess and I were required to do was to walk it out. With each step taken in faith, another page would be lived. That was that. We were going whether we liked it or not.

Three weeks later, we received another word of knowledge from a man who didn't even know what we were planning to do the following year. In fact, I'm not sure if he even knew our names at the time. He addressed us: "I just see you as arrows in a quiver, and God's going to take you and shoot you out. The moment you land, He's already got the next landing point in sight. Don't worry about any of it because it's all going to be taken care of. You're just going to walk it out."

*   *   *   *   *

Soon after, Jess leaned over to me during worship at church one Sunday and said to me, "God just asked me if I'd believe Him for a $10,000 check."

I responded: "That's nice, sweetheart. I don't. That's borderline 'Prosperity Gospel'."

We prayed about it and, like we always do when we're not

capable of creating results, we said "Lord, let your will be done."

Later on in June, Jess saw an image during worship of the two of us with a rope tied around our waists, being yanked backward as we tried to progress forward. When the image panned to the other end of the rope in her mind, there was a storage unit filled with everything we owned. She quickly shared this with me explaining that she felt like we were supposed to sell nearly everything. This included all of the things we registered for during our wedding season, most of our furniture, our movies, books, everything from our bathroom towels to our gently-used clothing. It was all to be sold except for our bedroom suite, our holiday decorations and some clothing.

Jess then added another desire of her heart at the beginning of August: to have our plane tickets to Bangkok, Thailand purchased by Labor Day (her birthday that year). It would be used as a sign from the Lord that we were most definitely to go. Between the $10,000 check, selling everything and the ticket deadline, I had to decide if I *really* trusted Jess' discernment. As always, I believed with her, even if I still questioned what she said she "heard" or "saw."

Reality check: We had quit our jobs in early June and had gone on a fundraised mission trip to Alaska for 7 weeks. This would easily allow ample time to build up my company to the point at which we could self-sustain. It would be perfect...until the internet receiver I purchased from a larger cell phone service provider didn't perform to the standard I was informed it would in that area of Alaska. Progress was minimal, and it often took over five minutes to load a simple webpage. I had to outsource almost all aspects of my work because of my internet problems. The business was now *costing* me money, not making me money. We were riding our credit card for any bills that would allow for us to pay with it, and we would figure out the rest.

While we were away in Alaska, our church held a service to

pray for written declarations and place them in a bowl at the front of the church. We emailed our friends Steven and Kristen a list they could submit them on our behalf. We wrote down many items, such as the $10,000 check, that everything would sell before the lease ended, that my internet business would cover our bills, that the plane tickets would be purchased by Labor Day; you know, those financial things you worry about and "give to God" hoping they will actually come to fruition.

I remember returning home from Alaska dissatisfied and discouraged with the progress of my business. We were accruing more debt than ever (Surprise! We quit our jobs when our expenses exceeded our income...would you have expected otherwise?). Something we have always practiced with our ministry efforts, however, is that we have always kept our personal and ministry finances separated. Personally, we had to put a large chunk of our 2012 taxes that were due on a credit card, and our credit debt was growing every month. I also wasn't sure how we were going to pay our rent at the end of the month after returning from Alaska. The truth was, however, that ministry-wise we had received $1,100 through donations, and we only needed another $500 to book our tickets to Bangkok. Two weeks before Labor Day, someone gave us a random $500 check even though we were not asking for donations at that time. Tickets paid. Happy Birthday, Jessica.

*　　　　*　　　　*　　　　*　　　　*

September rolls around: the business was still not running as smoothly as projected. At the end of the day, I was netting about $8 an hour, and Jess had quit her job. What does anyone do at this point? I prayed for more orders. Jess took some cleaning jobs again to make up for the deficit while pushing items we could sell. Our debt ceiling was approaching fast.

I remember the Monday in September, two days before we would hit our debt ceiling: We had a mattress on a 0% card that we had $1,200 left to pay. On top of that, we had an interest-bearing credit card with a $7,500 limit, to which $7,380 had been used with a $140 car insurance payment to hit on Wednesday. Our card would be declined for that bill.

As I was cold-calling my way through a list of potential clients, Jess had a friend's mom over for coffee. She had made a donation for our trip to Alaska, and she wanted to hear about the trip. I remember being in my office while the ladies were in the living room enjoying their coffee date. At one point while working, I was distracted by a friend of mine who was fundraising for a significant need, and I said to God, *"God we have nothing left in the giving budget. Will you please send me some money so I can give some to this person?"* Jess and I adore giving. We know what it's like to receive, so how much more fun is it to give money to people who need it?

Jess was wrapping up her coffee date, so I went out into the living room to politely say goodbye, and I saw that Jess had an envelope in her hand. As soon as the front door closed, we opened it up, and there it was: a $10,000 check written to our names. Jess immediately fell on the floor crying. I started crying and praising God. There are moments when you just don't know what to do to thank God enough. All I could think of doing was ripping out our carpet and sprinkling it around like confetti. I wanted to physically high-five God. I know He smiles in a moment like this. Now we weren't going to hit our financial threshold. In fact, we had just enough to pay off our debts, go down to zero and take care of a few other necessary affairs. The best part was that we had $1,000.00 to give away.

*   *   *   *   *

A few weeks later, we went to church just like any ordinary Sunday. During announcements, we stepped outside to talk with our friends, Steven and Kristen. We hadn't seen them in a while and wanted to catch up. While we were outside, a lady who we had never met before stood up in front of the entire congregation and said, *"I don't know who the couple is that is going to Thailand next year, but the Lord says that you are going to be launched out like arrows into the nations and that God has you in his quiver. He has laid out every step for you, and you are not to worry about a thing because it is all taken care of, in Jesus' name."*

It was quite funny because we ended up talking for almost an hour and came back in nearly halfway into the sermon. Jess and I tried sneaking in, but realized *everyone* was staring at us. Pastor smiled at me which was out of character for him since he's usually "in the zone" while teaching. A few minutes later, Jess checked her phone. We had received a text explaining what had happened. All the staring made sense after that!

I don't know what it was about that fifth confirming word, but when the Lord confirms a something five times, through five different sources, you don't take that lightly. I usually trust when words come in threes, but fives were a whole new level. When we got into the car after church, I told Jess that I would never again question if we were supposed to go on the trip. Did I stay true to that statement? No, but I meant it when I said it.

When the end of September crept up, we knew that our trip looked like this: Jessica and I would be launched out like arrows into the nations. God would have us in his quiver and would shoot us out, pick us up and shoot us off again. We wouldn't need to worry about the finances, and everything was going to be taken care of. We wouldn't need to make plans or do anything (necessarily) in advance. The requirement was to simply, "go." Basically, we were being ordained to sell our stuff, buy a one-way ticket to Asia and travel around without a plan, not knowing people or specifically what to do. As nice as all of this may have sounded, I wondered if a lifestyle like that realistically places a person into a category called: Stupid.

CHAPTER THREE

WHAT'S THAT UP AHEAD? REALITY

October slowly rolled in with its perfect weather and delicious desserts. Fall is our favorite time of the year, and with it came a slap in the face that we were only a few months away from leaving and just weeks from moving out of our first home. Tuesday January 7, 2014 at 10:00 in the morning we would be on a one-way flight to Bangkok, Thailand.

I know that for most places around the US, fall time can be wonderful. That is especially the case for South Florida. It's the time that you can (finally) open your windows and get a nice breeze into your home. The yellow-orange glow on the grass and trees helps me admire nature more. Although the leaves hardly change where we live, it's the time of year most people spend outside. As northerners are covering their pools for the winter, we're getting into them for the first time since early spring. A motto Jess and I live by: We get tan in the winter and pale in the summer. All you want to do in the summer is lay in a cool, dark room because it is unbearably hot and humid, and by the time fall arrives, all you want to do is enjoy the outdoors.

Jess uses her bread pan more often, and we stock up on canned pumpkin as even our oven begs us to bake fall breads and desserts. Our favorite decorations come out of their containers, and most of all, I get quality time with my favorite friends: squirrels. I love two things in this world: squirrels and pistachios, and I love to share my pistachios with squirrels.

This year was different, however. We were busy. We had an agenda. There were deadlines. Our lease was ending November 1, and we would be moving into Steven and Kristen's house. You want to talk about an awkward conversation? Try asking some friends if you can live with them for 10 weeks! *"Oh yeah, so can we live with you guys for 10 weeks,"* isn't typical dinner talk. Jess had to turn the air conditioner down five degrees just to begin the conversation. Thankfully, they kindly agreed to host us.

The challenge we had was that we had to get rid of pretty much everything we couldn't fit into one bedroom by the day we moved out. We had a yard sale the Saturday beforehand, and we had one shot for it to be successful. Thankfully, we had some friends with a yard in a good location and my father-in-law's old van (the epitome of moving-day vehicles) to make countless trips back and forth to the apartment. We prayed and prayed for a great turnout, because everything had to go. Nothing could return with us.

*   *   *   *   *

I remember the days back at the beginning of our marriage when part of my daily routine was to worry about money. The stress and frustration from the lack of predictability regarding our monthly income absorbed me. There were perks to not being on a fixed income, however, since some months we would make a lot of money, but other months, we scraped our pennies together. I would rationalize, *"Well, if all else fails, we can sell our stuff."* I found security in the stuff that we owned thinking, *"if God failed us, we could always survive on this or that."*

You would think all the furniture and belongings you own would be worth a lot more than $3,200, but that's what all of our stuff came out to at the end of the day. We had a large, new, flat screen television, a whole kitchen full of relatively new, nice pots and pans, silverware and small appliances. We had hundreds of books and movies, nice furniture spread around the house, plus plenty of those $10-15 Craigslist items we could sell. At the end of the day, however, when it's time to get rid of the stuff and you are on a deadline, you find yourself selling a beautiful solid wood end table that you love for $10 or entire collections of great DVDs for about $20. Selling everything is a great way to find out what your confidence is in.

Believe it or not, seeing the items from my childhood and things that Jess and I had registered for waving goodbye and being driven to their new homes was not the hardest event to endure. Cash reinforced the decision to sell the item, so it didn't sting horribly to see anything go. It was two nights before the sale that I had difficulty enduring. In fact, I still refer to that night as one of the most emotional nights of my entire life. I couldn't sleep, so I wrote this blog post:

Tonight I get to be more personal with my readership: something I'm not generally accustomed to being. We are just a few days away from moving out of our home. To one degree there is excitement, and to another, there is sadness and mourning.

Jess & I am having a yard sale in two days to get rid of the majority of the things that we own. We took down the photos off of all our walls, making our apartment stripped and bare: a constant reminder of the stripping of our "things" that is going on in the next few months. The picture frames we bought for over our couch were so special to us. Jess worked 3 jobs on the side after she was already exhausted in order to pay for them. We didn't even get them on the wall for over a year and a half, and in the same amount of time, they have come down. On the wall in the dining room, we had pictures hung on clothespins displaying the exciting adventures we had shared throughout the past 4 years. Those memories are only digital once again.

The shelf above our kitchen cabinets which used to be full of cookbooks now stands bare only with Jess' dried up wedding bouquet implanted in our unity sand sitting next to one of the few items we will keep: our ceramic cake stand. Our TV and dining set is sold. Everything in our kitchen is sold, and it really comes down to just the couch, end table, chair and lamp.

I remember when we moved into our apartment. We didn't know if we could afford the rent. I didn't know the area of town, and I didn't have a job yet. I remember unpacking all the goodies we received for our wedding and getting set up in our new home. We were so excited about our world map shower curtain, yellow tea kettle, and most of all, a place that was our own. We didn't have any money for the dining table that we somehow paid for. All we knew was that we were in love and that we were together for an unknown purpose.

I remember our first meal, first Christmas, the time we realized how quick the electric bill adds up when cooling the house below 70. I remember the many pizza and cookie nights. I remember the nights we spent with our friends here and never wanted them to leave. We could have talked all night many nights. I remember arguing over who would get to open the mailbox...and the many days we only had our weekly credit card offer or nothing at all. I remember the nights we cuddled up on the couch at 7:30, got really quiet and reminded ourselves that in 5-10 years we would beg to have the house that quiet with nothing to do.

I remember all the nights we would spend at the hot tub and pool.... We dreamed so much there. We dreamed about the very things that we are doing now. We dreamed about traveling the world one day before we had kids. When would we have kids? We dreamed of where we would visit and why. We dreamed of our futures and talked about what we liked about our lives and wanted to improve on. I openly talked about truly missing my mom there for the first time since she died. There are many nights we would swim, look up at the stars through the palms, and think about how the stars are the same on the other side of the world. I wondered if we would swim at night overseas, look up at the stars and remember those times and all the people that we care about.

When we walk out of this apartment for the last time in 2 weeks, I am sure that many tears will be shed as the comforts of having our own home, the security of the things we own and the thought of future memories in unit 1613 are stripped and dissolved into memory. Jess and

I have spent the majority of our relationship in this home. The secrets of our hearts lie inside these walls.

The nostalgia that I have shared with you just now is wonderful, raw and real, but it is sad that I am even going through this. No – it's not the fact that I'm being emotional and have real feelings I am open to, but it's that this is the true reflection of my heart. The reflection of memories is not what I discuss, but it is the stripping of those things that define me. The fact that I gain my security in having the desk that I do, the TV that I do, the USF coffee mug that I do, the granite counter tops that I do, is simply pitiful. When did I become so defined and owned by the things that are to be luxuries that I should be grateful to have? Was I a day old? Was I 12? Was it yesterday? When did I begin to donate areas of my security to the things that I own?

Jesus said not to store up treasures here on earth....things that can (and will) be destroyed. "...For where your treasure is, there your heart will be also." (Matthew 6:19) That's darn right. Currently, as I sit in my home and stare at the blankness on the walls, my heart aches in a very similar way to how my heart aches when I am desperate to see God. It is so sad to me that this is my natural response. Who is my God? Is my God security and money, or is it the God of the Universe?

Tonight, I'm not sure. To a small degree, I'm considering putting nails back in the walls, hanging the pictures back up and calling this whole thing off! I could just get a job, live an average life, watch football every Sunday like I want to, and not have to live out of a backpack in uncomfortable homes with food I don't like to eat. I want to live near a Chipotle and eat there every night. I don't want dragonfly and fish eyes with a side order of cow nose with lukewarm Coke!

Shame on me for even going to that place, but I am doing it so you can see the reality of the decision that we are making to sell everything and go! AND READ THIS: It's not the reality of the decision that we will have nothing and "oh it's a crazy, stupid, 'life-threatening' decision," but it is the decision we have made to follow what Christ has called us to do that is more important than the decision I can easily make to stay here. I'd rather know that I'll be caught on God's narrow path and eat dragonfly for breakfast than to be stuck outside of his divine purpose so Jess and I can eat Chipotle when we want. The cost is high, but the reward is higher: I get to see people fall on their knees, be delivered, healed, and changed forever on a regular basis. I get to watch God come through again and again and again, even when I don't want to be in a place where he has to come through anymore. I get to see the world and win the world.

At the end of the day, I choose to keep the pictures off of my wall. I choose the dirt. I choose the life of the other person, and I choose to sacrifice my comforts. Too many people have tried the American dream and the Western church has too long ignored the need for God to penetrate their lives and the very necessity of His existence! I get to be a part of the club of people that can show the western world that conformity to the comforts this nation has created often only brings a life of dissatisfaction, sadness and lack of purpose.

Now I look up at the wall, and although it still stings a bit, I am reminded of the very results that will come as a response to my choice, and now I smile.

Everything was stacked under the bar top ready to be loaded into the car the following evening. The office shelves were empty, no longer displaying our favorite books and souvenirs from past trips. Our magnet collection from the fridge was stored, our bathroom was bare, and we felt like we were visitors in our own home. The process of beginning to get used to having "nothing" had officially begun, and it hit really, really hard and all at once.

After a stressful moving day and a sad good-bye, we locked the door of our first home for the last time, and we were happy to be done with it. We had felt in our guts when we moved into our apartment that we would only be there for three years and would be moving out that week either way. The move had been planned for nearly a year and, frankly, we were tired of thinking about it. We were ready to stop talking about our new lives and simply start living them. There were still ten weeks to go.

*   *   *   *   *

The second weekend in November, we got the call: my last living grandparent, my mom's mother, was dying and only had a short time left to live. She was 87 and lived a great life. I was happy for her to make it that far, especially since she was dealing with severe medical issues towards the very end of her life.

I had talked with her at the beginning of July right after she had turned for the worst. I asked her the question that was important to me and was thick in the air at the time:

"Grandmom, do you still have a desire and reason to live, or are you just waiting on the clock?"

She replied, "You know, Christopher, I just...don't...know. If anything, I just want to make it to [my younger cousin's] wedding in September. After that, I'll be okay."

Not sure if she would make it to my cousin's wedding at the time, I said one of my last good-byes to her.

Sure enough, she made it to the wedding, and she did great. In fact, it was one of the best nights she had had in years. Her stride was strong, she was getting groovy on the dance floor, and she had great energy. Unfortunately, it was that very confidence that brought her down. There was a slope on the edges of the installed dance floor, and because she wasn't using her walker and was still weak in her legs (despite her confidence), she tripped and abruptly fell. It was one of those "DJ stopped the music" types of scenarios. I was sad for her because she was embarrassed, and I felt really bad for my cousin since it happened during her wedding reception.

To be honest, I only heard the fall, but when I turned

around, I thought she had died right there. The initial response in my mind was, *"Well, she made it to the wedding."* I wasn't sure if she was dead or alive. At the end of it all, she had broken her arm and weeks later found out she fractured her spine as well. She spent some time in the hospital during her recovery, and contracted two illnesses while staying there. Those illnesses are what ultimately took her life.

We celebrated Grandmom's life on our third wedding anniversary. I was the only grandchild out of all of my cousins to have each of the grandparents I grew up with able to attend my wedding. All three of the ones that had been alive throughout the majority of my life had died within the three years of our wedding.

Why is this important? Frankly, it's because I am thankful that we were around.

*   *   *   *   *

"Sissy! You're going to Tigerland!" This was the general understanding of Jess' four-year old adopted sister, Makenna.

"Yes, and do you know what Sissy and Chris are going to be doing in *Thai*land?"

"Telling people about Jesus! Aaaaahhhh, ahahahaha." Makenna laughed loudly and fell back onto the couch.

"That's right, and Sissy and Chris are going to be gone for a really, really long time, and we're going to miss you very much."

"Sissy?" Makenna asked.

"Yes, sweetheart?"

"There are no cats in America!" She laughed at her wisdom.

Okay, so Jess' four adopted siblings, Justin, Makenna, Juliana and Jasmine, didn't truly understand what we were doing and how long we were really going to be gone. I don't know if that made leaving any easier for us.

One of the hardest conclusions we had to come to while deciding if we would risk everything was that we were going to miss events like weddings, the births of our friends' babies, and most importantly, Jess' siblings' growth.

Jess' family has dedicated their lives to fostering and adopting children through the local foster care system. They had adopted four little ones whom were 5 years, 4 years, 22 months and 16 months old at the time we left, and we were going to miss some critical parts of their lives. Would the youngest two remember us? Would the older two still recognize us the way they did when we left? We were so close to them. Thankfully technology could help keep our relationships going, but we could only do that so often.

I barely remember much before I was five except for a few highlighted events. As a result, we determined we would most likely have to remind the kiddos later on in their lives that we even left. At least, that's what we told ourselves to believe. Our motto was that we wanted to teach them at a very young age to go after the things that the Lord calls them to even if they have to miss out on a few special things in life. Hopefully they will be able to look to us as an example later on in their lives.

Not only were we committing to stripping ourselves of our belongings but also to stripping ourselves of events and relationships we thrived off of. Would it only be for one year? We weren't fully sure. All we knew was that we would be missing out, and we had to commit to it no matter how much guilt or sadness we felt. At the end of the day, we committed to a life of "no regrets," and this was a portion of the cost. The relationships could always be restored.

With all this said, when my grandmother died, I was relieved. Her funeral was the one event I knew I would miss if it didn't happen before we left. She got to see all of her engaged grandchildren married off (something that was really important to her), she was in a lot of pain, and for me personally, I got to say goodbye well. We were able to jump into the car, drive up from Sarasota to Jacksonville and enjoy some of her last conscious hours with her. Not only that, I witnessed a complete miracle with Jess and a cousin of mine.

The nursing staff clearly told us that Grandmom was experiencing three-hour waves of pain. She was only legally allowed to get a shot of morphine every three hours at the hospital until she was transferred to a Hospice facility. Because of that rule, the pain was excruciating during the last hour, and she would scream out until the nurse could administer the shot.

Jess, my cousin, and I stayed for one entire segment. We wanted to make sure Grandmom got the next shot on time. During the last hour, Jess and I passionately prayed in the Spirit because we knew it was going to be very rough. Grandmom went in and out of sleep, but not once did she scream out in pain. In fact, she slept for the majority of the hour until she got the morphine and perked up again. God really comforted her during that moment. After she woke up, that was the last time she would be conscious. I was beyond thankful to be standing at her grave that next week knowing I didn't miss that last moment with her.

CHAPTER FOUR

THERE'S NO WAY I'M GETTING ON THE PLANE

Growing up in Florida, Walt Disney World was only a 3-hour drive from home, and my brother Trey and I were spoiled with the ability to go every July. My dad taught an annual continuing education course that allowed us to stay on Disney property absolutely free for three nights. With the cash my dad made from teaching the course, the theme parks, food and travel were covered, and he would walk away with a few hundred bucks at the end of the week. My mom would take us to one of the parks in the morning, and then after nap time, my dad's class would be over, so we would go to a different park as a family in the evenings. They were amazing trips.

If there's anything I remember about them, it's the night before we left. I could *never* get to sleep out of the excitement of going to see Mickey and the gang. I may as well have been given three cups of coffee and a bowl of ice cream before bedtime, because I wouldn't fall asleep until late in the night. It was a recipe for disaster in the backseat of the car during the drive to Orlando the next day, because my brother and I would pinch, kick, and annoy each other much more than usual as an outlet for our grouchiness. *"Mom, Chris hit me." "Trey hit me first!"* We'd always stop at the Daytona Beach Chik-fil-a since it was the midpoint and crash hard afterward until waking up to the slow traffic of Orlando, excited to see the skyscrapers.

I figured I would experience something similar to this while on the 10-week countdown to January 7th. Truth is, it was the exact opposite. Those weeks absolutely flew by, and if I had to attach a movie title to our experience, it would be *Rat Race*. Funny movie. Not funny in real life.

You know those projects around your house that you always

say, *"Yeah, I need to do that someday,"* but you never get to them? When you decide to leave the country, that "someday" comes, and you have to complete all of them. Just between organizing our documents and data, scanning all of our childhood pictures and going through junk boxes we had just stored under our bed, we had enough to fill a lot of time. We went even further, though. My brother became our Power of Attorney so we could make sure that anything could be handled at home base if necessary. Tax season arrived earlier than usual, so we had to file our taxes, and since we were at it, we went ahead and made a Last Will and Testament full of medical, financial and funeral directions. We concluded that we didn't want any of our family members to have to make decisions they weren't prepared for in the event they had to make them. Needless to say, our ducks were in a row upon preparing to leave the country.

Simply setting up the right bank accounts so international fees could be avoided was a challenge in itself. If you have ever been to a bank to set up an account, you know to brace yourself for a 1.5-hour experience. This happened multiple times at multiple banks. Then, calls had to be made to get all of our cards set for our travel itinerary. Additionally, other people had to be given permission to access our accounts if we couldn't get something done. The banking aspect was days of work in itself!

Black Friday marked the starting point for us to purchase any gear we felt we needed. Thankfully our friends Jordan and Stephanie knew how to pack as little as possible but live well. They helped us pick the right backpacks and design the packing structure to maximize our space. I had a 25L backpack and Jess had a 39L backpack, and we only carried about a week's worth of clothing. There was a lot to get outfitted with, so after returns and exchanges, we ended up being $1,344 in debt.

The final two months were abundantly stressful. Between the endless to-do lists, my company barely staying profitable, all of the dinners and get-togethers we had set up to say goodbye to our cherished friends, the holiday parties, and most of all, our families, we were both emotionally and socially spent. In the meantime, Jess was running tables at multiple events for her organization Hazina Life. We hardly saw each other.

Between everything going on, Jess and I were at one of the worst points in our marriage. I can thankfully say that our worst was not really *that* bad, but we don't function well as individuals when we don't function well as a couple. Our connection to the Father had diminished because we didn't make the time to seek Him amongst our never-stopping schedule, and we were frustrated about that. Jess and I came to a place where we would apathetically conclude, *"I'll see you in Bangkok."* There was no time to deal with our relationship with everything we had on our plates at the time. It became the same with the Lord. We all have these types of times in our lives, but it seemed a bit ironic for us to be leaving for a trip led by God, yet we were pretty much forgetting to pack Him in our bags.

The weekend after New Year's had arrived and seemed to go by at a turtle's pace. Almost every night was spent with Jess' family. Our bags were mostly packed and ready to go, and our days were spent tying up loose ends and finishing more to-do lists. Every chance we would make time for the Lord, some fire would pop up that we would feel required to put out. Many fires occurred between me and Jess. We regularly argued and weren't on the same team. Our love wasn't *gooey.* Trust between us was low, because we would hurt each other's feelings often. It was good timing for the enemy to strike heavy, right? We were proof that when you're not founded on prayer, everything is penetrable.

Thursday January 2nd: One year from my meltdown, Jess and I were at our lowest.

I said to Jess after another argument, "If some of this stuff doesn't get worked out, I'm not going. I refuse to get on a plane and go into ministry when we're in this condition. I'll go get a job and we can get an apartment again and figure it all out."

I was serious, too. Sometimes the best idea, however is to simply stay away from each other, keep your mouth shut and start using that wasted time in prayer. That was the case here.

There were two paramount declarations that I had made to the Lord at the beginning of our journey that I said had to happen or I would not get on the plane, and God had not come through for us. The first was that we were to be completely debt free. I didn't care if we only had $5 in our pockets, but we were to be debt free. Roland and Heidi Baker were missionaries who left for Indonesia over 30 years ago with $30 in their pockets. George Müller was feeding and caring for 2,400 orphans by only trusting in the Lord through prayer for the financial provision. No child *ever* went hungry under his care. Either way, we had to be living in what I refer to as a "cash society." We were $1,344 short of that.

The other thing I had required of the Lord for me to get on the plane was that our car was to be sold and paid off. We owed about $8,500 on our Toyota Corolla and market value was about that through a private sale. We put our car on the market in mid-October, and it hadn't sold as of the beginning of January. I ended up going to the DMV to get a special Power of Attorney for Jessica's dad to deal with the car once we were overseas. There was no buyer in sight, especially for the amount we owed, and I wasn't going to take a $1,500 hit just to get rid of it.

It was a challenging time. 5 days to go.

Tuesday the 7th was our departure date, so the last Sunday at our church was the 5th. Pastor Vin had us get up and talk about the trip and what we were (planning on) doing. It was our way of saying good-bye. At that moment, even though I was telling everyone we were leaving, I was not planning on boarding the plane. Even though that night we were going to have a going-away party that two of our friends honored us with, I still was not going to drive to the airport. Jess and I whisper-argued before getting up to talk at church.

"You're not serious, Chris. We're going on this trip."

Whispering back with my index finger pointing towards my knee cap, "Yes I am serious! God hasn't come through for either of my declarations, and if we can't have the home-front taken care of, then I'm not going."

After service, the church lined up to pray for us. Throughout the process many gave us envelopes with cash and checks, and I pocketed them while people were praying for us. When we got in the car and counted how much was given, it amounted to $1,344! That was the exact amount we needed to go to a $0 balance on our credit card. We were debt-free, completely cashless, had gas in the tank, and we were bought lunch!

After driving for just five minutes after leaving church, we got a text from a man saying he was interested in the Corolla for his daughter. The only condition of the sale was that he had to pick it up the next day (Monday), and he would drive 1.5 hours to pick it up since we had to pay the balance off at our local bank to get the proper paperwork. He offered us $8,975. When he showed up the next morning, he barely even looked at the car. He just handed us the cash, and I walked into the bank to pay off the loan. We celebrated with a doughnut and walked away with about a $450 profit.

Between the sale of the car and the generosity of many of our friends and family at our going away party, we were headed in Bangkok with just over $2,700 in our bank accounts. Needless to say, I boarded the plane.

*   *   *   *   *

The problem was, however, that we weren't able to board the plane we thought we were going to. No international travel itinerary ever goes wrong, right? Very unfortunately for us, it was on the wrong side of the trip: the beginning.

One of my close friends, Tyler, had driven 3.5 hours from West Palm Beach to attend our going away party. He's a brother to Jess and me, both. I am so beyond thankful for him canceling his plans that Monday to stick around and be my rock. He was there for the sale of the car, my last American haircut for quite a while, and a few final errands. I remember the moment we told him how much monthly support we had "promised" to us at that time (which was $650 per month). He about pooped his pants. The cool part was that we had never asked for that support. The Lord just provided people who wanted to give it.

Tyler was there at the very moment I about pooped my own pants. It was a cold, blistery Monday afternoon in Sarasota; an odd occurrence for South Florida, even in early January. I was thankful for the cold weather because I was making countless trips to Jess' dad's van (again, the epitome of moving vans) to get the things over to Jess' parents' house that we would keep in their attic. It must have been 45 degrees! That weather, however, was the result of arctic temperatures in the northeast US.

The news was fixated on the cold, icy weather in the northeast, and we had a layover at JFK in New York City. Our flight was scheduled to leave Tuesday at 10am from Sarasota, so I decided I'd check to be sure everything was still good to go even though I hadn't received an email alert. It was cancelled.

Normally, this wouldn't be that awful of a situation, other than the inconvenience, and since we didn't have a set itinerary, it shouldn't have been a problem for us. The problem was that we booked a separate airline for our flight from Sarasota to JFK to save a ton of money. Had we missed our flight out of JFK, we would have been in big trouble. We had to be there by 10pm

Tuesday evening for our 1:00am Wednesday morning flight. What were we going to do?

Back in our cleaning days, Jess and I had something we called "bust mode." It was when we went full-throttle on a job. We didn't miss things in terms of quality, since we did the same jobs all the time and knew many of the homes better than their owners, but we could cut down the time through walking quickly, not talking and being extra-efficient. As I sat in front of the computer screen knowing what may have to happen, I took a deep breath, called Tyler into the office and closed my eyes. I was exhausted from the weeks of go-go-go, the relationship struggles between me and Jess, the lack of strength from not spending time with the Lord, the shock of having to leave the US and all the emotions that came from that. I muttered to him, "it's about to get crazy." I handed him a pen and paper and spat out things for him to do, using my best delegation skills.

I yelled out to Jess, "Hun, go put everything you have on their chargers, make a soda, and meet me in the kitchen in five."

Those five minutes were spent with me searching for flights from Tampa to JFK. $1,500 per person! That's out. Let's try a train. Sold out. Let's try a bus. Sold out. Ugh! Five minutes up.

I walked into the kitchen, and there she was waiting for me. I simply said to her, "You want something to stress about?"

She looked at me with a bit of caution. "Oh no, what?"

"Our flight is cancelled and flights to New York are $3,000."

"Chris, what are we going to do?"

After some time, it came to the only option: a $550 rental car. We were going on a road trip to the Big Apple. I calculated the time it would take to get there.

"I can do it in 18 hours, Jess, but do you have enough in you to drive the 2am-5am shift? If so, that would mean we would have to leave no later than 10:00 tonight to be on the safe side."

After a few tears of frustration and sadness out of Jess

because we were going to have to say goodbye to her family earlier, along with an additional pep-talk, Tyler, Jess, and I got into complete and utter bust mode. Looking at various options, we found it would cost about the same for Jessica's dad to drive with us to New York and return the car to Sarasota since it is always cheaper to return a rental car to where you rented it from. What a relief, because I was way too tired to pull off that kind of drive on a whim. I was planning on sleeping when I got on the plane in Sarasota. The thought of doing a nonstop road trip to Brooklyn was overwhelming.

It was bust mode galore and rat race at its finest. Phone calls. Scanning documents. Emails to our friends. Packing our last containers. Zipping up our bags. Our last good shower and shave until only God knew when. We had until 7pm to get to Jess' parents' house to say goodbye. Thankfully they lived only ten minutes down the road.

Something clicked at 6:15 when I had done everything that I could do at our place and all that was left was to shower, shave and get dressed: I finally relaxed. That's when I knew people were praying for us. I took a long shower. I took my time, in fact, and I didn't care anymore if we made it to Jess' parents' house by 7:00. "This is my time," I said to myself.

Somehow, after taking our time saying a heartfelt goodbye to Steven and Kristen, thanking them for letting us live with them, and loading the car with our backpacks, it was 6:49. Just enough time to get there at 7. A grace I would come to know so well on our trip had just displayed itself, and we hadn't even left yet.

*   *   *   *   *

I grew the closest to my father-in-law, Joe, than I ever had during the drive to New York. We had taken two long road trips together in the past, but this one was special. We talked about a lot. One of the main things we talked about was the fact that he had never seen Times Square.

Jess and I had vacationed to Manhattan a few years prior, and I know the layout of the city as well as how long it typically takes to get around. After some discussion, I told Joe, "Let's do it. Let's go to Times Square. We can take the subway line that goes there from JFK, see the square, get some New York pizza, and get back to the airport in time for the flight."

I'll be honest and say that our average speed increased a bit to make sure we'd beat rush hour traffic Tuesday afternoon. Sure enough, we pulled into the airport parking lot at 6pm. We had four hours to get back with plenty of time to check in. All I can say is thank God we *only* had four hours.

Remember that blistery winter weather that cancelled our flight? Well, little Florida-boy could barely handle New York City that evening. It was 6 degrees with 20mph gusts. It easily felt like negative temperatures, and we were going on a city tour without proper clothing. We weren't dressed for much under 15 degrees, and certainly not to be outside for long periods of time. As Joe was getting his jacket out of the trunk, I remember saying, "Jess, I really don't think I can do this."

Something about me: I get quiet when I have a hard time handling something. Complaining usually makes the situation seem worse, so I just quiet myself and work through it knowing it will all be over soon enough. This time, I spoke up to Jess and told her I couldn't do it. The normal Chris would say, "It's only a couple of hours, so suck it up, Chuck." Not this time.

Jess looked back at me and said, "I know." We just knew we had a little boy at the entrance to Disney World waiting for us to get out of the car. There was no backing out of this one.

We froze our nubs off.

There is no doubt that this memory will be frozen into the depths of my mind forever. It's frozen solid just as much as

Hans Solo was frozen in carbonite. My feet. Oh my feet. Floridians don't understand the concept of the ground being cold, because it never stays cold long enough. Genius me, I wore my destroyed Vans with holes in the tread because I was going to throw them in the trash when I got to the airport. I remember sitting at dinner, banging my feet against the floor, trying to get them to thaw.

After some pictures and a mixture of walking, stopping in a store to warm up, then walking again, it was time to head back to JFK to say goodbye. I never wanted to get onto an airplane for 17 hours more desperately. I'm not kidding when I say that I finally warmed up by the time we reached the Pacific Ocean.

We thought it would be an easy ride back to the parking lot to grab our bags out of the car, but our plans got challenged. For those of you who are used to local trains, visitors get very confused when the line that you are on all of a sudden splits off into two different tracks, yet are the same color line. Tourists can't always figure out where the end destination of a train is as quickly as it comes and the doors close. There was a 50/50 chance of going the right direction, but we guessed wrong.

After three stops, the train would turn around and go back to the station where we could switch trains to get back on the correct track, but not without a break first. We sat on the train with the doors open, the wind freezing what warmth we had left in our bodies, just waiting. We didn't know how long the train would sit there. We just waited. 5 minutes. 10 minutes. 15 minutes. Finally, the train started moving, and we made the proper switch to go to our stop.

Once we exited the platform to head back to the car, we learned our first basic lesson of traveling: write down the place that you parked your car. We had forgotten to do this since we literally ran from the car into the subway station to warm up on the front end. Now we got to pay for it on the back end with everything we had left in us.

Time was ticking, and now we were behind schedule. The first place we thought the car would be wasn't right. Then we tried another area. It wasn't there, either. Before we knew it, the three of us were running around the parking lots in negative temps with frozen feet, trying to get a beep out of our Impala which every New Yorker seemed to drive that night. I eventually yelled out without hesitation with everything I had left of my frozen lips, "God! Do you want us to go on this trip or not!?"

I ran further, and within 30 seconds, something clicked. Although the parking lot was enormous and looked the same everywhere we turned, it's as if I became a human GPS and remembered exactly where we parked. I caught up with Jess and Joe and confidently yelled, "It's over there! Go that way!" We were finally in the car after 15 minutes of running around.

Jess and I had to change into clothes we were actually going to take with us, and I almost didn't change because I was so cold. I could barely talk, and the idea of changing into a pair of ice cold pants that were a bit snug because of those few extra Christmas cookies I ate seemed like volunteering to get multiple shots. Eventually, we got ourselves situated and had just enough time to get checked in and to our gate for boarding.

A quick hug and goodbye to Joe, and we were off to our gate. We were both flustered from all the running around, but we had finally arrived to our resting place for the next 17 hours: seats 32D and 32E. I slept 15 hours. Jess slept 14 hours. No Xanax required. We were *that* tired.

See you in Bangkok.

CHAPTER FIVE

HELLO ASIA

"If we are going to believe in the Lord for the entirety of this trip, then why can't we have the faith to believe that there's going to be someone waiting for us at the airport in Bangkok on January 9th with a sign that says 'Chris & Jessica Gunn' on it?"

We had decided throughout the preparation period that we would begin to search for the line between faith and stupidity, and there would have been no better way than to jump in head first. This meant no planning whatsoever. The only compromise we made was to take snapshots of various maps of Bangkok on my iPad. There are two airports in Bangkok, and I'm pretty sure the person holding a sign with our names on it went to the other airport by accident because there was no one holding that sign at our airport. As a result, we did what any other couple in our situation would probably do and settled in at the entrance of the airport studying a tourist map in order to figure out what may be the best approach for us to begin.

There was a metro line that would drop us into town and was the cheapest way to get there. From a fairly populated inner-city station, we would begin walking until "something happened" or we found a hotel. And we did that for four hours. In our defense, I don't know what it is about Bangkok, but the way they post their street name signs is downright chaotic, and there is little to no clarity regarding what is considered a hotel. I found myself getting lost very quickly as we began to learn how Asia functions (and much of the world for that matter). If you want to buy bread, you go to the area of town where there are bakeries. If you want furniture, you go to the part of town with furniture stores. This rule applies as a general rule for many and most cities overseas. It is difficult for someone from a "survival of the fittest" culture to understand how putting fifty car maintenance shops next to each other is smart for business.

Our experience on this day would be the beginning of a deeper understanding of what we refer to as Murphy's Traveling Law: You will not be able to find the type of place you are looking for, no matter how common it is, when you want or need to. When we wanted to find a coffee shop: none. When we wanted to pick up something from a 7-Eleven: forget it. When we would look for a restaurant: hardware stores everywhere. When searching for a hotel: we found ourselves in an office park. The entire duration of our trip consisted of learning to get used to seeing great restaurants just after finishing a meal and then being unable to find a place to eat when we were hungry. This was also a by-product of not having devices that had data so we could research.

A hotel that looked okay and had a decent rate was located, so we booked five nights. One of the few things we did right despite our attempt at a crazy faith story was plan to sleep as much as possible and begin a restoration process with our bodies. We had both dramatically aged from our jobs, our stress levels were at all-time highs, and we were simply exhausted. We slept. We slept some more. We woke up, ate and went back to sleep. A twelve-hour time difference was a difficult adjustment for us, but we had quickly begun to experience the fact that it didn't matter when we slept. During the day, we experienced a freedom many books and blogs we read before leaving talked about. It looks like this:

"What do you want to do today, Jess?"

"I don't know, what about you, Chris?"

"I want to get a coffee, sit outside and read. Then I want to eat. Then I want to take a nap."

"Sounds good. I want to walk around a little bit, too."

"Cool. Whatever works."

This was the level of freedom we now had, and it felt great because we needed the rest, and we weren't going to feel guilty.

*   *   *   *   *

The one topic that those books and blogs didn't talk about was a very critical subject to us, specifically. It involved traveling the world on a 100% faith-based budget. Budgeting is the most difficult part of any faith commitment because it not only requires the belief that the money you need to accomplish whatever "the Lord has called you to do" or "what you need to do" will come, but it also requires trust that the decisions you make now will be graced down the road. Where was the line of financial grace regarding a situation such as ours?

Through the process of the year prior, we had come to the conclusion that we were going to travel the world and do ministry wherever we went, completely in faith for the finances. Additionally, we were not going to ask for money or even hint for it. Our prayers and petitions would be taken to the Lord for the needs we had, and, better than that, we were going to do what we felt the Lord had said to do, which was "not to worry; that it would all be taken care of." This was going to require an entirely new level of thinking because we only had a small monthly income from a few donors that desired to give to us.

As I discussed in the preface to this book (many of you may want to go back and actually read it), I still haven't exactly worked out the mechanical and dogmatic kinks of the setup of our trip. How do you guarantee God will come through for you? Is faith the only ingredient for something to be successful? I'm not sure there is a set way to dogmatize our methods.

The difficulty for me came when making day to day purchases. Can we buy this Snickers bar we would like to have, or should we save the money? Do we go to this restaurant that we want to eat at that costs $2 more per plate, or do we eat at that one over there that costs less? Do I book this hotel for 3 nights or 2 nights? Should we fly or take the train? Should we take a $1.50 taxi or walk the four miles? We didn't know where our next dollar would come from, so how would we know the right answer? All of these types of questions came up at some point, and we played around with our choices. Every time, however, our financial situation was taken care of at the end of the day. When a Snickers was purchased, we made out fine. When we didn't, we still made out fine. If we flew, we still paid our bills just like we would have if we chose the cheaper travel alternative. When we used local transportation, we spent more money than walking, but everything still worked out.

We could have very easily blown through our credit cards and purchased a wonderful Asian adventure, but we had committed to live in a cash society supplied only through God. If our money ran out and we had no food, shelter or random options to keep sustaining, we would pull the plug and go home. It was very simple.

I think at the end of the day, there are a few practical answers regarding how to handle a financial setup similar to ours. First, it was clearly because we were faithful with little. We often gave a quarter of our income away, even at times when we felt that 10% of our income was a major chunk of what was left in our bank account. We trusted, to the best of our abilities, that God understood our situation, and He would rescue us if we cried for help. If He's the one who called us out, then we believed He was responsible to follow through.

The second and more obvious answer, in my opinion, was prayer (I will elaborate more on this in chapter 13). Prayer is the only real physical activity you can do when you have committed to not fundraising, casually asking for money, or taking temporary or online jobs, and trusting that the Lord would provide every cent from beginning to end. Even prayer is difficult, however, because you have to constantly check your heart to make sure you're not having a "works mentality." I had to ask the question often: "Am I praying for a paycheck, or am I praying because my friend, who happens to be the God of the entire universe, wants to know 'what's up'?" After all, He created me. God wants us to rely on Him, but he doesn't want us to come to Him out of obligation. How many parents out there want their child to hang out with them because they feel like they have to?

The key was also to not beg for money. We firmly believe in having a heavenly view and not a view from our circumstances. Sure, it's easy to talk about the current needs, but we were more concerned that the proper people and resources would cross our path, and as a result, the financial end would be taken care of.

It's hard to believe what we tell ourselves is truth based on biblical standards. *"God is my rock."* Is he, really? *"I can do all things through Christ who strengthens me."* Really? You believe that you can do all things? Didn't you just complain about your neighbor's dog; how it has barked all night, every night, for six months, and you're too afraid to confront your neighbor?

Our goal with sharing our story is to encourage you to get out of your boat and get wet, *not* to quit your job and travel the world. Even today, I wouldn't dare wish you to go through some of the personal challenges that we did. Sure, elements of our experience were awesome, but I can't endorse this style of living on a black-and-white level or develop a step-by-step approach to it. Therefore, I say: "if it hasn't been made clear by the hand of God that it is for you, then by all means, don't even consider following our footsteps." What I do want to make clear, however, is that although you may not be able to dogmatically or biblically explain the journey that the Lord may have you on, it doesn't mean you should write off the possibility of living it out because you don't have everything worked out.

I can't tell you how many times we had to alter our story in a way so other people could grasp why we didn't have a "church covering." Sure, we have a church, and they supported us, but I wasn't about to trust my pastor's judgment all the way back in Florida about what our next step should have been in Thailand. He'd be living the life that Jess and I were supposed to be living, and although we trust Pastor Vin's judgment dearly, he's not our Holy Spirit. There are many times, even with general life circumstances, when we take our problems to our leadership and not to God. We'd often rather get a free counseling session (or the answer) from the person we can see in front of us rather than abide in Jesus. "But...there's also having wisdom," people would often suggest. Where does true wisdom come from in the first place?

If I may interject a final approach to living on a faith budget: with every decision that needs to be made, whether it's a decision to buy bananas or buy bananas *and* apples, or where to book the next flight to, you have to simply ask God what He thinks. Yes, we have the free will to make the decision, but by including God in process, we invite Him to interact and co-labor with us in the fashion He originally designed us.

There is a practicality to living a spirit-led life like Paul talks about. If Jess and I accomplish anything, other than encouraging you to step out of your boat with this book, it's to bring balance to the concept of "being spirit-led." There is a "spiritual backing" that is provided when we are trusted by the Lord, and by simply including Him in the everyday decisions we make, we create space for Him to move. The moment we don't need Him anymore, we have varied from the straight and narrow path.

So many churches focus on the relational aspect of God but often run from the Holy Spirit while proclaiming belief in the Holy Trinity! We don't need to run, but rather, embrace God's fullness through simply including Him in our lives and allowing ourselves to be included in His. Being spirit-led on a relational level allows God to interact with you to the point that *you know* deep down in your heart on an experiential level that He wants you to enjoy both bananas and apples. A simple question of "should I buy the apples as well" often produces the response from the Lord: "do you not trust in my ability to provide for the apples I want you to have?" The discussion shifts from a position of questioning the purchase to developing the way you think of Him as a father and yourself as a son.

We definitely felt we were often walking on egg shells with our finances and didn't want to screw them up, but at the same time, we knew we would fall into God's grace. It is a daily walk that requires you to evaluate each decision you make, and if you struggle internally with the balance between the power of your free will and the predestined plan for your life like I do, this is where the biggest challenge comes when trusting fully in the Lord. Let's face it: without the funds, the trip wasn't going to move forward. We truly had to learn to let the tomorrows worry about themselves.

*　　　*　　　*　　　*　　　*

I remember the experience I would always have on the first day of school. I was usually tired because I couldn't go to sleep the night before from of all the excitement of starting a new season of life. The uniform I wore still smelled like the factory. All of my pencils and pens were in abundance and organized. There was also an excitement for learning about new subjects. This was how we felt during our first week in Bangkok.

Our backpacks were clean, our clothes were new, our toiletries were all at maximum capacity, we were in an unknown environment where only strangers surrounded us, and there was an abundance of cash at the time. The weather was warm, the food was outstanding, and we were ready to experience what we had spent over a year preparing for. If it wasn't the freedom of time or the reasonable financial freedom at the time, it was definitely the moment when we were riding down the river in a longboat and touring famous wats (temples) on a weekday afternoon when we acknowledged the reality of what we had just done. Many people save for years to fly to Asia to marvel at the large reclining Buddha in Wat Pho, the huge and iconic Wat Arun and the marble of Wat Benjamabhopit, and just like that, it was at our fingertips.

What goes up must come down, though, right? I had remembered very quickly one of the repercussions of a long summer vacation: the lack of structure. When structure lacks but freedom reigns, chaos often occurs in the household. Sometimes a healthy "chaos" released in church brings revelation but also highlights areas needing a tighter configuration, and this was valid for our personal lives. We had time to read, study, learn and develop. There was time to enjoy and be free for a change, but it allowed for introspection and the ability to evaluate our lives.

Jess realized very quickly that she had a problem letting others down. This meant that she would commit to things that she probably could have avoided by learning to say "no." It also meant that there were micro stressors in many areas of her life that were completely unnecessary for her to experience on a day to day basis. I realized that I had an inability to relax. I come from a family of workaholics who don't know how to rest or understand the necessity to do so, and I had to begin learning to rest, guilt-free. This is a mentality that Americans are increasingly struggling with, and one that round-the-world trips like ours naturally break. Uneasiness settled in our hotel room as I consistently felt I had a multitude of projects to complete, but there was nothing to be done. The last order for my internet company that we decided to close, so we could be in full faith for our finances, had been completed.

Instead, our world was about experiencing Bangkok. The food is outstanding and extremely cheap. I could get a huge plate of pad Thai for about $1.50 along with some of the sweetest mangoes, papaya, watermelon and pineapple you can eat. Jess and I were also looking forward to a famous Thai massage. An hour massage ran us $6 after tip. The Thai people themselves make the trip worth it alone. They are friendly, caring and genuine. Every person we met had a sincere interest, in us getting the best experience out of their country.

The great food, relaxing massages and friendly people of Bangkok helped us refocus on our marriage that was lacking trust. Although I love Jessica very much, I had to fall in love with her again, and her with me. As much as I was in love with her at the time, it was still weeks into the trip until our trust in each other was restored, and we had a generally "great" marriage of only three years. I can't imagine having been in a marriage 13 or 23 or 33 years where a lack of trust had settled in years prior. We must recognize that rest allows us to turn *on* our brains and open our hearts, not shut them off. Rest allows us to deal with ourselves and calm our souls so we can listen to God. As a result, we can deal with each other and the challenges that come with everyday living by staying calm and listening to what the Father in Heaven has to say about how to address these issues.

Gender roles we had developed such as "she's the cook" and "he brings in the money" had to be adjusted as well. Traditional household duties became irrelevant, even if we prefer to live by them. We could only rely on what each other brought to the table and God. Nobody else could relate to what we were going through. I knew how Jess felt when home sickness was overwhelming, and she understood when I felt helpless.

*　　　*　　　*　　　*　　　*

As exhausting as it was, our 4-hour trek around Bangkok the day we had arrived was well worth it. We approached a canal with a bridge full of traffic. Posted all around the walls of this particular bridge were many signs saying *Shut Down Bangkok*. It had a Monday January 13th date on it.

Jess and I weren't exactly sure what that meant regarding the stability of the city, so we asked around to find out local opinions. Our hotel management suggested that we stay in our room for the day, that it "could get pretty ugly," so that's what we prepared for as a result. Sunday night, we ate a large meal and picked up some food to eat in the hotel room the next day.

I walked outside our hotel door Monday morning to evaluate the situation. It was a beautiful, clear, blue-sky day. Cars were driving normally, people were walking as if nothing was going on, and life was, well, completely normal. Perhaps it had been a complete fail? Either way, Jess and I decided to go across the street to a Starbucks to have a quiet time and enjoy the weather, rather than being cooped up in the hotel room all day.

Then it happened: about 30 minutes into our coffee, waves of noise began to echo from the distance. A crowd of motorbikes swarmed down the street followed by trucks carrying hundreds of people cramped in the truck beds. Whistles were being blown and people shouting political agendas through the use of megaphones. My first reaction? Grab our stuff, throw it in the bag, and move inside Starbucks. Jess' first reaction? Grab the camera, run to the edge of the street, and take pictures. Why? Because it looked like a parade. I love my wife.

This *Shut Down Bangkok* movement was a parade of people wearing red, white and blue, waving Thai flags and blowing whistles. It was nothing more than a typical, patriotic 4th of July celebration. As everyone passed us, they were excited to get a wave from the white people. *Stay in your hotel room? Really?*

There was certainly a display of anger towards the government through riots, bombings, and killings for months after, but they were limited to a specific area of town. We were completely safe as long as we stayed away from government buildings. This would not be our last taste of *Shut Down Bangkok*, but it was definitely not at the level that the media portrayed it as throughout the planet.

*   *   *   *   *

Bussing your way through Asia is often the cheapest means of transportation, and it rewards you with being able to see more of the country. Flying, although advantaged with speedy travel, doesn't give you the full experience of a country. Even trains can miss a lot of "more experiential" areas as the tracks are often off the beaten path.

That cheap price is covered in other ways. Depending on the country, it could be whether or not you actually have a seat to sin on. Many times it is paid in overall comfort. Most of the time you just pay the difference in the amount of time spent on the bus. Every bus, on the other hand, has its own experience that makes it a memorable trip.

Our first bus trip was nerve-racking, because we had no idea what we were doing. I didn't know how far down we could haggle the ticket, or rather, if we could haggle it at all. I was offered a first class ticket from Bangkok to Phuket for $10 a ticket. Frankly, it didn't bother me, so I paid the fare. After all, it was a twelve hour, overnight bus.

Upon boarding, we just went to the seats we wanted, but the bus driver kept signing for us to go to the top floor and to the front VIP section (hence that first class ticket part). We loved the view even though it clicked that we had been slightly taken advantage of due to looking like tourists. We could have paid much less if we had bought a regular seat. Boy, I wish we had.

The bus was arctic, and all of the air was being blasted from the front of the bus to reach the rear. We had read about some bus rides in Asia being freezing cold, and our first experience was only confirmation. Thankfully they provided a blanket, but it only covered half of our bodies. I had a light sweater covering the top half of me and the blanket wrapped around me like a dress. It was a long twelve hours of shivering!

Across the aisle from us was a middle-aged monk. This was our first long-term experience with a monk, so as foreigners, we were interested to see "the difference" that this man brought to civilization. I'm not sure how he did it, but he sat cross-legged (aka Indian-style) for almost the entire length of the trip. If I sit that way for ten minutes, my back burns like fire, so I can only imagine his level of flexibility! Despite his ability to keep his mind aligned over his body, the monk was definitely freezing as well. When I looked over in the middle of the night, I saw his blanket over his head! It was quite entertaining to see the empty seat next to him get filled a few hours later. The person who boarded the bus looked at us with a confused laugh as we smiled back at him.

I don't know what it is about bus rides, but it seemed that every overnight bus ride ended with us getting dropped off at 5am somewhere. Everything's still closed; the weather still slightly chilly or damp, and we are nowhere near where we need to go. Once we got dropped off at a bus station in Phuket, we picked up a taxi to go to our next place of lodging: a middle school. It would be in its boarding house that I had to learn a frustrating lesson: I can't save the world.

CHAPTER SIX

HERE'S YER SIGN

"Then Jesus came to them and said, 'All authority in heaven and on earth has been given to me. Therefore, go and make disciples of all nations, baptizing them in the name of the Father and of the Son and of the Holy Spirit and teaching them to obey everything I have commanded you. And surely I am with you always, to the very end of the age'." (Matthew 28:18-20 NIV)

There are two gospels being taught in modern Christian churches today, and I can quickly categorize a church by listening to a pastor talk for just a few minutes. The concept of the American dream has lowered the standard of the responsibility of the modern Christian so much that Christianity has been devalued from being a practical, applicable and necessary lifestyle to being a categorical way of describing what one's moral standard is founded upon and developed.

The modern church often portrays this: "Jesus died for your sins. He paid the price on the cross so that we can be forgiven and go to Heaven. Confess your sins and sinful nature, and accept Jesus into your heart. Then, you will be saved [the end]." Even many "spirit-filled churches" teach this simple concept as the full gospel even though they believe in the Holy Spirit. Although what is written above is true, *it is incomplete*. When I hear this gospel preached, I usually roll my eyes in frustration. The idea that praying a simple unbiblical prayer enters someone into Heaven when they die has been spread across the globe, and it's not accurate. In actuality, professing the belief in Christ's resurrection should be a reflection of a person's heart[1] starting to understand that in Christ, we become a new creation.[2]

Christians who have a more mature understanding[3] of the purpose of Christ not only understand that He was the ultimate sacrifice for all, so that the sins of the world would be forgiven, but they also believe that through the power of His resurrection and release of the Holy Spirit on Pentecost, we now carry the same power and authority that He did while He was on the earth.[4] It is incredibly difficult for us in our humanity to grasp this concept, and we often filter truths that are reflected in the Word of God through natural worldviews rather than understanding them through a supernatural lens.

It is through the acceptance of Christ's death *and resurrection*,[5] our baptism into a new system, and the repentance and forgiveness of our sins that we are regenerated[6] so we can live in Christ and Christ in us.[7] Everything of ours (our body, soul and spirit) now has the ability to work in tandem with what the Lord is doing and wants to do in the earth. Our spirit is meant to be the overbearing portion of our existence, and it is our job for our body (the way we think and use it) and our soul (who we are, our emotions and feelings) to reflect the new creation that we are.[8,9] Our spirit not only allows us to function out of the freedom given to us through the forgiveness of all our sin (past, present and future), but it allows us to move in the same authority and diplomatic immunity in the earth that Jesus does because we are now a renewed product of God (a new creation).

When we accept Christ into our hearts, we accept the responsibility to put aside our own desires and beliefs in the physical, and as we go throughout the world, we are to make disciples as if we are Jesus himself.[10] We are to show them and tell them that the Kingdom of Heaven is accessible today, here and now. We can enter it freely and know the heart of God just as Revelation 3:20 suggests. We are to heal the sick, raise the dead, cleanse those who have leprosy and drive out demons, but we do this as we say what the Father is saying and do what the Father is doing.[11] Freely we have received Christ; freely we should share Him,[12] and we can do this outside of the confines of the natural world.

By accepting a gospel that only requires you to accept Christ, your job is done as you've checked off the box "guaranteeing" your ticket to Heaven upon death. Unfortunately, being a "follower of Jesus" isn't about following a belief system or even getting to Heaven.[13] There are plenty of religions and spiritual leaders that claim to know the right way to live, and they all require some sort of higher standard of morality. Christ, however, promises everlasting and abundant life (now)[14] because we have *already died with Him*![15] If we really begin as individuals to understand and believe what Jesus accomplished through His resurrection, I'd imagine we would be focusing more on what it means to live under the law of life in Christ Jesus and completely disregard the law of sin *and death*.[16]

*　　　　*　　　　*　　　　*　　　　*

Jess and I have always seen ourselves advancing in the area of signs and wonders. We see signs and wonders on a very regular basis, and our level of belief for them is different than for someone who has never experienced them. When people suggest "we're just not living in a time where miracles occur anymore," it is only because they have not been educated by those who see signs regularly. Due to common belief, churches pray the superficial, "God, take this sickness away" or "God comfort this person through this situation," when Jesus has given us the authority to take care of the situations ourselves.[17] God is our commander, not our controller. He doesn't control my next step; I have a choice to what that will be. Proverbs 16:9 (ESV) says it best. "The heart of a man plans his way, but the Lord establishes his steps."

God is not in control. I can't go a week without hearing someone say, "Well, you know, God's got it. He's in control."

We say He is without understanding the true identity of who He is. If He were in control, then I can promise you that there would have never been the need for a Messiah, everyone with sickness could simply ask God for healing and get it instantly on the spot from Him, and He would intervene in every situation that could be disastrous to humanity. If God is in control, and your problem isn't solved by Him, then what are the chances that you are going to blame Him for your problems or believe you deserve your problems because you did something bad?

God has control over eternity (He is eternity), but he is not micromanaging it. If He were meddling through all of humanity's issues, there would be no requirement for anything on our part as a follower of Christ. God is ruler over all the earth and all authority over the earth has been given to Jesus who lives inside of us. Therefore, *we* must go and make disciples.[18] If God is in control, then Jesus is wrong in telling us how to live our lives, because we could in fact do nothing but pray "God, save that person. You are in control." There is no scripture in the Bible that says He is. The scriptures only infer to the greatness of His power. The fact that this cliché resolve to life's challenges has made it so deep into the dialect of the church is astounding.

*   *   *   *   *

My first experience with signs and wonders took place February 19, 1999 at home as an 11-year-old boy. Dad, my brother Trey and I were in the living room watching TGIF when mom *walked* into the house. Most Friday evenings, this would have been a normal occurrence, except that the Friday before, my mom had slipped and shattered her kneecap so badly that it looked like a spider web on her x-ray films. It was going to inhibit her ability to use her knee for a couple of months. The x-ray negatives from Monday February 22, 1999 show a perfect, pearly-white kneecap as opposed to the shattered kneecap in the Friday February 12, 1999 x-rays.

"Jesus healed me at the church service I went to tonight. I was sitting there, and they laid hands on me. Then I felt heat go up from my foot, all the way through my body, up to my head, down through my other leg, and then back and forth. All I could think about doing at that point was running around, but they wouldn't let me. They wanted me to take it slowly."

As she was in the living room testing her leg out, twisting it and bending it, she continued to testify about her experience.

"I've never felt anything like that in my life! God healed me! God healed me!"

I know that the three of us were probably not the most exciting audience to tell her story. After all, we were Catholic, and a new episode of *Boy Meets World* was on. Even though I can't really remember how I responded to her, there is no doubt that was the demarcation point for a lot of changes in our household, and a seed to see more signs and wonders was planted inside of me.

*　　　　*　　　　*　　　　*　　　　*

While in Phuket, Thailand, I had an urgency to perform signs and wonders. My level of faith, however, was specifically limited to certain cases. For me, the situation had to be perfect, or else I wouldn't go for it. It had to be an ailment that prohibited movement, but the person could only be wearing a removable cast. I wanted to see clear proof of a healing from the lack of pain and the ability to move in a way the person was incapable of prior to prayer. With a hard cast, it prohibits evidence of a healing, because we can't remove it. I wanted that person to undoubtedly leave the situation as walking, talking proof of the existence of Christ being alive today.

I talked about the subject of healing fairly extensively in Phuket with the couple that we were staying with. There were some clear disagreements on the issue, and no matter who argues about signs and wonders, without the power of the Holy Spirit intervening in a situation, the skeptic will always settle for their ways.

There was something that was said to me that week that stuck and shouldn't have: "It shouldn't be all about signs and wonders." I don't know why this got to me so much, but for whatever reason, that comment was a direct hit on my desire to see more signs and wonders while overseas.

"I've seen how signs and wonders have become the focus of many ministries," I convinced myself. "The focus should be on people meeting Jesus, not always on healing." Although there is truth to this statement, one of the ways to which you can show the Kingdom of God and introduce people to it is through the manifestation of signs and wonders. Rolland and Heidi Baker of Iris Ministries use this approach very often, and I believe they do it well.

Rolland and Heidi have committed their lives to the country of Mozambique and experience signs and wonders everywhere they go. They walk so powerfully, and they believe that they achieve it through their committed level of intimacy with the Lord and by simply "stopping for the one." Whenever they go to preach in an unreached village, which is usually either a completely Muslim village or a village with various tribal religions, they take the same approach, and it works every time:

First, they call out the deaf. They tell everyone to go get the deaf in the village. This is a smart tactic because they probably wouldn't have heard about the event taking place. After sharing the gospel, they show the power of the Holy Spirit as proof that what they are saying is true by healing the deaf. Usually this will cause an uproar of people believing in Christ because everyone knows Deaf Doug and Deaf Diane. Many of them were deaf from birth, and the village has the proof of time for that. Then they call out the blind. When the blind get healed, more people come to Jesus because when Blind Ben, who has spent the last 10 years on his mat, completely useless and probably a burden to the other locals, can see, it is really clear that Rolland and Heidi are telling the truth. Then other ailments are healed, of course, along with those who are hurting, possessed with demons or looking for comfort. There is no doubt why many mosques have been given to Iris Ministries to be used as churches and why it is no surprise that as of writing this, Iris Ministries runs over 7,000 churches in Mozambique!

*   *   *   *   *

Although there was quite a bit of insecurity within me to pray for signs and wonders during ministry with the couple we were staying with, I told Jess I would push through and pray for people to be healed even though it may have made things uncomfortable. The moment of truth came for me at Bangla Road in downtown Phuket.

Bangla Road is one of the largest red light districts in the world. It is the second largest district in Thailand, and it is a place I never knew even existed until visiting. There are few bar districts that are as large, yet this area is dedicated entirely for prostitution. Every waitress is a prostitute. Most of them likely lived in a village outside of the city and were either tricked into prostitution or told it was the highest paying job they could do. One of the sad parts is that they send most of their money to their families still living in their home villages.

The surrounding area is similar to the size of an IKEA store. There is a lot of ground to cover, and there are a lot of different bars and strip clubs. Many bars are sectioned off in alleys with horseshoe-shaped bar tops on either side of the alley that continue for many blocks. Each horseshoe represents one bar, and all have "creative" names. They also have a madam overseeing the girls to make sure they are pulling their weight. A lot of times, the madams are family members such as an aunt.

Once the four of us had scouted the majority of the area, we prayed for the Lord to send us to the right bar. It was very overwhelming, and the thought that there is such a market with a steady demand should make the world tremble. Continuing down one of the alleyways, we found a bar to stop at so we could buy some drinks. That would buy the girls' time to talk. As we settled in, we began to read the names of each of the surrounding bars. When we looked above at ours, it was named "Freedom Bar." It had a picture of the earth with two doves on either side of it. We knew we were in the right place. After talking with one of the girls for a while, we asked her if she wanted a different job or if she liked hers and she said, "Nothing pays better."

The idea of a career change was discussed with her, and she essentially said "no" to the idea. According to her, she likes the attention she receives regularly more than the poverty she experienced back home. We encouraged her that there is a better way, a more "free way" to live, and if she wanted out, to connect. We discussed Jesus, prayed for her and moved on.

Jess and the wife of the couple we were with wanted to go a little deeper into the district to some of the more risqué alleys, so the husband and I stayed out on the main road. We walked around for a little while, and then I saw a someone standing out in the multitudes of people passing by. It was a younger guy on crutches without a cast! I wanted him to get healed.

Then that awkward moment came when I had to decide to leave to go to an unknown location to lay hands on some guy.

The girls simultaneously came around the corner in the distance, so by the time I had hesitated, he was gone.

I told Jessica what I had seen, and I was intently on the lookout for the same guy. We walked further down the road and parked ourselves on the side of the street where I could keep watch like a lion waiting for the right moment to attack its prey. That's when we saw a young white girl holding a sign while wearing a festive, European dress. The large sign she held said "European Girls" with an arrow pointing into a club.

Phuket, surprisingly, is 80% Russian. To see European girls for sale shouldn't have been a surprise to us. When you begin to understand the system and recognize that *all* of the girls in that building were kidnapped, raped repeatedly throughout the day, drugged up and tied up like dogs for the enjoyment and greed of men, it was a bit mind-blowing to see the result in person. The truth was displayed through the facial expression of this beautiful girl who was probably not even twenty years of age. Her eyes were hollow, and her grin was faked. I got angry as men and women walked into these clubs together!

While standing there looking over this area of the world that makes Vegas seem pure and unblemished, I saw a very tall man swinging his way down the street on crutches. I made a signal at Jess to find me down the street and pointed to the guy. I wasn't going to hesitate this time, so I simply chased him.

When I caught up, I asked him and his girlfriend if they spoke English. The man was very tall, thin and bald; definitely Russian and definitely drunk. He responded "a little bit," which I have found to be plenty for Europeans to communicate well since they have high expectations to learn secondary languages. I explained to him that I may be able to drastically speed up the healing of his leg and asked him what was wrong with it. He showed me that he had pins placed into his leg in 6 different spots. With that said, I asked him his pain level from 1 to 10.

"What are you? A doctor?" He asked while laughing at me.

"No, but I know someone who can help you." I responded.

Vlad couldn't get past the fact that I thought that I could fix his leg. We all know the truth is I couldn't, but only the Holy Spirit working through me could. He thought I was crazy.

"Whatever. Try your magic," he responded in his thick, Russian accent.

After explaining to him why I believed that his leg could be healed, I prayed. He was having a hard enough time standing with all the alcohol in his system, and he couldn't really feel because he was so drunk. It was difficult for him to gage his pain level unless the Lord took away his drunkenness as well.

I was impressed that he had enough faith to try to walk after praying for him. He trusted me, and I was thankful for that, but he just couldn't get past why I had stopped for him. Finally, I told him, "I just stopped because I care. I couldn't let you pass knowing that I may have the solution to you walking perfectly fine." Vlad melted. It clicked for him.

After a few rounds of prayer, a lot of laughter pointed in our direction, a police officer getting involved wondering why the guy in crutches was on the ground and a large amount of skepticism from Vlad and his girlfriend, I decided to walk away from the situation with a handshake and a declaration.

"Vlad, how long are you going to be walking like this?"

"6 months."

"Wow, 6 months? That's a long time!"

"Yes. But it will get better."

"I'm sure. Let's make it 3 months. Would that be better?"

Laughing hysterically, "This man is crazy!"

"Three months, Vlad!" I laid hands on him one more time.

"Vlad, I pray in the name of Jesus that you will be completely healed and off of crutches in three months, and if you are, you have to thank Jesus."

"Three months? Doctor said six."

Laughs continued as we said goodbye to each other. Looking back, I should have said an even shorter time frame.

I'll be honest in saying that it's very intimidating to be in the spotlight in front of thousands of people like that. I wasn't there to put on a freak show. I just wanted Jesus to touch him. It was probably the first time in my life, however, that I truly didn't care about what anyone else thought about me. Frankly, at the end of the day, all I felt was compassion for Vlad, and I still think about him, often wondering whatever happened to him.

The four of us went back to our hotel room for the night to debrief about what we saw and experienced. We talked for over an hour about the sadness that overcame us, especially when we saw the European girls. We prayed for solutions, for those working underground in that area to shut down the brothels and stop illegal trafficking, for the girls to experience the Lord even in the midst of the horrors they live, for those who are already committed to helping to stay committed and for those who were planning to commit to the area to be fully covered and blessed.

Then we talked about the situation with Vlad. Although he didn't get his healing, which I really, really wanted him to get, it didn't seem to bother me at that very moment. I was just happy he felt cared for. At the end of the day, however, the discussions we had about signs and wonders still troubled me. Something died in me that night, and Vlad was the last person I prayed for healing for by simply walking up to someone for nearly two months.

*　　　*　　　*　　　*　　　*

Have you ever had a great idea? An invention or business idea that would surely work? Maybe you sat down, created a business plan, had a solid SWOT analysis, made a conservative, realistic budget and sincerely looked at the pros and cons of moving forward with that idea. Then you discussed it with someone whose opinion you highly value, and their response to your idea was negative and disapproving? This is how most dreams die, and people miss out on the greatest opportunities of their lives.

There is a powerful meme that occasionally floats around the internet that displays interesting tidbits about "famous failures." For example, Michael Jordan went home after being cut from his high school basketball team, locked the door and cried. The Beatles was rejected by Decca Recording studios because "[they didn't] like their sound, [and] they [had] no future in show business." Steve Jobs was 30 years old when he was left devastated and depressed after being removed from Apple Computer, the company he started. Walt Disney was fired from working for a newspaper for "lacking imagination" and "having no original ideas."

Oprah Winfrey was demoted from her job as a news anchor because she "wasn't fit for television." Albert Einstein wasn't able to speak until he was almost 4 years old, and his teachers said he would "never amount to much." KFC's Colonel Sanders couldn't sell his chicken recipe. It was rejected over 1,000 times. Heidi Baker laid hands on every blind person she could find and didn't see one blind person healed for years. The Apostle Paul wrote the majority of the letters of the New Testament in prison after taking multiple beatings!

Thomas Edison said to those who asked him about his failures to invent the light bulb, "I didn't fail 1,000 times. The light bulb was an invention with 1,000 steps. Great success is built on failure, frustration, even catastrophe."

I wish I could write the next chapter of this book saying that I didn't stop praying for people because I wasn't going to base my success level on the result of my prayers, but I did. Somewhere through the experience with Vlad and the fact that we traveled overseas with a sub-goal to minister specifically through signs and wonders, I had thrown out the countless words declared over my life that said I would be gifted for signs and wonders. I threw it all out, and I gave up after one shot.

Take it from us; the fear of failure only prevents you from moving forward. We've experienced it firsthand! There are plenty of people who have gone with the flow of the traffic, swam with the same group of fish and stuck to tradition. Why should you and I be another statistic? Why not try the other way; the way that all the people who win at life go?

*   *   *   *   *

If there's anything that the enemy should have done from the beginning of our trip, it would have been to shut us down. You can be a Christian all that you want, but that does not affect the thoughts that guide your decision-making process. It is when you decide to act and speak out of a heavenly perspective that things get shaken up. Satan's goal is to create stagnancy in all areas of your life. It's emotions like guilt, shame and sadness that fuel this stagnancy. When we are focused on our circumstances and how awful they are, we inhibit progressive movement towards our destiny and the creation of change on this earth, but when we speak and pray from a heavenly perspective, we declare things as they are supposed to be, even though they don't look or feel that way.

Satan's desire is ultimately to take your eyes off of the Kingdom and put them on the earth. He wants us to develop an intent focus on it, a desire for all it brings and the desire to fit everything within the confines of the limitations this earth has (physics, science, humanism, dogma and the elimination of the spirit). By accomplishing this, *nothing* fruitful and eternal will be produced. If Satan accomplishes his goal in your life, you will certainly be facing the response Jesus rightfully gives of, "I never knew you. Away from me evildoer!"

Look at some people and businesses we know made a difference with next to nothing: Google was started in a garage. St. Theresa started out with a small school in the slums of India. Ford Motor Company was started with a $28,000 loan after two failed companies and Henry Ford filed for bankruptcy. Kevin Plank, founder of Under Armour went into $60,000 of debt to get his product off the ground. Jess and I were $1,344 in debt with a $380 car and insurance payment the day before we left the United States.

There is no reason why you should end up in a position in your life that is stagnant. If you are committed to looking at every portion of your life and heart, by dedicating yourself to heavenly-minded prayer and asking God to do the impossible in your life, stagnancy will be avoided. Jesus said in John 15:5b "...without me you can do nothing." Nothing sounds a whole lot like stagnancy! Go back to your last word, pray hard and wait patiently. If you don't have a word, get under the shadow of the Almighty and ask and believe for one. Deal with the things that you can address and eliminate in your life and heart, and make a plan with the Lord to do something great. After all, Jesus says that we will do even greater works than in his lifetime![4]

Vlad unfortunately marked the end of an attempt to be world changers and the beginning of being world travelers who do "comfortable ministry" for the Lord. As long as we sent some good news home on occasion that God was moving in our lives, we could sleep at night. The truth was we were both sincerely scared to take a risk that required a large amount of faith.

*   *   *   *   *

Perhaps I should give us a little more credit. A lot of lives were touched in Thailand. We impacted people in all types of situations from those being sick in the slums, being a prostitute, simply lying on the side of the road, being tired and homesick missionaries, even for those simply needing strength. Our job of praying for people and connecting with those around us was enjoyable as long as we weren't walking up to a stranger hoping to see a healing. Ministry had to be set up, or we wouldn't move.

Our time in Phuket came to an end, and we had booked a flight to Chiang Mai, Thailand. We were told by multiple people to visit there and that there are great ministries in place. Peace followed the decision to go, so we booked a flight. We had the money at the time to fly, and the idea of a 24-hour bus ride versus a cheap, three-hour flight didn't seem appealing.

Chiang Mai was refreshing. When we landed, we couldn't help but simply feel like we were in the right place. The sun was shining, the flowers had just bloomed, the weather was comfortable, but most of all, internal peace reigned, and that was a nice feeling. It's always a good feeling to know you're right where you need to be at that moment.

A nap followed check-in to our hotel and after some research, we decided to connect with the local Youth With A Mission (YWAM) base the next day. YWAM is an organization of Christians from many cultures, ages and denominations from all around the world dedicated to serving Jesus through missions. They currently have more than 1,000 locations in over 180 countries. Each YWAM base throughout the planet serves a different need specifically catered to the city it is located, but the goal is the same: to share the love and knowledge of Christ to everyone. YWAM bases are a great place to begin ministry work in a city, because they typically have a finger on the pulse of the area they are in. Although we have never been through one of their Discipleship Training Schools, we are certainly YWAMers at heart and are connected to the worldwide family it has developed into.

The YWAM base in Chiang Mai focuses specifically on the local red light districts and slums. Jess wanted to get more experience doing ministry in the red light districts of Thailand, so Chiang Mai was a great starting point as there was an area of the city with a half-mile stretch of bars.

We were offered a room at the base's guest house for $9 a night, so we didn't hesitate to jump on that. When we were introduced around, we met Sarah from Austin, Texas. She and Jess instantly clicked while she walked us to the guesthouse where we would be staying.

Sarah is an incredible individual and quite fearless. Fairly tall with blonde hair, she definitely sticks out among any foreign culture, yet she was traveling on a journey with the Lord completely alone. Sarah is a people-person, and she didn't hesitate to meet anyone around her. Most people would try to tame her social skills to prevent her from being raped or kidnapped, but it's the attitude that she has about life that opens up the door for amazing relationships to be created and abnormal opportunities to be experienced. She is the epitome of someone who has absolutely no fear of man.

As she showed us the guesthouse, we met a few Americans in their early 20s. This was no surprise for any YWAM base as there are a lot of college-aged students and many from the United States who work through their programs. Hours of conversation along with multiple cups of coffee followed as we got to know each other. Later on, a large group of young Germans and Americans arrived at the guest house, and we also connected with them. It turned out after talking about each other's lives, we all had a mutual connection: Sarasota, Florida.

CHAPTER SEVEN

A PREMATURE RETIREMENT

The Sun Coast of Florida has some of the most beautiful beaches in the United States and is a top destination for many tourists. It has a diverse blend of history and Hispanic culture along with an emphasis on the arts. Sarasota is known for the famous Ringling Museum and for being home to John Ringling's Ringling Brothers Circus which became one of the United States' dominating circuses before shutting down in 2017. St. Petersburg, Florida holds a Guinness World Record for the most consecutive sunny days ever recorded: 768! Siesta Key Beach was rated the best beach in America in 2011 and #2 in 2016 by Dr. Beach and has won multiple "best sand" awards for the white baby powder feel that lines the side of the clear turquoise waters of the Gulf of Mexico.

Just short of a million people visit Sarasota annually, but the only ones who actually stay are those who retire to the south for the winter. Few move to the area to establish a ministry. Yet, this is what a group of Germans decided to do.

The story that has floated around was that someone at the YWAM base in Herrnhut, Germany had a dream about Florida and felt like they were to establish a base with an emphasis on arts and media. A few individuals then flew to Florida, got a rental car and drove around to each city praying about where they felt the Lord was telling them to plant their base. They returned to the Sarasota area multiple times and began to establish a base in the fall of 2013.

One of the first logistical issues that any YWAM base needs to deal with is where to house all of the students. Many of the facilities they choose require some form of renovation in order to comply with fire codes, make the best use of space and most importantly to keep costs down in the long term. A close friend of ours, Nathalie was able to provide this through her home. By renting out her home to YWAM, she and her son were able to move to a smaller home and earn a rental income. It was a win-win for everyone.

The night before we left the United States, we had an amazing going away party at Nathalie's house hosted along with Jess' maid of honor from our wedding, Leslie. Not only did it have a fantastic variety of foods, but the atmosphere was fun, travel-themed and, best of all, nearly all of our friends were there. It was just what we needed to affirm the feeling inside that the beginning of our journey had arrived. The day after the party, Nathalie didn't just take down the party decorations and clean; she began moving out to make room for the YWAM team from Herrnhut to move in and begin ministry in Sarasota.

As we discussed further with our new German and American friends at the Chiang Mai base in Thailand and had established that we were from Sarasota, a lot of excitement came over them.

"We have many friends there! We're based out of Herrnhut," they explained to us.

It was a really confusing setup for non-YWAMers like us. Herrnhut, Germany is basically a ministry hub that focuses on ministry through media and art. People from all over the world who want to understand how to develop their artistic skills as ministry tools travel to that specific base in Germany. They are then sent out to different bases around the world that focus directly on ministry through the arts as well, such as Sarasota. One of the other bases that Herrnhut sends students to is in Suzhou, China (pronounced Sue Jo). Our new friends were from the Suzhou base, visiting Chiang Mai to attend a conference.

Very quickly, we penciled in plans to visit the Herrnhut base to see if any other connections could be made. If we could pull it off, we would visit in the middle of August at a time our new friends would be there as well. It was very clear that there was a distinction between the Sarasota team living where we had our going away party and the fact that we were in Northern Thailand talking to people with whom we were mutually connected. It blew our minds. We weren't sure what it was about the town of Herrnhut, which few have ever heard of, but it was now a place being highlighted in our lives, and something bigger was happening.

*   *   *   *   *

I remember it as if it were yesterday - it was a beautiful Tuesday morning, and the sun presented a beautiful glow over all of Chiang Mai. I wanted us to experience it, and the best way I knew how to do that was to drive around.

"Chris, there is no way you're getting me on that scooter."

"It's a motorbike, Jess, and you're letting fear get in the way of you enjoying an awesome day!"

"Not doing it."

"That's fine, but I'm going to rent it. It's only six bucks a day. You can sit here at the guesthouse or come with me."

"You are not going by yourself. What if you get hurt?"

"Then come on! Let's go!"

The thought of renting a motorbike to travel around town brought a wave of excitement, but a reality check surfaced right at the time the paperwork was being signed. The reminder that I had never driven a motorbike nor ever driven on the left side of the road was knocking on my conscience as I nervously tried to play off to the rental shop owner that his bike would be returned in one piece.

We walked across the street, dodging swarms of traffic to our new ride and were handed two bright, lime green helmets. The shop owner showed us using broken English how to start the bike and how to fuel it up. I nodded to let him know that I understood and had it completely under control. He walked back across the street to his shop, we jumped on, turned the key and...nothing.

I had to call him back over to show me what I was doing wrong. Meanwhile, Jess was on the back of the bike nervously laughing out loud at me. Usually I could play it off and pretend that I knew what I was doing, but between Jess laughing, not being able to start the scooter and the fact that the shop owner was going to watch us drive away into a busy traffic circle, my nerves started to get the best of me.

The motorbike may have been extra bumpy for the first five minutes of our drive, but then again, it could have been my nervous shaking lifting the bike off the ground. Either way, after a few stops at some traffic lights, some turns and lane changes, I got acclimated. Before long, I understood the motorbike traffic patterns, made a few risky lane changes and even drove on the sidewalks like the locals do.

We found our way to the west side of town to a mountain that had a tranquil drive under beautiful lines of trees that had changed color for the cooler time of the year. There was a slight breeze keeping the cool areas at a nice 70 degrees along with a balance of warm sun to keep us comfortable. Every three miles or so, there would be a pull-off to capture a great shot of Chiang Mai or a Buddhist temple to admire.

It was driving up that mountain that "the moment" came for us: We had done it. We had completed the process of selling everything and fulfilling life choices that naysayers would have told us to avoid. We were outside, enjoying our free lives on a Tuesday morning. All of our family and friends were back home, at school or working, and we were living our lives how we wanted to. Yes, we had made sacrifices. Yes, we had sold everything. Yes, we couldn't guarantee how long we were going to be able to do it, but that moment of freedom is one that few have the pleasure of experiencing in their lifetime.

Financial freedom is the most expensive purchase on the planet. It costs money and time, and in the West, if you don't have the money, you don't have time. The majority of the western world consistently lives in bondage, chasing the next golden carrot. The next promotion is often taken by the younger, less qualified, cheaper individual. Many times, the next bonus you were counting on at Christmas is cut in half or allocated elsewhere. Promises that exist to keep you holding on are broken. Inflation eliminates your discretionary spending, so you can't enjoy the money you earn. For those who decide they want to live their lives the way they want to, they must sacrifice many of their own desires in creative and large ways.

There is a staggering difference between the average western Christian's lifestyle today and what Jesus promises to a follower of Him. Western civilization generally suggests that the amount of life a person is able to live is based directly on the amount of resources they are able to acquire. The truth of this statement is proven invalid, however, when applied logically with numbers. This is not a new revelation to confront, yet the materialistic mindset of the West has only worsened. If we take this rationalization and apply it mathematically, it suggests that I am able to live a greater life if I have a home that is larger in size and better in quality. It would also suggest that by having one dollar more saved in my bank account tomorrow, I will be able to look back and suggest "I have lived my life because my security and the inheritance of my children is greater than before." The problem with this mentality is that there is no life produced or consumed, whatsoever, which is one of the very essences to which Jesus was necessary for humanity.

This was a chosen time for us to be in complete faith for our daily needs as well as our marching orders. As we became more comfortable with an identity aligned with "world travelers with Jesus," we learned that we did a variety of things. One day, we would be out on the streets ministering to the street workers of the area, and the next day we would be reading a book that we wanted to. Then we would tour the city on other days. We did what we felt like was right for that day, and we enjoyed what we did even if often we felt like we should be "working" more. Jim Elliot is credited for saying "wherever you are, be all there," and we reminded ourselves of this constantly. Yet, it seemed inevitable that the typical guilt that most Americans feel for taking personal time would sweep in.

The beginning of February arrived, and our 30-day visa for Thailand was about to expire. We felt like Myanmar (Burma) was going to be the next country we would visit. Jess' organization, Hazina Life had some funds that had built up, and we had contacted a friend who had connections to an orphanage in Myanmar that could potentially have needed some pillows, blankets, and mattresses for the home. Our contact lives on the border of Thailand and was willing to send us in with a trusted friend in ministry there.

If there was anything we learned how to do in Asia, it was how to sleep anywhere. We learned how to sleep with our necks in any position, at any hour of the day, with anything as a pillow, but most of all, with any level of noise. Asia is a great place to practice. Our last night in Thailand, we stayed at our contact's home which had a very comfortable and large futon Jess and I would share. There was only one thing that would keep us up - their Great Dane.

Just on the other side of the wall was the kennel that they put their Great Dane in for the night, and this particular dog was very social. Street dogs were so prevalent in this area that Disney could make countless talking-dog movies for children with plenty of personalities. Those dogs would talk trash from the street, and get our dog riled up; barking and jumping inside his kennel all night long.

There is truly no greater feeling in the world than having traveled on a bus all day and not having slept all night followed by a visit to an orphanage with kids eager to play! I am sure it's very similar to having to host your kid's birthday party with a bunch of active toddlers after being up all night with a newborn. Nothing says "I pulled an all-nighter" like face painting, playing nonstop tag and giving piggy-back rides in the hot sun.

Once we crossed the border of Myanmar and were escorted to the orphanage, we spent the day running around, painting and playing. The real purpose for us being there, however, was to provide pillows, blankets, and mattresses to this orphanage. It seemed that when we would bring the subject of our purpose up with the owners of the home, however, they blew off our offer. At the end of the day, they made it clear that they were in fact not interested in any financial support.

This is very a typical response of Thai people, and we found out the hard way that it is also the case in Myanmar as well. It is rare that people there do something without looking for something else in return, so they tend to believe that free things are not valuable. When we visited the sleeping quarters, the bedding was fairly new and didn't really need to be replaced. This orphanage, unlike many we have visited, had most of their needs met.

Although we were sad we couldn't help financially, it ended up working to our advantage. Every country does life differently, and if we were going to buy mattresses, pillows, and blankets, we were going to have to figure out how to do it, set up the transportation, and do it in another language. Additionally, the currency was extremely difficult to get a hold of, so if we needed more cash than we had, we were out of luck.

The border town of Myawaddy is about the size of a mid-sized suburban neighborhood. It is there for one purpose only and that is for people making visa runs. We definitely had bordered "stupid" during our time there, because we had no ability to get what we needed, no place to stay, and no transportation.

What do people of faith do when they do something stupid like not researching what they needed to before entering a country that is still being introduced to the internet? They usually pray. This time, however, God beat us to the punch. He provided two friends.

The first one, unfortunately, is nameless, so I'll call him Manny. I remember him by the conversations we had. I have no picture or name reference. All I know is that he used to work for the orphanage, and he owned a car. We became his project. Manny took us to one of the two hotels in the area to get checked in and got someone to exchange some USD for Burmese kyat. My two, twenty dollar bills got me a handful of kyat. I was very careful with it because you can't bend it (it must be perfect to be accepted) and you can only pay and receive it with your right hand (for semi-obvious reasons). Once we were settled in our room, Manny said he'd come back at 6pm to take us to dinner.

5:55 – we were down in the lobby and were thankful to be able to connect to decent Wi-Fi. By 6:15, I realized what kind of country we were in. 7:30 rolled around, and in walks Manny.

"Are you ready to eat?" he asked.

We were starving.

We hopped in his car and drove about five minutes down the road to a restaurant that had just a few light bulbs hanging from the ceiling. A young girl and a teenage boy seated us and were really excited that Jess and I had come to their parents' restaurant. It was one of the few moments we had where we smiled with each other because there was nothing to say. They wanted to know who we were, but we couldn't tell them.

"What are you in the mood to eat?" Manny asked.

Something told me we weren't going to be eating Chick-fil-a for dinner that night, so the natural response was to ask what is good. This excited Manny. It sounded like he ordered for a party of eight. We trusted his judgment, so we let him lead.

"I am excited you come to my country. Is so great and beautiful here," Manny said.

"We're glad to be here."

"We have many bad years."

He continued to talk to us about his life and experience in Myanmar. There was a tone of hope in his voice for his country that clearly had grown through confidence built over time, yet was on a shaky foundation. He asked how much America knew about Myanmar and the struggles they've had [to break away from the heavy hand of government to a democratic state].

"If the US does hear anything about your country, it's a quick story somewhere between sports and the weather. After that, everyone forgets," I explained.

Judging by Manny's face, you would have thought I just told him his wife had cheated on him with me. Mouth dropped, and in complete shock, he responds, "You not hear what happen here?"

"Not really." I think a heat wave blew through the restaurant as I said that. I started to sweat.

Manny had studied world history and knew so much about American politics, history, and culture. When we showed up, he was excited to apply what he knew about America to what we were like. Hearing that a country that has had access to free and limitless information hardly knows anything about Myanmar, let alone it's geographical location on the planet, was disheartening. Manny had to work hard to get resources where he could learn about the world because they were limited, restricted, and prohibited for most of his life.

There's nothing like food to cheer up a moment, and ours had arrived. It was *a lot* of intestines in a soupy, curry-like presentation. We were not excited.

Jess and I are open to most new foods, but that doesn't mean that our bodies will accept them, and that was the case with this meal. To this day, we are not entirely sure of all the things we ate, but we do know we had a really, really, really gamey venison along with ibex intestines. Then we were told that Manny had already eaten with his family, so we were responsible to eat a meal made for at least six people. It was a long dinner.

When we returned to the hotel and said goodbye to Manny, we were overwhelmed. We were in a city that was pretty much in the middle of nowhere, and we were around a different type of people that we could hardly communicate with. We had no access to transportation, and the area was clearly not safe for us to walk around. The orphanage didn't want our help, and we found ourselves questioning what our next step should be. We went to the most comfortable place we could find: Facebook.

Although I can't stand Facebook for the amount of time it wastes of people's lives, I certainly cherished it during the times I needed a taste of home. I could "escape" the times that were difficult and keep up with our friends and family. This was one of those moments. So we sat in the lobby and enjoyed ourselves, stomachs grumbling.

That's when the Lord showed up with comfort. In walked our second friend Samuel.

CHAPTER EIGHT

IF TSA SHUT DOWN FOR A DAY

One of the most difficult adjustments while living overseas was not having a phone with data. This meant that when we planned to meet someone who we conversed with via email, and something changed in the plans, we found out by waiting around or by getting stood up. If we needed to find a place to eat or use the restroom, we often walked a long time until we found one. Overall, we learned to relax. We just read, wrote, or talked to other people and stayed content with all of our circumstances.

Our bus that took us to the border of Thailand and Myanmar from Chiang Mai was running significantly late, and we needed to let the people who were hosting us that night know that we were behind schedule. Sitting next to us at the bus stop was a college-aged boy named Samuel, and Jess asked if she could borrow his phone to send an email. He ended up giving us his password so we could connect to the internet via his phone's hotspot. Jess was really thankful, because we had a four-and-a-half-hour bus ride. Samuel talked with us until the bus arrived, and he told us all about his life at Chiang Mai University.

*   *   *   *   *

Samuel walked into the lobby of our hotel at a really difficult time for us; a time we needed a friend to talk to in English that would "get us." Excitement beamed from his face when we made eye-contact, and we felt immediate relief. It was as if we had seen an old friend after years of missing each other.

He was visiting his girlfriend who had met him in Myawaddy.

97

She attended college in Yangon (the former capital which is a 24-hour bus ride from Myawaddy), and they were in a long-distance relationship. He introduced us, and all four of us immediately hit it off. Hours of talking flew by, comparing lives and cultures, belly laughing, and becoming great friends.

I finally asked him, "Samuel, you're different than anyone we've met in Thailand (he is a Thai citizen, born in Myanmar) What is it with you, man?"

"Well, it's because I'm a Christian." He suggested.

That's when I looked at Jess and I said to her, "I knew it!" Samuel has the light of Christ on him. He looks physically lighter than most do in that area of the world, and I now understood why: he represented the 1.2% of Christians in Thailand. I couldn't put my finger on it, but it made sense after he told us. People who know Christ often look physically lighter.

Since our experience in Myanmar wasn't looking so promising, we asked him where some of the best places were to visit. He told us Yangon is beautiful, but since it was a 24-hour bus ride one way, we considered going back to Chiang Mai to refocus and pray about our next step. With that said, we asked him to help us talk with the front desk to explain the bus process.

"Oh, the only bus leaves at 7:30am."

"Okay, how long does it take to get to and through the border; then to the bus station?"

Samuel translated for us: "You can take a taxi, and it is less than five minutes, but we will need to call them now, and you need to get to the border by 6:00 because it will be busy."

After some explanation, we were also told that they don't have taxi cars in Myawaddy but only motorbike taxis. I immediately pictured Jess on the back of a motorbike with some random guy and then them turning off onto a random street where she is kidnapped and trafficked.

"How long is the walk?" I asked.

*   *   *   *   *

5:20am. It's dark, foggy, chilly, and eerie outside.

We started trekking down the road to get to the main highway that would take us straight to the border. Neither of us felt safe. The smells were unbearable, the sides of the road were trashed, and there was a lovely crowd of folks out at that time. The hairs on the backs of our necks were telling us to keep a watchful eye.

Upon reaching the main road where everything was more lit up and local shop owners were opening their businesses for the day, we found ourselves in a unique position. The sidewalk was tight, and before we knew it, we were walking behind a single-file line of monks ages 5 to 50 organized by age. They each had their own bowl and the business owners met them outside with pots of rice as their daily offering to the monks. They would stop and the person offering would pour a scoop of rice into their bowl. Leading the front of the line was a monk with a gong he would bang every few seconds as a call to let everyone know they were there and hungry. Jess and I found ourselves chuckling at the fact we were bringing up the rear end of the line and shaking our heads at the randomness of our lives.

We arrived at the border a few minutes early, so we parked ourselves to the side of the road to prepare our immigration paperwork. Then, we heard it. Out from the depths of the quiet came a riot. People were yelling, screaming, fighting, shaking the fence and doing whatever they could to get to the front of the line. They were trying to be the first ones to cross the border into Thailand to get work for the day. The sound being reflected in the distance was the sound of desperation. The people of

Burma/Myanmar have been oppressed by their government for years, and this was clearly one of the outcomes.

Jess and I let the mayhem settle before going to the immigration window. Once we were in line, however, we kept getting weird stares and points. It was a normal occurrence to us to receive stares because we were white, but these weren't the same types of looks. Eventually two people started to talk to us and point, but their words meant nothing but gibberish. Finally, a man came over to us, grabbed us by the hands and pulled us out of the line.

I'm surprised my first reaction wasn't to rip my hand out and plant my feet since I'm usually tense at a country's immigration checkpoint, but I trusted what was happening. He took us across the street to a different office, pointed at it and nudged us to go in. Then it hit me that everyone was just trying to help us.

I had a moment of realization during this time that most people have other people's backs. When a child is unattended by their parents, the people around watch from a distance to make sure the child is safe. When someone looks lost, someone tries to help them find their way. When two foreigners are in the wrong immigration line, people tell them to get in the right one. The West isn't so much like this anymore. The western parent gets reprimanded for leaving their child unattended, the lost person takes an extra hour to find the place they need to get to, and the two foreigners stand in the wrong line for thirty minutes until the immigration officer tells them to go to the other line. #merica

*   *   *   *   *

Many people have heard the piece of wisdom that suggests "when you aren't sure what the Lord is doing in your life at the moment, go back to the last word you received and continue from there." Although I completely understand the reasoning behind this statement, and also why it would be considered "wisdom", I have concluded that is not always the *best* advice (even though I have given it in this book). If I've learned anything about the Lord, it is that He is constantly speaking fresh words. Sometimes we need to simply adjust our hearing so we can pay attention to what He is saying in that very moment.

It is *not* that anything has, in essence, *changed*. It is that *what* He is saying will pierce our hearts more directly in order to produce the best end-result. Let's face it, a word or something we experienced in April of last year may not have the same impact on us now as it did then. Often by *only* going back to the words of our past, we are choosing to ignore or forget to acknowledge the fresh word that the Lord has for us right now in this very moment. This is not to forget the power of our testimonies and the times God has come through for us in the past, but it is to develop upon what He has already spoken to us. Our destiny hasn't changed, but it's that the approach to getting us there could be more effectively administered, and God is more than willing to show us more!

Had we continued our trip deeper into Myanmar, I'm not sure what would have happened or where we would have ended up. Who knows, we could have ended up back in Chiang Mai at a later date, but as far as I'm concerned, it was because we returned to Chiang Mai that we received a daring mission.

Upon arriving back to Chiang Mai, we decided to connect with a missionary whom Jess had known from a mission trip years prior. We met for dinner and told them all about our journey. After spending some time with us, we had earned their trust and were asked if we'd be willing to go on a special mission to smuggle Bibles into a closed country. There was no doubt that we were open and willing, and we were honored to perform the task. The risk was high, but the reward was far greater, especially when we heard the story behind these Bibles.

They told us a couple had spent most their lives overseas translating the Bible into a certain language fit for a specific people group, and they recently finished the translation. Now it was operation "get the Bibles printed and in the hands of the nationals." The area they needed to get to was not a very popular place to travel, so what could be more perfect than two naive and daring Americans without an agenda. Excitement filled us at the thought of transporting the Bibles.

That afternoon, we booked a bus ticket to Bangkok and a round-trip flight. Our contacts told us that someone would meet us with the bags of Bibles at our bus stop before we left and to be on the lookout. They were very serious about what we could say and what we should or should not do.

Sitting at our dark, dirty, sketchy bus stop, we were filled with nervous anticipation. A man met us in a dark corner of the parking lot, handed us two large, square, paper-thin rice bags with forty Bibles each in them along with a couple of other items, and then he prayed for our journey. Some brief and vague instructions about what we were to do once we arrived in country were downloaded to us, but we were on our own.

After a long, exhausting bus ride, followed by an expensive taxi ride, we arrived at the airport. As we were emptying one of the bags out of our taxi, the top of it completely ripped open as we were lifting it to carry it inside. The Bibles were on display for everyone to see. To say that we panicked inside was an understatement.

We conducted a quick search through the airport to try to find a store to buy a new bag, and then we saw the solution out of the corner of our eyes. As if God put it there knowing we would need it, the airport had a luggage saran-wrapping machine. We were stunned and confused. America won't let you lock your bag, but overseas it is very common to have your luggage saran wrapped to prevent tampering and theft from the workers in the airports. It was the best $5 we could spend, and the bags were wrapped tightly. We didn't want anyone looking in them for any reason.

Jess and I had worked out a story and a plan in case we had been caught smuggling Bibles. "We thought it was *Pride and Prejudice*" was what I was sticking to. Jess not so much. "They're souvenirs" was her go-to answer. Either way, as we descended into our destination, I would be lying if I said we weren't shaky while going through immigration. Actually, we were freaking out.

As we were directed through the different immigration rooms, we could feel the heaviness that was thick in the air. It was cold, the people were stiff and if the officers could have had lasers in their eyes, they would have. We signed our paperwork carefully and tried to be lighthearted to calm our nerves. Then it was off to baggage claim and customs.

A sign pointed us to customs, and as we headed that direction, a man dressed in military-like attire was directing us to take a different turn. When we followed his direction, we entered a large, empty room. The lights were out, the screening machines inside were unmanned and completely shut off. The realization started to sink in: that room was customs, and it was shut down that day. God had His hand on us in that moment.

Our luggage, rather than being collected at customs and inspected was collected from the domestic flight conveyor belt at the entrance of the airport. We picked our bags up while looking at each other in disbelief, wondering if that was all we had to do. Was it really that easy? It seemed too good to be true. Either way, we quickly got out of the airport and hailed a taxi.

Upon arriving at our hotel, we knew two men would be waiting for us in the lobby. While checking in, we made eye-contact with them. Thankfully one of the men looked to be an

American, so when the eye-contact was made, we were pretty positive he and his partner were the two we were to connect with. After check-in and a few minutes of getting settled in our hotel room, we heard a knock.

I slowly opened the door, and the two men from downstairs were there. They introduced themselves and asked if they could come in for their gifts. They were carrying two medium-sized, black duffle bags.

After closing the door, the Bibles were quickly emptied out from the rice bags into the black duffle bags as if they were stacks of cash and kilos of cocaine, and the deal needed to be completed before someone else may have caught wind of any type of trade taking place. Within about a minute, the bags were zipped up, and the non-American carried them on each of his sides down the stairs to the back entrance of the hotel where a sedan was waiting to retrieve them. They were loaded in the trunk, and the driver sped off with them.

After the deed was done, the intensity in the room began to die down, and we were asked to go to dinner and coffee. Not long after, we were learning all about their ministry and hearing amazing testimonies about what God had been doing in their region. We connected closely with two men we knew we'd never see again.

One of them had asked if we had ever been to Vietnam, and we told them we hadn't considered going there at all. It hadn't even been on our radar. He shared about how beautiful it is, and he recommended a few specific places to visit, so we booked a flight to Hanoi, Vietnam from Bangkok.

*   *   *   *   *

Money had now become a bit more of an issue since we had taken three flights, purchased multiple visas and were visiting a metropolitan city where everything is typically more expensive. There were few things we were not willing to compromise in Vietnam, however, such as visiting Halong Bay and the Dau Go cave which were worth flying to Vietnam just to see on their own, so we had to stick to free things other than those tours.

Have you ever had those times when you have a hundred dollars to spend on dinner and you can't pick a place you want to eat, but when your budget is empty, you can think of a million places you would like to eat? Then when you have no money to tour a city, some of the world's most exciting things to do are right in front of you. Since there were many times on our adventure that we were cash poor, we prayed for God to intervene in creative ways. As we were walking in one of the more touristy areas of Hanoi one day, we were approached by an attractive woman, a cameraman and a microphone.

"Excuse me, sir. Hello. I am from Hanoi TV, and we are interviewing visitors to Hanoi about local amenities we offer. Would you and your sister like to give an interview?"

"She's my wife."

"Oh! I sorry. You so young." She giggled.

"Sure, what would you like to interview us about?"

"Have you taken the bicycle carriage tour through town?"

Jess and I looked at each other and smiled. There was nothing too special about these bicycle carriages. It would be like doing a carriage ride through town, but between thousands of honking motorbikes. Nevertheless, what this reporter didn't know is that two days prior, we had prayed for a free ride.

"No we haven't ridden one."

"Oh, you must! We will pay for you to ride if you and your wife would give an interview about your thoughts of it."

The cameraman called two of the carriages over and paid for both of them. Not only were we going to ride in one, but they would be in the other one filming our ride. Off we went.

We sat in our red velvet carriage being biked around town soaking in the moment, in awe of the Lord and all that He had done in our lives. Those are the moments we step back and laugh at how random it was that we were riding around in the middle of Hanoi getting interviewed for the daytime news. We could have been back home cleaning toilets.

Jess and I worked the camera, faking interest in random signs and buildings. An occasional laugh and dramatic pointing of our finger at the perfect angle would woo the cameraman and his shot around every corner. Vietnamese people all around town thought we were famous white celebrities simply because there was a camera following us. In hindsight, this would've been an ideal scenario to be kidnapped, but it was a win for us!

* * * * *

Thanks to some friends of ours back home, we were connected to some additional places in north-central and northwest Vietnam that we bussed to. Like I said before, driving is, in my opinion, one of the best ways to see a country, and boy, did we see Vietnam! Bussing is the cheapest approach, and for about $40, the two of us were able to take a bus to three different places, each about five hours apart. I'm still not sure how anyone actually made any money off of us.

People ask us all the time what we thought were the most beautiful places we visited. Vietnam takes the #1 spot on our list without a contest. Someday we hope to return to Vietnam to travel more southward. The deeper and further inland you go, the more stunning it gets with its plateaued mountains, terraced fields, flat valleys, and rice farms.

Working our way westward, we stayed in a beautiful guest house made of bamboo overlooking a rice field and enjoyed a simple life. While hiking one day, we came across a fabric shop and decided to look around. Inside were women with all kinds of special needs and disabilities. The owner told us about how she "adopted" each of the women working there, taught them how to sew and the sales of their products in Hanoi go to fund a house she runs to care for them. There are amazing people all around the planet, and this woman needed encouragement the day we met her. It was an honor to spend the afternoon talking with her.

A family so graciously offered to host us in another area of Vietnam as well. They own a coffee farm that they took us deep into, and we drank the most freshly-roasted coffee we've ever had. Three cups of black coffee later, we were energized and ready to cook a traditional Vietnamese dinner over a live fire.

I enjoy analyzing how people live life. Cooking dinner consisted of three generations of women working together next to the family of cats who were licking their paws by the open fire. Every time we finished our drink, it would immediately get refilled, and if we didn't drink fast enough, they'd prompt us to drink so they could give us more. The post-dinner festivities weren't much different than any other western family, however. You'd think being in a village in the middle of nowhere, television wouldn't be too popular, but we found ourselves watching Vietnam Idol with the family while adding each other on Facebook. We enjoyed each other's company even though only one person in the family spoke English.

The stars were by far the most amazing experience we had in rural Vietnam. There was hardly any street light, so you could look over the coffee fields and mountains and see nothing for miles. I could sit outside for hours looking at the sky at night.

*   *   *   *   *

One of the things I think is most interesting about faith, in general, is that most of the time you can separate those who truly know their God and trust Him for everything from those who have pumped-up, fluffy "faith" without any trouble. It's very easy and usually reveals itself when someone doesn't have any money.

Why is money often the most used tool by the Lord to challenge us? I think the obvious answer is something along the lines of, "duh, because without it we can't do anything we need to or want to." I should point out two key words from this natural response to the question – "We can't." Getting into a situation where we are literally without the means get the very things we need (or think we need) to move forward seems reckless. It puts our soul in the middle of a frustrating tug-of-war where we are forced either to choose between the reaction our body exhibits when being without resources or the response our spirit expresses when attached to the Father.

We can't. We can't make something appear. We can't fill up our gas tank. We can't eat. We can't pay the electric bill that allows us to cook, stay warm or cool, see at night, check our emails, etc. We can't make a phone call. We can't do anything, and it's really frustrating. What has the world done as a response? We've created a system based on credit, allowing those who can handle relatively disciplined financial habits to do what they can't at the cost of accrued interest. We have come as close as we can to being financially invincible at the cost of our slavery to the banks.

What do we do when we can't do what we need to? I could give a variety of answers, so let me ask the question in a manner a little more relative to our situation and the subject matter of this book: What do we do when we can't do what we think God tells us to do, yet we can't make it happen in our own power? Stupid says go home. After working through a bit of the surface responses, however, I resolve with the very answer that keeps me moving forward during these times: I anchor my faith.

The concept of anchoring your faith throws your emotions for a loop. One minute you are completely trusting, loyal, and excited to see what the Lord is going to do in your life, and then the next minute, you're a wreck, face in your hands, crying out "what in the world am I doing?" Like I said, it's a tug-of-war that you can't allow your emotions to win. After all, many times, it's by your choice that you're in the situation that you're in, and this was the case for us. Jess had to keep me in check, just as I had to keep her in check, and when we were both in check, our eyes were on what the Lord had for us. It was the joy of the Lord that gave us strength, and the only place to get that was through keeping our thoughts and hearts close to Him.

*   *   *   *   *

Working our way into Laos, we stayed in the city of Luang Prabrang. This was one of the hardest times at that point in our trip. It was the end of February, only seven weeks in, and Luang Prabrang brought us suitable comfort that we could have on a $25 a day budget for two people. We had hot showers, a quiet room with a comfortable bed, a good-enough fan to keep us cool, two fulfilling meals a day and (my favorite) fresh pineapple and mango smoothies for a dollar. There was nothing to complain about. Since we had just bussed our way through Vietnam the week beforehand, we were ready to rest for a while.

"Rest" comes in many different forms. For some, it's going to the beach and plopping down in a lounge chair with a cold drink, a book, and a plate of fruit as they toast under the hot sun. For others, it may be doing an outdoor activity or getting some fresh air. The rest we enjoyed consisted of sleeping late, grabbing lunch, spending the 2-hour limit we had on the internet getting our fill from back home and walking around town, depending on how hot it was. Then we would take a nap, go to dinner and return to the guest house to read, pray, write, talk, and go to bed early. We did this just short of week. Sometimes life calls for this, but looking back, I'm not positive this was the best choice for our time in Laos. Either way, it had been a busy month leading up to that.

One of the perks of resting is that it often gives you time to think about the things you don't have time to think about when life is moving fast. When Jess and I have time, we dream. It's when we think about our future; what we're going to do; what we're going to create. We'd start thinking about where we would live someday and the jobs we might apply for along with how many kids we're going to have. How we were even going to get to that point?

We've had to learn the hard way that the freedom of time to think about our futures isn't always what the doctor should prescribe. During this time, the grass on the other side of the planet began to become extra green. Our future lives back home so easily slipped in to our minds, because we're both natural planners. We want control and confidence regarding what we will do in the future. It's a difficult thought pattern to break.

The reality of the situation was that we were seven weeks into a year-long trip. During the times we were sick of Asian food, staying in hotels and not being able to have a "normal" life, that fact wasn't something we could fully anchor our faith in. We had a long way to go. We knew it, but why were we truly thinking about everything back at home and the future? The truth was, we were running out of money.

When you dedicate yourself to a life focused on unadvertised faith in finances, the game changes more than slightly. We didn't allow ourselves (by our own design and trust in the Lord) to fundraise via social media or call home and cry for help. This was part of discovering how long the Lord would keep providing for us, and we also knew that our friends and families were watching us. Don't get me wrong, this wasn't a situation of pride where we were too stubborn to ask for money. Our hearts leaned to the other side of the argument; to the side that wanted to see the Lord come through at the end of the day. When we were out of money, we were literally done. Game over. An airline ticket home could be booked on credit and, we could face our friends and families then. I could see us shrugging our shoulders while rationalizing with the cliché, "I guess we weren't in the Lord's will, but God uses everything for good, right?"

It wasn't a simple "oh we're out of money, let's go home" though. To us, it was that we couldn't prove the existence of our God, which was one of the very things we wanted to do with this trip in the first place. Hopefully I will help develop an argument for God through this book, but when you're trying to make a "budget" in faith during week seven in the middle of Laos, you can imagine stresses were high. It was easier to think about the job I was going to make money with when we moved back home rather than how much money we wouldn't have by the time week nine rolled around. Provision had to arrive. Too many people, believers and nonbelievers, had an eye on us. God had given us too many words about this trip. He had us overcome huge financial situations prior to the trip that had given us convincing validation that we were in His will. How could this be the end?

John 15:5b: "Apart from me (Jesus), you can do nothing." Again and again I'd have to remind myself of the truth behind this completely radical statement Jesus makes. We're not trained to think this way, yet it's how we get closer to our designer! It was critical that we anchor our faith on every testimony we had leading to that moment, even though all of them seemed like ancient history. Then, matters became more difficult.

At the beginning of our trip, I found out that Heidi Baker

was going to be holding a conference in Singapore. I wasn't fully sure why, but I really, really wanted to be there. Our mental itinerary as a result was to try and be in Singapore for the conference in the middle of March.

While surfing the web during lunch one day, I thought to myself, "I hope there isn't a ticket system for the Heidi Baker conference. In that case, I better go check it out to make sure that we've secured a seat." When Heidi comes to Sarasota, it is usually free and ticketless, but the seats fill up very quickly. Researching the matter would have been "going the extra mile" considering the history I had attending her meetings. Upon finding out more, I realized that it wasn't just Heidi who was to speak at the conference, but there was going to be five other big names speaking, and it was a 4-day (all day) conference with classes and multiple sessions of worship and teachings. It sounded awesome. However the price tag didn't. It was going to cost $347.50. On top of that, lodging in Singapore is pricey. The week easily became a $600-week pre-food, pre-transportation around the city and pre-bus/train tickets to get there. I was really discouraged. Our bank account had less than $300.

"I really felt like we were supposed to go, Jess." I kept saying.

I know God knows the desires of our hearts, and one of the words we consistently received before leaving was "don't doubt the path/plan." We were planning on going to Singapore and paying the price whether or not the conference was free, so we decided to keep moving towards Malaysia which would be our "pass-through country" and finish up our 10th week in Singapore. We immediately declared, "God, if you want us to go to this conference, then we want to see you come through with a $350 check in the next week. Not $500. Not $50 and $300. $350 to the dollar." Then we said we were going to head south in faith, but we would not go to Singapore unless we had that money. There was a little over two weeks until the conference began, so it had to come fairly quickly.

That declaration was made on a Thursday, and that Saturday we FaceTimed Jess' parents. Her Dad said that we received a $350 check in the mail that Thursday. It was already in our post office box as we made our declaration! I booked our spots that afternoon, and we were left with $2.50 to put towards dinner that night. My questions about free will and predestination really get challenged with this story. Was the idea to declare for the $350 our idea, the giver's idea or God's all together? If it was God's idea, how much free will do I really have?

CHAPTER NINE

BREADCRUMBS

The week before knowing if we would be able to go to the conference in Singapore brought a roller coaster of emotions. There wasn't just the obvious question of, "what the heck were we doing," but with our finances dwindling, we were going crazy inside. To add to the struggle, we had no clue where we were going in Malaysia, and I wasn't about to pick Kuala Lumpur because it was the largest, most popular city in the country. We prayed our hearts out for connections to reveal themselves.

I don't know what it is about living in the spirit, but sometimes it seems like God is out of the office when needing some very important answers. One week, things are going great, and everything clicks into gear. The next week, it's like He takes a vacation to another planet! That's the week you can't hear anything, see anything, and it often feels like He doesn't exist. Oh yeah, by the way, you're on a deadline. The week leading up to the $350 donation, we would pray and seek and pray harder and we wouldn't receive anything. Not even some feeling of, "hey guys, just hang tight."

Literally the same Saturday we found out about the $350 check, we received FOUR random messages or emails to go to the Youth With A Mission base in Georgetown, Penang, Malaysia all within a couple of hours of each other. Explain that!

Neither of us had announced we had plans to visit Malaysia. No inclination was passed around that we were even on the move. We simply prayed, and God showed up bigger than ever. Breakthrough had come. Relief had arrived, and confidence was more deeply established. It is so difficult to believe for what you cannot see right in front of you. All the more, God delivered at a great time, and I wouldn't have changed any part of this story.

*　　　*　　　*　　　*　　　*

We (finally) arrived to Penang that next Friday after an overnight bus, two overnight trains and a night in Bangkok midway through. Boy, did that come with quite the experience. Picture this: you get on a bus from Luang Prabrang to Vientiane, Laos that is considered a "sleeper bus." Based on a prior experience, we pictured there being three columns of seats that recline almost flat with two of the columns against the windows and the third one in the middle creating two aisles in the bus. Add various neon lights in the cabin, and you have yourself an Asian sleeper bus. No, this bus was way different.

As we stepped up into the bus, we could hear a great deal of laughter. Then we saw the inside. The walls were painted lime green, and lined against both sides were full size mattresses bunk-bed style. Add fuzzy Angry Birds blankets and Minnie Mouse sheets, and you have yourself a Lao sleeper bus. Jess and I were on the top bunk in the middle of the bus, and it was a long night of twisting and turning through the mountains with absolutely no bar to block us from falling off the bed onto the floor! It was as if we were on a magic carpet riding through the mountains. As much as the experience was worth it, the sleeper trains to Penang were much more comfortable.

It was nice to be around people (somewhat near) our age and with a similar heart and understanding of the Kingdom of God at the YWAM base in Penang. We spent our days helping out with a homeless program, worshiping at PenHOP (Penang House of Prayer) and evangelizing on the streets. It was refreshing to have somewhat of a support system that we could rely on and be in ministry with.

One night during the week, we went to a worship set at PenHOP led by an amazing man named Josh Yeoh. It was four hours long, and it was one of those nights I was reminded that

God can often do more in a few hours than years-worth of counseling sessions. I found myself with my face on the floor bawling my eyes out. Snot was all over the floor, my face was soaking wet, and just as I would get myself together, I would go for another round. The Lord was speaking about a lot of things to me and showing me a lot of images, and my heart was receptive. Then, something weird happened. I'm "having my moment," and Sean Feucht (pronounced "foit") pops into my head. Sean is a worship leader who establishes Kingdom foundations prophetically in places all around the world. You want to talk about travel? Sean travels everywhere, and his itinerary is completely bonkers.

I thought to myself, "Why in the world am I thinking about Sean? Right now, in this moment?" Then I prayed a little more, and Sean pops into my head again. "Chris, you've got to focus right now. Stop thinking about some singer-guy you've never met," I said to myself. Again, a third time, I thought about Sean. "Sean, get out of my head. I don't even know you," I said to myself. By that time, it was almost midnight, and the session was wrapping up. After dismissal, Josh got onto the microphone and said, "Hey guys, before you leave, I wanted to let you know that Sean Feucht is coming to PenHOP at the end of March. It's completely free, and it's a big deal that he's coming here."

Jess looked at me immediately and said, "I feel like we need to be here for that." I looked at her and told her that I had been thinking about Sean all night long, and it was freaking me out. That was that. We believed that we needed to return to Penang after the conference in Singapore to make sure we were there for the time Sean would be. Then confirmation followed. An American girl who was interning at PenHOP came up to us in the amount of time it took to get from our seat to the door and said, "Yeah, the Lord told me you two are supposed to be here for Sean Feucht." I don't even think this girl knew my name, and there she was, telling us that we were supposed to drop everything we had planned to return to oven-hot Penang to see some worship leader. Okay!

Even though returning to Penang made complete sense to us and felt right, it put a huge dent in the plans we had in our heads at that point. Frankly, we had planned to be in south Vietnam or Cambodia following a flight to Japan to do a week in Osaka (even though we still had no money). Changing our plans either erased this part or pushed it forward; one of the two. We didn't know.

When you have a "God-moment" to anchor your faith to, you view events that happen in your life with a drastically different lens. Our plans to go back to Vietnam and work into Cambodia and Japan were our own, but we were told never to doubt them, so we didn't. We just had to decide what we felt was right at the time and go with it, all while hoping the Lord would carry us along the way.

We had to be flexible. When you go through a life-shaking night where the Lord, not only tells you and your wife to return to Penang, but also tells some stranger the same thing, it changes the questions you ask. It alters what you put your faith in. It changes everything. Looking back, had we not received that word, we would have definitely gone to Singapore and boarded a plane home after the conference, and God knew it.

*   *   *   *   *

Before our wonderful night at PenHOP, Jess and I had a very difficult time the day before. That morning, reality had hit us hard. No donations had come in, funds were dwindling exceedingly fast, and based on my budgeting, we were going to hit our financial threshold either midway through or towards the end of our time at the conference in Singapore.

During this particularly difficult morning, a local family that we were getting close with had called us to go over to their house. While we were walking there, Jess had told me she was done and over it. She wanted her life in America back and had concluded we were finished.

Money was slipping out from our hands quickly. It was difficult to enjoy the days we did have our needs met knowing that next week, we could be in serious trouble due to poor decision-making. Hopelessness had settled in that morning, and we didn't have enough money for a place to stay in Singapore for the conference. "God paid for the conference, so we'll get the lodging taken care of," we'd remind ourselves. We had contacted over 15 people on Couch Surfers and messaged friends with potential connections in Singapore, and every person either had friends or family in town or weren't willing to host us. We were going to have to go into debt to pay for a hotel room, so emotions were high.

Within two minutes of Jess telling me she was finished, we walked into our friends' house, and in the living room was a man named Rick. Rick, a very tall, middle-aged American man, looked at us with sincere interest. We tried to put up a fairly good front so we didn't give the aurora that we were just having an emotional moment. Rick started to ask us the traditional questions everyone asks a westerner overseas. *Where are you from? So are you guys backpacking? How long did you save to do the trip?* Since finances were on the forefront of our minds, we opened up about how it was very difficult believing in God, and God only, to somehow connect all of our financial dots and tell the world to support us. Through our discussion, he could see we were definitely in a moment of struggle as I made heavy, compassionate eye-contact with Jessica and shrugged my shoulders in concern.

Without hesitation, Rick asked to pray for us. He gave us a

word of encouragement and prophesied three words we had already been told and had been holding onto already. He reminded us yet again that everything we were going to do was going to be taken care of and not to worry and that the Lord hears even our most radical prayers; even the ones that we think He doesn't catch. Within ten minutes, Jess was crying, I was on the verge of tears, and we were restored to confidence yet again.

I know, I know, you're probably sitting in your chair wishing you could reach through the page and shake us saying, "Look at what the Lord had told you and was doing the whole time!!" I know. I would suggest, however, that it was a completely different experience when you have all of the emotions that came with the choices we had made. It was the next night that Jess and I had our Sean Feucht experience.

To add to this moment of encouragement with Rick, our friends came downstairs to greet us and offered us lunch and dinner to go. They told us to come back the next day for lunch. By the next evening, Jess and I had completely stopped spending our cash for the exception of lodging, and we were filled with the binding words the Lord had given us (again). Additionally, that weekend, we got an email response from a friend's cousin that we could stay with them in Singapore, and they were relatively close to the Expo hall where the conference was to be held. That confirmation came just two days before we were going to arrive.

Our last night in Penang had come, and I had to pay 400 Ringgit for our room. It was really difficult to hand that cash over. I knew what that $132 dollars could do for us. As I handed the money over to our friend who managed our room in Penang, he counted all 10 nights' worth. He stared at it for a moment and then gave us 100 Ringgit ($33) back. We were blown away, because not only had this family fed us for about five days, but when it was all said and done, they had given us a huge chunk of money to work with in Singapore. It was truly humbling to have that money returned to us, because we were at the end of our financial rope.

$106, I counted. Before that, it was $73. What a difference! Every dollar we had was taken out of our bank accounts. Our bus tickets to Singapore were paid but not local transportation or food. We were going to walk into the most expensive country in Southeast Asia for five days with nearly nothing.

I don't know if you can put yourself in that position emotionally: You have no home. You own next to nothing. You have no debt, which in my opinion made us richer than most Americans, but you don't have any cash to work with either. It's Tuesday, and you know you'll probably be able to make it to the end of the week by eating fairly light and can count on some regular, bi-weekly support to come in enough to pay for a bus ticket back to Penang. The question is: Do you get on that bus? Stupidity says yes. Even faith says yes, but reality says it'd be smarter to take your credit card, book a flight from Singapore to Tampa and start a new way of living (because this ain't working out). It's those two words we had received from the Lord, however, that kept us going: Sean Feucht.

*   *   *   *   *

I'll tell you what though, the Lord knows exactly who to hook us up with and for what purposes. There were times we didn't even know we would need help, yet the Lord sent it. Thanks to our very, very slow bus driver from Penang to Singapore, we got to the border too late to convert our Malaysian Ringgit to Singapore Dollars. Because of the openness of Malaysians to receive Singapore Dollars, we figured that would be the case on the flip side, but it was not, and it was too late to learn that lesson.

As usual, we made a multitude of stops on the bus ride. We'd pick up people on the side of the road, hit bus stops in a bunch of cities and then stop at rest stops in between. Once going through immigration at the border of Singapore, we were told by our bus driver to transfer to a different bus. That bus would then take us to a bus station in town, and we were going to have to figure out how to get to the house we would be staying at from there. Figuring out somewhat complex itineraries wasn't too concerning as we were getting used to them. Usually we could just ask locals and get a close-enough answer to what we needed.

We were both tired and wanted to sleep until our final stop, but a really nice Muslim lady came and sat next to us and started talking. Jess is typically the one who likes to talk to people and find out everything she can about them, and I'm the one who likes to clock out and drool on them. The tables were turned this time, however, because this was my first official conversation ever with a fully covered Muslim woman. After telling her a little about our travels, she told us how to get where we needed to go and that we would have to take a taxi that only takes cash. She offered to exchange some of our Malaysian Ringgit for Singapore Dollars after she asked if we had the proper currency. Without us knowing it at the time, we would have been a very miserable (taxi-less) couple without this woman striking up a conversation with us. God uses everyone, even without them knowing. Thanks to her, we were able to get to our host's house without any issue, and she gave us a favorable exchange rate.

Our host in Singapore was fully responsible for making our time in Singapore successful. Something tells me he and his family were shocked we were surviving and taking the risks that we were. No matter how crazy the stories we had were to them, we know their family was impacted in some way, shape or form.

When we arrived, we asked our host if we could convert the cash we had for Singapore dollars. He asked us, "how much do you need for the week?" Out of my pocket, I pull out a mixture of Malaysian Ringgit, Thai Baht and USD, and I said, "about $100 Singapore for now." There was obviously a bit off shock on his face, but he tried (unsuccessfully) to hide any reaction. We did the trade, and that was it until we ran out of money or God came through. Who knew where in the world we were going to be a month from then.

The next morning, we were told that we needed to take not only the bus, but also the metro train (MRT) to and from the Singapore Expo every day, costing us about $8 roundtrip. Since that was nearly half of our money over the period of the week, we decided breakfast really wasn't an option; that we would eat a large lunch and skip dinners. The main problem: lunch would cost $20-$25. Either way, we would be out of money very quickly. Thankfully, our generous host gave us two local transportation cards filled with enough money to pay for the bus and the MRT, free of charge! He may as well have handed us a free pass for another week of life.

Due to an error on my part, registration the first day started at 4pm, not 7:30am like I originally thought, so we had some extra time. Across the street was a mall, and we headed that way since it was air-conditioned. As we sat outside a McDonalds that we couldn't really afford to eat at, we watched as hundreds of professionally dressed businessmen and businesswomen walked past us. It's amazing how nicely people in Singapore dress. All the men wear nice button downs with dress pants and shoes (often with French cuffs and ties), and the women wear classy dresses and professional clothing. Insecurity hovered over us like a thick cloud as we were dressed in our "missionary clothes" and trekking shoes. We stuck out like a sore thumb, and it wasn't just because we were white.

The corporate American dream was being smashed in our faces like a cream pie. Jess' desire to wear cute clothes and dresses was tearing her up inside. We had eight very long hours to think about how we were down to $88 in our pockets and what we would have been doing back home if we had real jobs like normal people. Add the spiritual warfare that comes right before God has to show up (or else), and that Tuesday was a wonderfully awful day. Neither of us had ever simultaneously felt so close to rock bottom. What the heck were we doing?

We were attaching ourselves to the words we had received, and no matter what we wanted to do, we were going to walk that out. Each day we had to remind ourselves that we were not finished with our trip even though the numbers made zero sense.

We knew we were supposed to be at the conference. Promises through many words of knowledge that we would never have to worry about finances had been made. We knew that God had not brought us to the other side of the planet for us to fail so He could point and laugh at us. We also knew that we had to be back in Penang for the meeting with Sean Feucht.

The second night of the conference we decided to go home early instead of attending the evening meeting. Exhaustion had hit us, and to add to the stress of the week, I got a cold. Our hosts offered us dinner, so we didn't hesitate to join them since we were planning on skipping it. It was a scrumptious meal of lamb with mint sauce, homemade macaroni n' cheese, baked pumpkin, sweet potatoes and a variety of chocolates for dessert! There we were, easily the poorest tourists in the country, eating lamb and high-quality chocolates. It felt as if I was in a bathtub with boiling water and a mountain of ice was poured in.

During dinner, we asked what the process would be regarding buying a bus ticket back to Penang. Even though we didn't have the money at the time to purchase the tickets, we knew to research this on the front end of our time in a new area, because we had many experiences where we had to actually go to the bus station in advance to buy a ticket. Our host got his computer out and started researching for us. Since Singapore is on the developed side of Asia, we learned that we were able to buy our tickets online.

After a few moments, he asked for our passport numbers. We then knew what he was doing, and realized that we had reached decision time at our personal fork in the road. He purchased the tickets for us without even hesitating. "Well, I guess we're going back to Penang," I whispered to Jess. The deed was done, and we were confirmed yet again through the way God used the people around us that we were to keep moving forward. That man may not even have realized that he was probably the key instrument for us to not call the entire trip off and book a flight home.

Jess and I went upstairs at the end of the night completely stunned. Just hours earlier we had almost become content with going back to the US, and now we were back up on the horse and headed to Penang for at least another two weeks. It is a constant roller coaster of emotions: one minute you're freaking out about the next step, and the next moment you're slapping yourself in the face saying, "You idiot, where's your faith?!"

The final night, our host sent us off well by taking us to an amazing Mexican restaurant. Mexican food ministers to Jess' heart, and it is through simple gestures like this that remind us that God cares about every need, desire, and step we take. It was a peaceful bus ride back to Penang as we slept quietly knowing that we had been taken care of.

Upon arriving back in Penang, we counted 85 Ringgit or $28 USD. In order to save money in the long run, we picked up some very basic groceries when we got there, leaving us with $11 USD by the time we got back to the YWAM base. We were dirt poor and had no prospective donations coming in. Even if we did have a donation come in, by the time it got to the bank and cleared in our account, we wouldn't have enough cash in hand to eat by the end of the week. God had to move, and that was that.

The night we returned to Penang, Jess decided to unpack her backpack. This used to be a great challenge for her. I'm the guy who unpacks my bag for a one night stay in a hotel because it helps me relax. Jess could live out of a suitcase of a disorganized mountain of clothes for a month without any problem. That lifestyle got old for her after living out of a backpack for 10 weeks. We knew we were going to be planted in Penang for a while, so it was worth her time to unpack and organize everything. Our rule of thumb eventually became that it was worthwhile to unpack if our stay was at least 3 nights.

Two-thirds of the way through unpacking her bag, I heard Jess say, "Oh my gosh!"

"What?" I asked her.

"There's cash in the bag!"

"What?"

I skeptically wondered if I had given her cash at some point and she had put it in her backpack without remembering. As I saw the cash, I realized what it was. It was a mixture of Thai Baht, Malaysian Ringgit and USD. It was the very cash we originally gave to our hosts in Singapore. Those sneaks (angels) put the cash in Jess' bag while we were headed out to dinner the last night! Right then, we knew (again) that we were covered.

After counting everything up with the returned money and converting the math, we concluded that we had only spent $20 USD from the time we left Penang to the time we returned. We had been to our most expensive country yet for the least amount of money, and it was all because of the generosity of our hosts and the faithfulness of our God. We were truly blown away and knew that we were absolutely supposed to be back in Penang.

*   *   *   *   *

Many times in your experience with God, you will receive knowledge about your future or calling through a certain means. Each person receives differently and often to the degree you believe that you are capable of receiving it. I am currently not much of a hearer, but I often see pictures. Jess sees, but often the Lord will drop something into her Spirit that is spot-on, such as "Will you believe me for a $10,000 check?" I've learned to trust what she hears. Others are knowers or feelers. We both are feelers as well. It is important to know which are your strengths.

On another level, I am someone who the Lord talks to through materials, very often. I'll read a book on a certain subject, and something will catch my eye. Then, in the next day or week, I'll watch something or read something else that I feel like I'm supposed to, and that same topic is being elaborated. It's possible that I'll also have a random conversation with someone that brings up that very subject. That's usually my cue to pay attention. It's how the Lord grows me.

One of the few ways that God rarely speaks to me about my future is through getting prayed for, falling on my knees in shock and awe and crying my eyes out. It's only happened a few times in my life, but then I found myself on the floor of PenHOP…again.

CHAPTER TEN

FORK IN THE ROAD

It seems that about 99% of the time when you think God is going to do something in your life a certain way, it doesn't actually pan out to be how you pictured. This was definitely the case at the meeting with Sean Feucht, and I wasn't sure why. Frankly, nothing happened.

I had come to the conclusion after the meeting in Singapore that we were to return to Penang to get connected with some new people. In fact, we met a handful of new individuals that have become lifelong friends. The Malaysian people, out of every country we visited, are our favorite of all, without a shadow of doubt. Malaysians are caring, generous, proactive, empathetic, compassionate, and, most of all, hungry for God to show up in their country. They taught us about community, and we were specifically able to connect with them as if they were our family. Although they have many cultural differences, they are easy people to connect with.

Additionally, some of the connections we originally made in Chiang Mai visited Penang as well. One of them, Josh, showed up at the front door of the YWAM base we were staying at, and we were shocked to see him. Even our friend Sarah visited at the same time as well. The four of us became great friends during that time.

It was two nights after the meeting with Sean Feucht that God showed up big. That night, a team from Bethel School of Supernatural Ministry in Redding, California was visiting PenHOP, and the leader spoke and had prayer ministry afterward. Jessica was talking with a few people, and I could tell that the conversation would last a little while, so I visited with a few individuals in the back part of the room. I was then tapped on my shoulder.

"The man up front wants you to go see him," I was told.

"Sure, no problem." I figured he needed an extra man to help him out with prayer ministry.

As I arrived, the speaker told me to stand next to the spot he was at as he was praying for someone else. I turned my body around to face the audience and he chuckled.

"No, I want to pray for you."

"Ohhhhh!!" I obnoxiously and nervously expressed.

I had never experienced someone never having known me before to literally pick me out of a room of people to get called up to receive prayer ministry. I wasn't expecting it, nor was I sure what to think about it, but I was excited to pray with the speaker. He was obviously a man of God from watching how he functioned and by listening about the fruit of his ministry. As he turned to face me, he looked at me very intently and said, "I *never* give the word the Lord wants me to give to you."

He looked at me straight in the eyes. He was clearly apprehensive because he was about to say some things to me that he personally restrained from telling others at past times because of the weight of the responsibility that would then lay on his shoulders if he were wrong. It was the fear of the Lord. Then the moment came while prefacing his motives to me that he decided inwardly he would take a huge risk in faith for himself. It was as if something clicked in his pupils. Determination to follow through with what the Lord was telling him now superseded all of his concerns.

I can tell you without a doubt that it was a bit awkward to have your mail read that much by someone who didn't know who you were. Things I hadn't even shared with Jessica about what I thought the Lord is going to do with us in our lives were being confirmed by the Holy Spirit through this man.

For about an hour after he prayed over me, I was curled up

in a ball on the floor receiving image after image from the beginning of my life to that point and with each image an experience in my life was shown along with the explanation of why it happened. The Lord was walking me through each piece of my life that was presented, showing that even in the darkest times of my life, He was there and that He used it for a specific purpose as part of a chain of events that would lead me to the very place I was that evening. I was in shock and awe as "everything clicked" for so much of my history and why things that had occurred the way they had. The times I would ask God through my challenging teenage years, "why me," were finally being answered.

* * * * *

"As soon as Jesus was baptized, he went up out of the water. At that moment heaven was opened, and he saw the Spirit of God descending like a dove and alighting on him. And a voice from heaven said, 'This is my Son, whom I love; with him I am well pleased.' Then Jesus was led by the Spirit into the wilderness to be tempted by the devil." (Matthew 3:16-4:2)

I don't think it takes a brainiac to acknowledge that some big things were spoken over me during that moment, and I pray that I am responsible enough with those words to see them through. Sometimes, however, there are other people looking to piggyback off of other people's promises, dreams and callings, and that's where Mr. Canada showed up.

Mr. Canada, an unnamed Canadian man who was at the service, was sitting on the floor next to me and Jess when I finally opened my eyes. He was excited for what the Lord had done in that moment and was eager to talk to me and Jess about an opportunity to minister with him in the Philippines. He had already been attempting to woo Jess over with his words, but it was his turn to work on me.

It was close to midnight, but like everyone does in the Malaysian culture, you go out for second dinner. We went to an outdoor seating area under a large white tent full of plastic patio furniture and blinding fluorescent lights to share some fried rice.

As Mr. Canada began talking to us, he told us all about how he had great connections in the Philippines with the school system. He is able to teach middle and high schools filled with thousands of teenagers as well as other large groups measuring more than 5,000 people. He shared a lot of testimonies about how great things happened at the meetings *he* held and the people *he* ministered to.

He talked about how great the opportunity was and that it would supply all of our needs. It was very clear that whatever he was offering was a paying gig, and we would be taken care of somehow. There was also the indirect suggestion of greater opportunities in the future.

Looking back, I want to slap my younger self and yell "run!" I spiraled into a deep, weeklong, wishy-washy consideration for flying to the Philippines to minister alongside Mr. Canada. It was a promising opportunity, and I could see how the Lord could have planted Mr. Canada right there in front of me at PenHOP as a marching order to say, "This is what I said, now here is your first order." There just wasn't peace, though.

There was too large of an emphasis on what *he* was doing and not what the Lord was doing, and I just had too difficult of a time wrapping my head around it. I can usually find out within the first hour of talking with someone who their Lord is, and Mr. Canada seemed to be Mr. Canada's true Lord.

"Without me, you can do nothing," I just kept reminding myself. That scripture was so important when making decisions. At the

end of the following week, I had come to the conclusion that Mr. Canada was using the church to develop a platform for himself and not an altar for knees to fall. After Jess and I decided to avoid the opportunity, peace returned.

Jess and I could have ministered anywhere, but it would have been stupid to follow through with the decision to go to the Philippines. I'm positive that we would have fared out just fine, but it was the right decision not to go.

*   *   *   *   *

Our friends in Malaysia are still constantly at the forefronts of our minds. We still connect with them today and will hopefully cross paths at another point in time. Although friendship was something we gained from the people there, an even greater gift we received was a lot of encouragement to begin believing to see more signs and wonders again.

When someone approaches me and suggests that signs and wonders are bogus, I'll usually ask them some questions about why they think so, but more importantly, I'll ask them how much they are around people who pursue it. Usually the answer is almost never, or they've had a negative experience to coincide. I like to use this example when defending signs and wonders:

I was a mac n' cheese, chicken nuggets, pizza and fries type of kid. You couldn't get me to each much else. The "spitting the broccoli into the napkin" approach was used often while my parents were not looking (unless it was being force fed to me before going straight to my room after dinner).

Today, I eat nearly anything, even if I don't like it. I love spices and hot sauce and flavors. I now love to mix my foods. Years ago, my foods couldn't touch, but now my plate often becomes one big mash of food. The way I experience food has completely changed, and I have been exposed to a whole new palette of foods as a result.

When I was a child, I would say, "I'll never eat that! It's gross!" Yet, I had never even tried it! Today, my taste buds have adjusted, my willingness to experience new foods has shifted, and as a result, I'll eat at any restaurant, take a bite (or at least try) almost all foods, and because of it, I love food now. I'd say we have a healthy relationship.

Let's apply that back to signs and wonders. If you're unwilling to experience what God has put out there for us to delve into, your understanding of them will be limited, and your belief for them will be as well. Start listening and working next to people who function in signs and wonders regularly. When you begin to see amazing events that can only happen by the hand of God, you'll never go back to chicken fingers and pizza as your everyday diet.

My experience with Vlad in Phuket back at the beginning of the trip had left me feeling alone and incapable, due to the lack of consistency of it in my life. My unbelief trumped my belief for his full healing. I knew *I was* incapable, of course, but the thoughts that I dwelled on in my heart made me believe that the Lord's grace wasn't sufficient enough for me in my life; that He wouldn't move through me. I wanted to get alongside people who had been regularly functioning in signs and wonders and understood their identity in Christ. Thankfully, Penang provided this for us. My experience with Vlad was quickly disregarded once I was connected with a local at a homeless shelter.

There was a 12-hour worship "burn" session at a homeless shelter, and Jess and I attended for the majority of the time. About an hour into the day, I connected with a young man named Matthias whom I ended up spending a fair amount of time with for the next few weeks. He and a friend of his were praying for a blind man. They asked if I'd be willing to join them to advocate for his sight.

It wasn't long before I took the lead. I prayed, listened to the Holy Spirit, and tried to find the key that would open the door to his sight. We kept hitting wall after wall. I would ask my translator to say certain things and get certain information out about his history, but none of it helped (like it sometimes does for a healing). Nearly an hour had passed, and I was getting tired. Prayer is sometimes exhausting when you keep hitting walls. Then, I remembered something specific that I had learned from other experiences.

I looked at the man's hands. They were covered in many different rings and jewels, and he had many bracelets on. I told the translator to tell him to remove them if he was willing. Some of the rings were on so tight, we had to locate some scissors to get them off. The marks on his hands were so deep because the jewelry had become a part of him, literally.

Many times a witch doctor will tell a person to wear a charm to fight off a certain sickness or to avoid a certain spirit. The witch "blesses" that jewelry with their demonic powers which is accepted by the individual. It's then that power that rests on the them, often bringing sickness or ailments such as blindness. There's been a strong correlation with the removal and renouncing of these charms and the ailment lifting off or then being prayed off.

When the man took the jewelry off, he accepted Christ. I'm not quite sure what had happened in his heart during that time. He kept to himself, and I couldn't speak his language, but his heart had completely changed. That's when I saw it: his face looked physically lighter as if he was ten years younger. This happens *often* when someone gives their life to the Lord. I knew we had made headway.

The man stayed the entire day. After a while, we'd pray again and then let him soak in worship, and pray again some more. It was very tiring, but we believed. Finally, ten hours had gone by, and the day was ending. That's when a teen boy who was blind in one eye walked in the door and changed everything. Someone started to pray with this boy in the other part of the room, and I approached someone else near them with excitement.

"Hey, you guys need to get both of the blind guys together and have them pray for each other," I recommended.

A few minutes went by, and the situation was set up. It wasn't long before the boy had a dramatic shift in his sight. He went from seeing nothing (like complete black) to having a fuzzy view of everyone around. He'd check his eyes out and get excited. Then the man I had been praying for began to see a difference. Their smiles and excitement lit up the room, and everyone involved got excited.

It's amazing what happens when a shift begins to occur and the amount of belief within the hearts of those praying gains momentum. It's as if a tug o' war match takes place with one person against an entire team. The person holding the rope alone is easily conquered. Within thirty minutes, it was finished. Both of the blind guys could see.

These are moments you remember your entire life. They stick with you forever and change the way you look at the world and the Kingdom of God. When unbelief in other circumstances starts to get the best of you, a testimony like this allows for repentance to take place and your faith to be anchored. These two men, that were blind and can now see, helped me break past the blinders put over my own eyes after my experience with Vlad in Phuket. I was thankful to be surrounded with people who wanted to see more signs and wonders like I did.

*   *   *   *   *

One of the cultural identities of Malaysia that we did not realize would be the case upon arriving was that it is a heavily Islamic nation. This was quite the change from the first countries we had visited because they were mostly Buddhist and Confucianist. It was amazing to us how you can literally cross the border of southern Thailand, where Buddhism is the main go-to religion, into Malaysia, where it is generally Islam. This means the people are different, the clothing is different, and the mindset and understanding of life is different as well.

Politically, Malaysia is an Islamic majority, although it is a "free" country. Even though a good portion of the population would consider themselves non-Muslims, the government is currently inching its way closer to enacting Sharia Law, which is a government founded upon the commands in the Quran and Hadith. Although constitutionally illegal to pass, growing corruption of the country's top leaders is pushing the people into a direction where Sharia is "the only option." This would send churches underground and force non-believers to comply with the laws of Islam.

Since the church in Malaysia is being persecuted more greatly today than ever before, there is a faith that is rising in the believers there like no other area in the world. There is a deep hunger and desire for the Lord to show up greatly. As a result, more people are seeing the fruit that is produced by abiding in Christ, and the ecclesia (the body of Christ) is growing at a staggering rate.

I was told recently of a statistic shared from a third party (so don't quote me on it) that it takes, on average, a total of nine years from the time a Muslim is first introduced to the gospel to the point of accepting Christ as the way to the Father. This is for a few reasons. First, depending on the country, they are most likely going to be kicked out of their home, their family or even their own town. They will even be restricted to the kinds of jobs they can work. Most importantly, however, they will be a target to be killed by committed Muslims. It's not that it takes nine years for them to decide if Christ is the way, but it takes that amount of time, on average, to decide that they will accept the potential consequences the decision could bring upon themselves and even their families.

It is illegal, according to Islamic law, to share the gospel to a person who is either born into an Islamic home or has converted to Islam at some point in their life. It is not only a risk for them to hear it,[1] but it is a risk that the person sharing takes as well. If a country has established Sharia Law, that government has a right and a responsibility to handle the situation according to the Quran, and the spreading of the gospel to Muslims is punishable by death. Malaysia is headed down this path, but not without a fight, and we got to be a part of it in Kuala Lumpur.

*　　　　*　　　　*　　　　*　　　　*

Our time in Penang had come to an end, and it was time for us to move on. We were sad to leave, and we had made great friends. After talking with some new contacts, we acknowledged that we needed to get connected to Kuala Lumpur (KL). It's interesting that just a month earlier in Laos, we had chosen not to visit KL simply because it was the largest city on the map. Nevertheless, we ended up there. The problem was that we didn't have anywhere to stay.

Some of our friends also making the drive had two spots left in their car, and they were willing to drive us for free to KL since they were headed that way. We had asked many people if they knew somewhere we could stay, but nothing had transpired until the moment we were about to load up the car. A young man named James said his cousin might be able to host us, and he'd text us if she agreed to take us in. He contacted his cousin as we were driving away.

Was it stupidity to get into the car to go to KL when we didn't have a place to stay? I don't really think so. Worst case scenario, we could have taken the credit card and bought a cheap hotel for the night until we could work something out. Was it faith to get into the car to go to KL when we didn't have a place to stay? Absolutely. We knew, without a shadow of a doubt, that KL was the next place on our agenda, so we went and believed God would show up. There was no other choice at that point but for Him to make something happen, or else we'd quickly run out of money and be forced to return home.

One hour before we got into the city limits, we received a confirmation text from James saying that his cousins would be happy to host us for the weekend. He included their address and names. We were told it was a nice part of town. When we arrived, we pulled up to the security gate of a very nice luxurious high-rise. It was as if we were going to enter a Ritz-Carlton. Jess and I looked at each other and got excited. It would be a much-welcomed change from YWAM base mattresses and time restricted A/C units.

One of the doormen took us into the elevator and told us we would be staying in the 26th floor penthouse. We were grinning from ear to ear, still having no clue who we were staying with or having even seen the apartment. When the door was opened, we were greeted by a woman in her early thirties and her husband, who was an American man.

Of all places we could have ended up in Malaysia, we ended up at a home with an American man! I have learned over the period of my life that there is no such thing as coincidence, and this was not a different case.

After talking for about an hour, telling our stories and getting the same shocked looks most people reacted with about our style of "backpacking," we shrunk our world even further and made a connection of a mutual friend we had back in the states. There we were, victims of the six degrees of separation, being connected to people "organically." When there were times we would wonder if we made the right decision to go to a specific place, it was connections such as these that confirmed a solid "yes" for us.

We were taken to our quarters and were overwhelmed with comfort as we entered the nicely lit, taupe room with an overstuffed king size bed topped with a rich, red velvet comforter on top. There was even a lamp! Through the blinds we could see a magnificent view of the surrounding complexes as well as the King's palace. We were told that when we woke up in the morning, their maid would make us breakfast and that we could enjoy their resort-style pool.

What if we had stayed in Penang? What if we hadn't taken the risk? Looking back, that would have been a stupid idea.

The following day was a very relaxing one by the pool. We hadn't vacationed or simply relaxed in over a month. God knew exactly what we needed, because KL was going to kick our butts in ministry.

CHAPTER ELEVEN

THE GLITCH THAT GUIDED US

I was interested to learn that in many Muslim countries, hospitals use a red moon as their emblem rather than a red cross like the west does. Frankly, I had never put together that the red cross may have been chosen as a depiction of hospitals being a place where you can not only be healed medically but restored by the power of Christ. I doubt that the full intent behind the decision made by the now named International Committee of the Red Cross was to depict the cross of Christ, but it is interesting nonetheless.

What I find to be truly hilarious, however, is that *if* the cross was meant to depict Christ, or even the power He carried, it is a completely foolish response by the Muslim population to stick a moon on top of their hospitals. Yes, in theory, it was done out of rebellion to represent the god that they serve, but the reasoning behind why they would change the symbol is not rational within the Muslim faith.

Those who understand the fullness of what being a Christ-follower is [someone who is to fill the earth with life[1] (the same Zoë life or ruach that Jesus says that he *is)[2]*] understand that they have supernatural power inside of them to change and redeem things in the natural realm. The Muslim faith, however, does not grant any type of power to its followers because Allah does not intermingle in human affairs.[3] He is to be believed in and praised and (hopefully) you will be good enough by the day you die that his mercy will forgive you of your sin and let you into "heaven".

I'll discuss this story in greater detail later, but I remember a group of Muslims allowing me to pray for them, but they would pray some kind of prayer under their tongue that would negate or cast out whatever I would say. Looking back, I wish I had addressed this activity, because Muslims don't have the power to cast out any type of evil because they have never been granted the freedom or authority to walk in spiritual warfare by Allah. Their response was based out of the goal of preserving their goodness in the sight of Allah, not the protection of their spirit from the power of another source. The act may be an attempt to not get on Allah's bad side, but if Allah looks at actions individually, I think he'd potentially be upset at the fact that the guys were interested in listening to my prayers.

With this said, to put a moon on the top of a hospital signifying that Allah will be (or is) able to take care of you (more) is simply not possible and does not follow the teachings of the Quran. I find it interesting that using the sign of a cross to highlight a location of medical help is a sign similar to the symbol that represents the man that saves you from death! The moon is only the representation of a belief system that *could possibly, maybe, hopefully, if you're good enough* give you eternal life and the moon itself is an object to which time (or a way to measure a limited life) is quantified.

*   *   *   *   *

Despite the red moon on top, we found our way into the waiting area of a KL emergency room, ready to encourage men and women of the Muslim faith to follow through with the unforgiveable sin of "shirking". That is, they would pray to another source besides Allah for help. In essence, if they were to die right after doing this, they would surely never enter heaven according to the Quran.[4]

Jess and I, along with a group of other young adults wanting to see transformed lives, headed into the ER to pray for people. All of the people in this hospital were Muslim, and they were all hurting in some way, so there were no excuses not to pray for someone. We went one-by-one, praying for the next person in the room. Some would stand by their Muslim faith and were absolutely opposed to us coming near them, but most were in a vulnerable position and just wanted their ailments healed.

My favorite example is of a man and his daughter. It's only my favorite example because it was one of the first times Jess had experienced a major touch of God right in front of her that was completely undeniable. As we began to question the man about what was wrong (he had a cane), he told us that he had a problem with his knee. I love knee problems because it is obvious when the knee is healed because the pain is gone. It's as simple as that. Cancer on the other hand is a more difficult ailment to pray for because you usually can't see the difference with your eyes. You can only trust what you think the Holy Spirit has told you about that situation in that moment.

We prayed for him (all eyes closed), but he didn't realize that I don't pray with my eyes closed. My current personal take on the idea of closing our eyes during prayer time is that it was established under the understanding that we need to close our physical eyes in order to focus on our "spiritual eyes." I believe we started doing this as a result of Adam's eyes being opened when he ate the fruit of the Tree of Knowledge of Good and Evil in the Garden of Eden, and thereafter believers began to close their eyes to try to see differently. Frankly, I'd rather be used to functioning in the spirit whether my eyes are open or closed, and so I often choose to (reverently) keep my eyes open. The man we were praying for didn't know this, and I saw him mouth to his daughter, "I felt something." That's when he began to smile.

Smiling is often a cue that something has taken place by the hand of God. It is usually either a reflection of the joy of the Lord filling the person up or the situation/ailment in the body being noticeably improved. The man's knee was better, and we shared about how and why Jesus had healed his leg.

The statistic I shared in the last chapter about it being a nine-year process to introduce a Muslim to the gospel and for them to accept it is certainly remarkable. Further developing that statistic, it also takes on average eight times of being presented the gospel before it is accepted as truth. With the case of the man we were praying for, it could have been his seventh time being presented the gospel in five years, so there is no compelling reason not to pursue forward with the presentation of the gospel and prayer despite any life-threatening rules and uncomfortable situational variables. What is most important is that we were there to not only present the gospel, but present our case by healing his knee.

Then the time came to pray for his daughter. She was the reason they were at the hospital in the first place, because she was experiencing severe abdominal pain. Jess asked if she could lay her hands on her belly and pray for God to touch her, and she agreed to let her.

Shortly after Jess prayed, she felt something the size of a large fist stick out of her stomach and move from one side of her body to the other. Jess looked at me as if something crazy had happened, but couldn't explain it to me at the moment.

"Did you feel that?" The daughter asked Jessica.

"You felt that too?" Jess seemed relieved.

"Yes! What was that?" She responded.

Some of the best moments, when praying for people, is when something that you weren't expecting happens and everyone is surprised by the response. Jess, who is someone who struggles with the courage to step out and pray for random people, was shocked and surprised that the daughter had been healed.

We left the two in the waiting room not sure if they were

going to follow through with their visit to the doctor. The knee pain was gone, and the abdominal pain had subsided. They had been touched, and despite their faith in Allah, they couldn't deny that they experienced something in that hospital waiting room.

Moments like these are not few and far between when you're constantly praying for people to be touched by the Kingdom of God. In fact, it is really difficult to pray for someone and they *not* get touched in some way. It's the dogmatic arguments of "this is the right way and yours is the wrong way" that destroy the family of God, encourage people to run from the church and distract us from what God is saying this very second.

*   *   *   *   *

Another healing which was a favorite of mine in KL was also at a hospital in the cafeteria. There was a woman and her husband eating a late dinner, and she seemed completely hopeless. She had been in a brutal motorbike accident and was wrapped up all over her body. Pain was something she planned on becoming close friends with for the next year or so.

Her husband, instead of praying with us or staying to the side decided to video us. It is typical of Asians to video events freely, but not necessarily the typical response of a Muslim when Christians were coming to pray for them. They would usually try to hide because they knew they were being watched.

As we prayed, a lot of pain was relieved from the woman's back. The most obvious change in her body, however, was that there was a massive (and ugly) swelling on her hand the size of a tennis ball, and it had flattened to the size of a cookie after prayer. Again, the smiles overcame her, and she couldn't withhold them. This is when we told her about Jesus. The response we received was surprising:

"I've already been healed by Jesus before." She said.

(Insert shocked looks.)

"A few years ago, I had shattered my leg in eight spots, and some people prayed for me, and Jesus healed me completely."

Sometimes I really wonder why this woman had never accepted Christ the first time she was healed. If I couldn't even consider bending my leg due to the immense pain and broken bones and could turn around a few minutes later and walk perfectly fine, I would probably accept the vessel to which I got that healing as at least some sort of truth. The Muslim world, however, has such a high price on submission to Allah, and it is incredibly difficult to break through the fear that comes with rejecting him.

Later on, we put it together that the woman's husband wasn't videoing us because we were a bunch of quacks praying for his wife, but rather, he knew what was about to happen because he saw his wife get healed the last time. That is a Muslim man full of faith in Christ! The more I hear stories like these, the more I recognize there has to be a huge population of Muslims who pray to the God of Abraham, Isaac and Jacob five times a day in the mosque. Although they don't have the faith to sacrifice their lives yet, God hears the prayers they are declaring over their friends, family and nations in their mosque!

I believe that intense breakthrough for "Muslim Christians" in the Arabic world is going to rise up, and when the faith in Christ of the region surges above the need to protect themselves, a radical movement birthed out of the community of believers will pour out into the Arabic nations declaring Jesus Christ as Lord. A breakthrough like that starts and continues by being bathed in prayer. What better place to pray for breakthrough consistently than in cultures that are required to pray five times a day!

The woman still did not accept Christ publicly that evening.

She left us with a wink and responded, "I'm almost there." I pray that we are not the last people to pray for a touch by God in her lifetime and that she will truly find Christ.

*　　　*　　　*　　　*　　　*

Remember the story of the Samaritan woman by the well in John 4? This is a story about a woman who had had five husbands and was trying to fill a void in her life with men. Jesus and His disciples came through the town, and Jesus stopped by a well to talk to her (which was inappropriate because Jewish people didn't associate with Samaritans), and He asked her for a drink of water. Jesus was setting her up to be touched by God.

The woman tends to state the obvious throughout the moment, but she responds by saying she was a Samaritan and it was odd that he was talking to her. Jesus replies by saying that if she only knew who she was talking to, she would be asking him for living water.

This "living water" is the water from the river that flows from the Tree of Life (Revelation 22). This water purifies our hearts and heals our souls. When we drink of it, we are filled with the kind of life that fuels us in a way that defies the level of time, aging, strength, abilities, weariness, hopelessness, and uncertainty that the average person experiences. As the Samaritan woman begins to see this throughout her encounter with Christ, she tells everyone in the city about how Jesus told her about everything she had done and that he was the Messiah. Many Samaritans came to accept Christ's call to believe in Him through her.

Why is this story important? It is to remind you that when you have faith, your prayers are never too large or complicated for God to answer. You will never earn your way to be good enough to receive healing in an area of your life by what you do or don't do. Your job is to drink the water Jesus offers.

One night we had gone out into a red light district to share the love of Christ with those in one of the most disgusting and enslaving professions in the world. We came across one woman, in particular, who was older (probably in her late 60s) and had problems with her back. She was very crooked, and in a lot of pain. We prayed for her, and within a minute, her back had straightened out, and she was without pain.

Often times, it is natural to think that a prostitute doesn't deserve the grace of God for the healing of her back. I mean, she's a prostitute, right? Chances are, she had been a prostitute for a very long time and is potentially still one to this day, but God still healed her. How could He respond with such a loving sign, when her soul was such a mess? Then, I remember the state of my own soul and how it was. Frankly, my own wasn't much different than this woman's when God got a hold of me.

Signs like this literally make you wonder. She will have to come to her own conclusion about Jesus at some point in her life, and I'm not sure she has the capacity to know how to escape her lifestyle or whether she could escape the grip of her pimp, but it's amazing to see Jesus touch people whether or not they have accepted Him as their end-all, be-all. This is how awesome the God is that we serve.

*　　　　*　　　　*　　　　*　　　　*

While in Malaysia, we lived off a range of anywhere from $5 to $110 at any given time. We never ran out of money, but the decisions regarding how to spend our money became very challenging. Thankfully our dollar went far in Malaysia, and it was a safe country to practice our faith in finances. It was still difficult to decide, however, if it was worth it to go out to a restaurant down the street for $3 or travel across town on the free bus to the grocery store where we could get food to cook for $2.

During this time, our finances were on some sort of cruise control. We would consistently be given a 50 ringgit note from someone, which at the time equated to $17. As soon as we would almost run out of money again, we would meet someone who would give us another 50 ringgit bill. It makes me wonder what would have happened had we spent our money more quickly. Would God have kept following through with another 50 ringgit? There was a part of us that wanted to know, but then the realistic side of us just wanted to make sure we played our cards right and stayed safe.

Finally, upon making new connections in KL, we experienced substantial breakthrough in our finances. Malaysians are some of the most caring and generous people on the planet. Once someone would hear about what we were doing, they would do everything in their power to make sure we were taken care of, fed, and had ministry work to do. We give mad props to our friend Grace, whose connecting and care for our well-being carried from late March all the way to the final day of our trip. It was because of our connection to her that we only purchased a hotel room for a total of four nights after the month of April. The rest were in someone's home for the exception of a few nights in a rental car (by our choice).

We were connected so well during our time in KL that we were exhausted by the end of our time there. In the morning we would lead some kind of meeting which would follow with a lunch with someone else who wanted to connect us with another person followed by a meeting and then another meeting. Then there was always a small group meeting or church service at night we would attend or speak at. We enjoyed ministering to all of the different people, but we were not conditioned for it at all, and it ran us ragged! Through that time, however, many places would surprise us with love offerings, and not before long, we had gone from barely being able to eat on a consistent basis to having over $1,250 cash in our pockets. That amount of money is a big deal for Malaysians because you convert your currency by multiplying the dollar times three. It's as if we were given almost $4,000 over the period of a couple of weeks. We were blown away at their generosity.

It was nice to be around people who had our backs for a few weeks. We didn't really have to think about where we would stay or worry if we could afford to eat. Very often, our schedule was planned out for us, so we didn't have to think about anything. The next city or country we were headed to wasn't on the forefronts of our minds either because we were confident that we would stay in KL for a few weeks. We were the most comfortable we had been all year, in some sense.

Then reality began to settle in, however, because our visa was soon to expire. It's not like being a member of our own country where you can go wherever you want for however long you want. Different countries have different lengths of time you can stay and only allow you to re-enter the country a certain amount of times per year depending on the type of visa. For a simple visitors' visa, 30-60 days was typical throughout Southeast Asia before you had to leave the country for, at minimum, one day.

Some connections to Cambodia had been established, but we didn't feel peace regarding the decision to go, so we continued to discuss the plan we had designed at the time, which had become a two-week trip in Taipei, Taiwan, followed by a two-week trip to Seoul, South Korea. These were monster flights in terms of cost, and we had to book both because Taiwan required us to have an exit itinerary in order to enter the country. It is, in fact, an island.

As time closed in on the 30-day mark, the pressure was on. For some reason, we just didn't have peace to book a flight out of Malaysia. We didn't want to leave the region yet, but at the same time, we felt that we were done in KL. The only way to renew our visa would have been to travel back north to Thailand or south to Singapore and then enter back into Malaysia. It was a confusing time as our hearts were saying "stay in Malaysia," but the visa stated "it's time to go." Jess came to the conclusion that we should just book the flights. I hesitantly agreed because we had to make a decision, but I wasn't offering up anything valuable. There just seemed to be a missing piece to the puzzle.

Each time I tried to complete the last page on the website to book the tickets to Taipei, the page would go to a bad link. It took forever to type everything in on my iPad, but I would do it again. After 25 minutes of typing, it went to the bad link again. Frustration began to build on the original stress.

"Lord, I don't even know if this is what we're supposed to be doing. Just let it go through, so I can be done with the decision process," I submitted. We had to be at a lunch meeting, so I would just handle it that evening.

It was at that lunch when our friend Grace told us a story about a bus ticket she was trying to book online, and the page kept freezing up just like ours was. The next day, she went to look for the ticket, and it was sold out. Not knowing what to do, she searched deeper and found a bus company she had never heard of before that was selling the same itinerary for about ten percent of the price she was going to pay. It was an encouraging story, and I decided I would look for other sources to book the flight hoping there would be a cheaper route than the ones I was able to find that morning.

After returning home in the evening, I thought to myself, "You know, you should go look at your passport one more time just to double check the expiration date on your Malaysian visa." As I did, the truth set us free. Malaysia gave us a 60-day visa, not a 30-day visa like what we were accustomed to with other countries. We still had another month until we had to be out! What a relief!

Our host at the time, Dawn, gave us some of the most practical advice we received all year. We were focused on such big places like Taipei, Seoul, Tokyo, Beijing and Shanghai, that we were ignoring the smaller places of the world. She shared with us that she felt like we should visit the town of Miri, East Malaysia. Flights were cheaper to get there, the food was cheaper, the transportation was cheaper, we had contacts through other connections there, and the Lord is doing a lot in that region of the world. It was a place worth considering in her eyes.

"It's not that you shouldn't trust the Lord for the bigger places, guys, but if you don't know that you know that's where you're supposed to go, why not start at a place where you know things can be great, and then continue from there?"

It was brilliant advice. As always, it came down to the test of peace, and the following morning we woke up with peace at the idea of going to Miri, so we booked the flight and made a connection with our contact there.

* * * * *

We were sad to leave KL. We had spent a total of six weeks in Malaysia, and even as I write this, nostalgia seems to overwhelm me. The friends we made like Lyn-ni, Melinda, Elsie, David, David & Grace, Josh, and Matthias, among many more are those we will stay connected with for years to come.

There we were yet again, getting picked up at the airport by someone we had never met and had only connected with via email by a mutual friend. We never knew what kind of situation we were getting ourselves into, but there was a certain level of trust that we kept until we had a reason to lose it.

Rachel is the daughter of a man who was, in-part, responsible for the beginning of a revival that took place in his East Malaysian village of Bario. Bario is in the middle of the jungle, and it is at the northeast border of Indonesia on the island of Borneo. An outpouring of the Holy Spirit took place on such a large level that not only do people outside the area still talk about the things that happened there, but the village is still 97% Christian to this day. As we met Rachel at the airport and got into her car, she told us she had booked two tickets to Bario and we owed her money for them!

At first we thought she and her family didn't want to host us, which may have been partially true, but anyone who visits the area should visit Bario. It is a place to literally get off the grid and clear your head. The day after we arrived, we went shopping for a weeks' worth of groceries because we were going to have to check everything in on our plane. There would be little access to food there, so we had to be prepared for everything. I even had a tray of eggs on my lap as my carry on!

Frankly, when I heard the term "jungle," I expected it to be a lot worse. The roads were paved in most of the village, and we had running water and electricity. English was minimal among the locals, and there wasn't any A/C, so at times it was borderline miserable, but the nights were cool and comfortable.

As we arrived to this jungle village, we weren't quite sure why we were there. Our friend Lyn-ni from KL had given us a book to read about the outpouring in Bario before we had made the decision to visit East Malaysia, so we felt that the reason we were there would be of long-term importance, but there was no direct reason for us to visit the place. We decided to just seize the week and enjoy it. We had no phone or internet, but we had stacks of books we had accrued on our journey and had no time to read. By the end of that week, I had read six books, and Jess had read five. It's amazing what you can accomplish when you have nothing to do but walk around and wave at people.

The star gazing was one of the highlights of our trip. Every night we would take a walk, let our eyes adjust to the darkness and just stand in awe. It's amazing how many stars the West cannot see due to having so much light. We just sat on the road and stared.

*   *   *   *   *

Our first morning in Bario was one of the freakiest moments we had on our trip. At around 5am (you know, that time your REM sleep kicks in) the person next door started a continuous drumming that began with long intervals, built up to quick beating and then back to a slow thumping. While this was taking place, all of the dogs in the area barked, the cats meowed, the roosters crowed, and I think Jess screamed. Were we going to be sacrificed? Surely the cannibals were outside our front door with torches ready for breakfast.

Then we heard what many people have historically said what sounded like the "sound of rushing waters." After a few minutes, you could hear the village praying. It wasn't being administered by an imam on a megaphone; it was spontaneous, earnest prayer from hundreds of people. Never in my life had I experienced a Christian culture that set times throughout the day to pray, and Bario stands out as the only place I have been to that commits to a daily lifestyle of prayer like that.

What would it look like if New York City had a call to prayer at 5:00 AM every morning? Could you imagine the difference in the culture and atmosphere of the city that would be present compared to today? It is sad that the group of people who know the one true and *living* God and who have the power to transform situations through prayer have such a poor prayer culture. This must change, and it can be changed through passionate followers of Christ and a band of believers who have decided they're going to pursue cultural and geographical revolutions to see the earth fully reconciled.

The most amazing part about being in an area of the planet that has been bathed in prayer is that it makes room for dreams to surface. It is out of the abundance of my prayer time that the craziest and most exciting dreams pop into my thoughts and make their way onto the pages of my journals. It was no different in Bario. It certainly helped to be entirely off the grid in a place we had very little to do.

After the stressful time of trying to figure out where to go next, we decided it was best for the two of us to not discuss the issue at all for a while. There was nothing we could do to book our itinerary in Bario, so we had a week to enjoy the fact we wouldn't have to deal with it.

The last day before we returned to Miri, Jess felt like we both needed to fast, which is something that she rarely does. Jess has a blood sugar issue, and after so much time without eating, she gets a horrible migraine, vomits, and spends the rest of the evening sleeping it off. To fast would be a major sacrifice.

At around 4:00 in the afternoon, I was getting cabin fever, so I suggested we take a walk and get some fresh air. An hour later, as we were almost home, I saw that Jess began to turn very pale, and she was running out of energy. When we got back, I decided she should break her fast and get something into her system. While I was in the kitchen frying up an egg, I heard her collapse in the bathroom. She quickly woke and threw up, and I would bounce between checking on her and the egg. Once we got some food in her system, she perked back up, but it took her a little while to work up an appetite from all the vomiting.

I have learned over time that it is often shortly after you break a fast that the breakthrough you are praying for often comes. This was the outcome in our case. As we were lying in our bed reading later that evening, I put my book down and asked Jess if she felt like we were finished in Asia.

"Yeah, I do, Chris. Honestly, after our time in Miri, I know we're going to be flying overseas."

We asked the question "where," and we both felt like the United Kingdom was our next landing point. When we had this discussion, however, we had it as if it was the easiest conversation we have had in a long time. It wasn't stressful or difficult to decide, and we felt nothing but peace. I had broken my fast at 8pm that evening. It was 8:20 when this conversation took place.

Just before we left for Bario, we had received a $1,350 donation from someone back in the states. We knew it would give us the ability to make the jump out of Southeast Asia, but we wanted to make sure we didn't squander that money in the incorrect way. When we returned to Miri and booked our flights to London, the total price of the itinerary came out to $1,342. We had just enough to purchase the tickets.

*   *   *   *   *

Have you ever stayed in someone's home without them there, but you didn't know the people very well? You may have seen their family photos, looked at all the different books and movies they have in their collection, even found some private information you wouldn't have known unless you stayed in their home. Then you meet them later on. This is how we felt with our new friend Rachel. Although there wasn't much in terms of valuables and family portraits in the home we stayed at in Bario, the culture and village that we experienced bonded us to Rachel and her family without having even talked much.

Rachel and her friend Sabrina were developing an extension

of a Singaporean church in Miri. Sabrina had been sent by her pastor to Miri to team up with Rachel and begin mounting everything into place.

Many churches, especially ones that are content, lack any form of evangelism whatsoever. It is often because the leaders are too scared or don't feel like carrying out the principles Jesus and the disciples modeled for us to do. It is also because many churches have a focus directly on self-improvement alone. Rachel & Sabrina have the desire to get into their city and disciple it from top to bottom while creating a community completely bonded in Christ. It was an honor to spend the week with them praying over the building they would be in that was under construction, holding meetings with their family and connections, and counseling them through some of the struggles that they were going through as two young women starting a church in a Malaysian culture.

But like staying at any person's house for free, we helped pay our way through simple labor, and that usually meant working in the kitchen. Food is the cornerstone of Malaysian culture, and they eat like hobbits. How the majority of them stay so thin is beyond us, because they eat all day. It was normal for them to enjoy a meal five or six times a day, and although the food was healthy and the meals were, on average, a bit smaller than American meals, it was still a lot of eating.

Jess and I would find ourselves in the hot kitchen, sweating everything away, peeling tiny onions and garlic and chopping green onions and other vegetables. We were always volunteered for the work the people we were staying with didn't like doing. I don't blame them. The area under my index fingers burned for a week! Malaysians work so hard to make meals, and it was like cooking for Thanksgiving every day. The end result, however, was beautiful.

I remember back to a time in Laos, in late February, when I

was venting to Jess about the food. Most of the food we ate was great (except for our experience in Myanmar) but I struggled with the way cultures outside the states cut their meat. It seemed like instead of having a nice boneless chicken breast, they'd just take a butcher's knife and chop that chicken up into a hundred pieces. You have to take your lamb, beef, chicken, pork, fish, or whatever you were eating, throw it in your mouth and go on a meat search. I finally reached a point when I was over it, yelling out loud:

"I just want a piece of meat without a bone in it! I'm not a freaking filter-feeder."

It's normal to get your hands dirty and slimy when eating overseas. Eating is an adventure, and it's a special time in which you lose your perfectionism and move to a level of vulnerability that allows you to connect with those you dine with. Without food, you don't function, and with hands covered in sticky, yummy sauce, you have to recognize the fact that you are human like everyone else. My favorite joke is one that reflects the eating culture of the West, and I've credited myself for writing it:

"Why *couldn't* the chicken cross the road? Because it was boneless."

Rachel and Sabrina took us on an eating adventure. If we had not been introduced to Malaysian food correctly prior to meeting them, then they made sure we knew their eating culture before we parted ways, and we would reach our tipping point in the country of Brunei - our last stop before leaving Asia.

CHAPTER TWELVE

FAITH AND SHARIA

I'm sure you've seen it on the news at some point in your life, perhaps when Saddam Hussein was in charge: someone getting their arm or hand chopped off because they broke the law. Yes, this happens all around the world, and specifically in Muslim countries because of Sharia Law.

Sharia Law has specific ways of dealing with situations of sin or those who break the law. When Sharia is adopted by a government as a country's guidelines, the system of punishment can become quite brutal. Many advocates for Islam are trying to work loop holes into British and American laws to be able to give the power to certain people to integrate Sharia Law into western government. Sharia, as a whole, may be unconstitutional in America, but depending on how loosely the US interprets the constitution for equal rights for various cultures and identities, with experienced lobbyists and the necessary individuals in office, it will not be long until it has become legal for a Muslim to handle a situation how they see fit.

Brunei, a tiny country in north Borneo in the north and central part of East Malaysia, is a country I had never heard of until Rachel and Sabrina mentioned that they were going to be speaking at a church in the capital of Bandar Seri Begawan for Mother's Day. We booked our flights to the UK after this weekend because we were excited to experience another country. Brunei has a Sultan in charge, and he is a very, very, very rich man who made his wealth from oil.

The Sultan has a large family and is known for living a bit of a promiscuous life. His money buys anything and everything and anyone. He fosters children from around the world, consisting of many girls, giving them all the things they may desire. He has his own zoo, amusement park, a mansion for his cats with a full-time staff, a supercar each day of the month, plus much more. The Sultan had signed Sharia Law into effect the week before we had arrived. The atmosphere was a bit tense when we showed up to the house where we would be staying.

On the coffee table of our host's house was a book with a list of all of the new laws and standards that the people of Brunei were to uphold. Although the country had been lax on some things, such as requiring every woman to cover their head, they were strict on how punishment would be carried out. I began to read through some of the things required out of interest, and some of the things, particularly in the removal of women's rights, were very concerning. The new law will be phased in more strongly over time.

Many believe that Sharia Law was passed because the Sultan is getting older and felt the need to prove himself to Allah in hopes that he will get into heaven despite the promiscuous life he has carried out. At the end of the day, however, the Sultan's family cannot fulfill Sharia Law because of the hypocrisy they carry from the lifestyles they uphold. The Sultan and certain members of his family should technically be punished under their own law, but I don't think anyone is going to approach them about it. For now, the people of Brunei who love their Sultan, despite his flaws, simply adjust and respect him.

*   *   *   *   *

Sunday came, and we went to our first "underground church" of the year. It actually was considered a community center, and everyone had to carry a membership card that would be displayed on their lapel. A new person would have to fill out an application as if they were signing up for a YMCA membership. Then a $10 fee was required to get a laminated membership card with your photo on it. We were mandated to wear our ID at all times, and if anyone forgot theirs, they were asked to leave.

Since Sharia Law is now in place, the "head manager" had to know that there were no Muslims in the community center. Each member had to sign a contract saying that they were not Muslim-born and had never converted to Islam. They also had to list any Muslim family members on the application. If the community center saw that an applicant was unfit for their program, they would not allow them to become a member. This was because you cannot legally preach to a Muslim on any level. If a person of question had made it into the meeting, the pastor could be charged heavily. The process was still new, and there was frustration that the new rules of the community center were in place, but everyone was thankful to still have a place to corporately and freely worship God.

It was Mother's Day, and it was a particularly difficult day for us to be overseas. My mom died when I was 18, and that always brings a variety of feelings, and Jess is very close to her mom, Michelle, so it was difficult to celebrate on the opposite end of the planet. Despite our touch of home-sickness that day, we were having the time of our lives and were amazed that the Lord was still carrying us financially.

As we sat in that service, however, I could only think about one thing, and it weighed heavy on me: The Great Britain Pound. At the time, the exchange rate was £1 = $1.68. It scared me to death. We were flying to London and didn't know where we would be staying. We had no contacts there, and everything is expensive. It would be an absolute shock for us to go from an area of the world where costs of goods were a third of the price of the states, to an area that was more expensive than the states.

One of the main things we had decided to do after our fast in Bario was to visit historical places of revival. We would travel around the United Kingdom to see what the Lord was doing in each place. It was a slight shift from our original purpose for being overseas, but it was what felt right at the time. Planning began for a road trip around the UK to visit a variety of spots, and we would run up a rental car and gas bill to do it all. There was about $650 left in our bank account at the time. Either our experience in Asia had been the product of a lot of cheap luck and coincidental meetings throughout our journey, or God was carrying us, and He would continue to throughout the rest of our time overseas.

I hate fear. I hate everything about it. I hate the courage that it destroys. I hate the bondage it keeps people in. I hate that people believe in their hearts that it can actually produce something positive. Some people define fear as false evidence appearing real. Fear more often prevents logic from seeing any form of potential in any given situation and therefore inhibits action to take place. Fear is inefficient, and for a man who seeks to be efficient in all his ways, it drives me nuts. Humanity actually believes that fear will produce positive results through worry.

How can I, through worry, add another second to my life? How can I worry my way to a filled bank account? How can I worry my way through the Kingdom of God when God's nature says not to worry? Worry and fear are unoriginal ways to respond to a natural issue. When your life motive is to seek a supernatural outcome (such as the completion of this trip free of debt), a supernatural response is required.

If we pick apart Philippians 4:6, "Do not be anxious about anything, but in every situation, by prayer and petition, with thanksgiving, present your requests to God," it not only says to take anything to the Lord in prayer and petition, but it also says to do it with thanksgiving. I believe that the word "thanksgiving" is not only referring to the past tense form of being thankful for what you have and what the Lord has done for you in your life, but that it is referring to thanksgiving in the sense that you have a level of thankfulness established in faith that God has already taken care of the means by which you are to accomplish the goal or receive a need, even though it hasn't yet manifested. We are to approach the throne of God with confidence that we are God's child and that He brings to completion the things that He sets us out to do. If going to the United Kingdom to visit places of history was what He put on our hearts, it was up to Him to make sure we could get it done.

The numbers didn't make sense for us to go to the UK at the time, and the exchange rate between the pound and the dollar were not favorable. We had a word, however, followed by peace and provision, to get to the starting point, and we were going to continue to trust God in faith. If there was any place I could be that Mother's Day to encourage my heart, it was in a room full of Asians pouring their heart out to the Lord in a country that had just been committed to a powerless god.

Our time with Rachel and Sabrina was very special. We met a ton of people, ate absurd amounts of food, and shared our testimony until we were blue in the face. Although we were sad to leave Asia, we were focused on the next part of our journey.

*　　　*　　　*　　　*　　　*

Sometimes when I had something special in mind that I wanted to save money for, when we had excess, I would hide money in the secret compartments of our bags. Maybe it was for a special thing we wanted to do or in case we ran out of food money. Either way, I occasionally put the practice into effect throughout the trip for some rainy day. The truth is, I actually forgot about the money sometimes (which was rare).

The payoff came when booking our flights to London and the cheapest itinerary was with EgyptAir. We had two layovers, one in Bangkok and one in Cairo, and the Cairo layover would be twelve hours during the daytime. Because I had set some money aside, we had enough to make a visit to the pyramids.

There were many things we didn't communicate to our friends and family on social media, and this one made the list. Had we told them everything we were going to do, many of them would have *begged us* to reconsider our choice, therefore inhibiting us from taking a risk or going somewhere that is uncomfortable for the typical American tourist to visit. Cairo, at the time, was definitely one of them.

I had visited Egypt purely for tourism purposes in 2006 before the revolution. It was "safer" then, and a lot more tourist-friendly, but I wanted to experience it with Jess. Going into Egypt this time, I knew the political atmosphere was a lot different and potentially life-threatening as an American. Unfortunately, there was just no possible way that you could have kept us in the airport all day knowing the pyramids were just a 45-minute taxi drive away.

We came to the conclusion that we would just let my brother (who was our Power of Attorney) know that we would be there. In fact, no one knew that we were even leaving Asia until pictures of us at the pyramids were posted on social media.

It's quite a bit freeing knowing that no one on the earth except for one person (and maybe the government) knows where in the world you are. Not many people have ever truly had the pleasure of experiencing that powerful feeling.

*   *   *   *   *

When we arrived in Cairo, it was five in the morning, and we were tired and greasy from our red eye flights from Malaysia to Egypt. We freshened up and got into a clean pair of clothes in the bathroom. Thankfully we didn't have our backpacks since they were still checked (all the more reason as to why we wanted to visit the pyramids). Then the moment came to find a taxi. This was always our least favorite part about airports overseas. Perhaps you can relate through a story from when I was fourteen:

My father was heavily involved with the Florida Institute of CPAs, and every summer through my teenage years, we would take a week vacation to wherever they decided to have their annual meetings at. It was usually somewhere expensive like Aspen or Vancouver, but this particular year we had visited San Diego, the city where Jess & I first met. All of the days on this trip were spent with the other teens and preteens of privileged families that reconvened every summer. It was a little rich boy's camp at the Hotel Coronado.

One night, the group was chaperoned to a semi-fancy Italian restaurant in the area, and someone whispered to me "that's Jason Alexander over there!" I, being someone who is awful with names, song lyrics, or anything trivia had no earthly clue who that was until I made the awkward, noticeable turn around to see who was behind me.

Realizing it was the bald guy from *Seinfeld*, I had a little bit of a freak out moment. I had never seen someone famous in a restaurant like that before. I just *had* to say something. It was the only thing I could think of doing for the rest of dinner. After all, this was before the Age of Selfies.

Then my moment came. One of his sons was being a bit ornery, so Jason decided to take him to the restroom to deal with the situation. It was in that moment the majority of the males in the restaurant suddenly had to use the restroom, including myself.

As I finished faking my business in the stall, I made my way out to the main area of the restroom where Jason had his son propped up on the counter, trying to pull out a loose tooth.

Obviously attempting this tooth removal a bit prematurely but all the while trying to console his son, I thought it was the perfect opportunity to add my own personal, empathetic moment of compassion for the two by saying, "I'm fourteen, and I haven't even lost my molars yet."

Jason looks and gives me a polite "this kid is weird" chuckle as I exited the bathroom face-in-palm. Since that very moment, I have had a bit more empathy and compassion for the very fact that famous people can't go anywhere without people trying to get their moment with them. They can't even go to the bathroom without getting hounded.

There's nothing like entering an African airport's taxi hire area. Jess & I felt like Brad & Angelina (RIP), working our way through the crowd of hungry, needy, desperate taxi drivers who have been directly affected by the destruction of the tourism industry in Egypt. Little (broke) Jess & I were the difference between one lucky individual out of tens, maybe hundreds of taxi drivers getting their next meal. And we're white, so we were obviously rich to them.

The winner of this chicken dinner was the one who chased us the most through the airport terminal because I ignored everyone as much as possible and even zig-zagged back and forth until I found someone who offered me the deal I wanted. After making a deal and walking out to the car, he asked us the dreaded question, "Where are you from?" When we told him the United States, he responded, "Oh, if I knew that, I would have charged double. I thought you were German." He was only a little off, me being Italian and Scottish and Jess being French Canadian. Netter Versuch!

*   *   *   *   *

Since I am always someone who asks people about their

lives, their politics, and their worlds, I did the very same with our tour guide at the pyramids. We purchased a 15-kilometer camel (and horse) ride to the pyramids. A guide and a young boy escorted our horse and camel.

"How many tours do you do a day?" I asked our guide.

"Before the revolution? About one to two a day. Now? About one to two a week."

I was shocked at his response. He was at one of the greatest tourist spots in the world, and he was working 15% of the time he used to. That would be a drastic pay cut for anyone.

"Before the revolution I had many camels, but when tourists stopped coming, I had to sell all of my camels because I had to choose between feeding them and feeding my family. Now I rent this horse and camel."

That was our guide's bridge into asking us for a good tip. He did a good job too, because we gave all that we had in our giving budget to him and the young guide. We have always enjoyed giving a significant portion of our income away, and if it's for funding a missionary to go after the lost or for a struggling Sunni Muslim man in Egypt, we do it knowing we're blessed in return with the opportunity. Unfortunately, we may have given precedence to the cliché that Americans are rich because we took care of them. After all, they needed it more than we did at the end of the day.

*   *   *   *   *

As we entered the Heathrow Airport immigration area, we could quickly tell we were back in the west. Out of the entire world, Heathrow was the third-most nerve-racking immigration office to go through. The other two were at London Gatwick and Dover, England. Notice a trend? The questions they would ask were highly personal, very calculated and meant to scare you into telling the truth. Nonetheless, we got through as usual. Although the question of "what do you do for a living" wasn't always the easiest to answer, having experience in the internet marketing field helps you convince them that you can work anywhere there is internet, so how much money we had (or didn't have) was not a large issue to discuss.

How do you tell an immigration officer that you have hardly any money, you've sold everything to see if God would carry you financially through prayer, and you're seeking out the line between faith and stupidity? And, oh yeah, you might be staying in the United Kingdom for a couple of days, but who knows? We would have been back in Africa the next week if the conviction was there and the transportation was available. There wasn't a soul that lived in the UK that we knew personally at the time.

In fact, that was a deep concern of ours, because the week leading up to our flight to London, we were concerned about the lodging prices in the city. For some (crazy) reason, however, Jess and I voted against sending up a flare to all of our friends to see if they had contacts in the UK that we could stay with. We simply prayed. As a result, two nights before leaving East Malaysia, we were contacted by our friend Grace asking us where we were staying in London. Within a few hours, we were connected to a Malaysian man who lives in the UK named Zach, and we were given directions to his house from the airport via the London Underground. We actually entered the country with a real address to write on our immigration form. What a change!

It was over an hour-long ride on the Underground, and we were nervous that we were going to miss our stop. Subways, metros, trains, whatever you want to call them; they all freak Floridians out. Few Floridians truly understand how they function and how to know if you're on the right one. After "rinsing and repeating" the learning process in many cities around the world, I can now pick it up easily. In fact, I can now clearly give someone directions in London, New York, and Singapore regarding train navigation from memory. I guess that makes me a subway nerd, and I'm a bit proud of it.

This odd feeling hit me once we got above ground next to Finsbury Park just before eleven in the evening. Red double decker busses and black hackney carriages were passing by us, there was a light drizzle sprinkling over us and our backpacks, and everyone around us was speaking English. I thought to myself, "This morning we were at the pyramids." In fact, there was still sand in my shoes. Then I thought to myself, "Yesterday, I was in Asia." What an odd feeling. It was similar to the feeling I had on the day I was able to say, "My mom died, yesterday."

It is rare and sometimes a privilege to have such a climactic, defining point of change in your life. When these types of moments come, whether forced or chosen, I try to close my eyes and burn that experience into my mind, because it will either be a reference point down the road for something bigger, or it will be a moment that brings reflection and gratitude when thinking about the amazing opportunities I've had in my life. It still blows my mind that you can be on an entirely different continent at the beginning of the day and on another by dinner time. That wasn't possible for the average individual very long ago.

As we walked to the front door of Zach's house, we had no clue what we were about to step into. We were once again about to walk into a house of someone we knew nothing about. Could Zach be a serial killer? Who knows? What we did know is that we had a free place to stay in the greatest city in the world, and we were excited to experience what we could of it.

*   *   *   *   *

The door opens and a tall, fair-skinned British man named Tim answers along with Zach who is short like me and was wearing a fedora hat (no peacock feather unfortunately). They invited us in, and there was a clear excitement upon them to meet us and hear our story. We were not surprised when they offered us tea.

We apologized for walking into the house as if we had been in the desert, and once the formalities were finished, we chatted for over an hour. From the start, Jess & I knew we had formed lifelong friends with Tim and Zach. They said they would introduce us to the other flat mates in the morning, but they would let us catch up on sleep first.

After carrying our bags up the steps and entering our bedroom, I saw it. It was one of the most beautiful things I had seen in months: my own personal wardrobe.

Staying in many different places with only enough to fit in a small backpack had taken its toll after four months. Any Type-A person like me would have a difficult time with all of the change and lack of structure, but I seemed to handle myself well. Jess was just fine struggling to get a pair of underwear from the bottom of a pile of clothes in the corner of the room. Having my own personal wardrobe was a dream come true, because it was the closest to an organized, controlled lifestyle I could get.

We took a hot shower after 48 hours of travel and a trip to the sandbox, and organized our belongings. Even Jess unpacked. There was an odd feeling that night because it was almost as if we nested in that room.

CHAPTER THIRTEEN

CONSTANT AWE AND WONDER

Most families, when pulling off some kind of vacation with their children, do everything they can do financially to make the trip perfect. This doesn't always mean that they get to check everything off their list, and although compromise isn't an enjoyable feature (especially when visiting a place very special and rare), it often must take place. There was a level of understanding that just because we were in a particular place, it didn't mean we would be able to visit everything we wanted. London, however, was going to be the most difficult place for us to compromise. There are too many amazing sites to see. Thankfully, the locals pay high taxes that are distributed fairly well, so most of the museum exhibits are free!

As we gathered our small, black daytime backpack filled with our camera, phone, local map and spare toilet paper, we headed downstairs to grab a cup of coffee. Since Malaysians tend to drink instant coffee only, I opted for tea. That's when Zach entered the kitchen and told us that he wanted to purchase us a city bus tour pass. We were shocked. He told us that he would take us to Piccadilly Circus to pick up the tickets, and he wanted to buy us lunch there as well.

We certainly didn't hesitate at the generosity of this man, and we had learned through experience at that point that Malaysians typically like to purchase you a meal as an expression of honor. It's in their blood to do so. Zach didn't skimp out either, because he took us to a Brazilian all-you-can-eat meat restaurant. We felt like a king and queen. That was the first of many meals with Zach, and there isn't much more in my life that I currently desire than to share a meal with him once again.

*   *   *   *   *

There is nothing that we could do but just shake our heads in awe in moments like when we were standing on Westminster Bridge in the evening time. There we were, at one of the most visited places on planet earth, taking selfies and listening to Big Ben sing his song. Who were we? What had we done to deserve this? Was this just the high before we would crash and burn? After all, we only had a few hundred dollars left. Failure seemed inevitable, especially since now we were in the UK.

Commitment was the word of the week. We were committed to the next stage of our trip. We were committed to seeing the Lord come through faithfully in our finances. We were committed to resting, touring London, and simply having fun.

It was so easy for us, however, to constantly be in the fight to "earn our paycheck" from God. I especially had a battle within arguing that if I wasn't working in ministry, then I wasn't "working for God", which meant that our finances wouldn't be taken care of. If that happened, then I would be a failure as a husband, as a provider, and I would have misled my household into some sort of hoax. The thought of facing Jess' parents with my tail between my legs was not appealing.

*   *   *   *   *

Living out of rest is incredibly difficult for the Gunns. I come from a line of alcoholics and workaholics seemingly incapable of rationally constituting rest. We always have to be working toward or away from something. It's in our blood.

It has been the most difficult task for me in life, especially as an American, to understand that when internal rest and peace is prevalent in my life, I become more cognizant of God's presence inside of me. It is when I am busy trying to make things happen, that I actually lose the perspective necessary in order to know the very next step the Lord wants me to take in my day. When we seek the place of internal rest, we enter the breeding ground for faith to develop more deeply, and we are more inclined to connect to the voice of God. The enemy is doing his job best if he is creating chaos in our life, thereby, preventing us from being in a stance where we can function out of the overflow of the Holy Spirit.

Worry is the expression of internal chaos. It is difficult enough to have everyday matters distracting us from the pleasures of life or by carrying out our tasks with pleasure, but it is taken to another level when internal chaos is prevalent in a moment of silence. Worry only removes us from a place of sensitivity to the Holy Spirit by redirecting our focus from the power of God onto the power of man. When our inadequacy becomes our focus through worry, striving settles in because we are overly-focused on the things we need to do to make the things we want in our lives happen rather than focusing on the effect we can have on the obstacles in our lives by simply co-laboring with God.

This is one reason why Jesus is the Prince of Peace. When we adjust our focus and make Jesus the center of our lives once again, His peace will then supersede chaos so we can function out of our proper identity in Christ along with the power of the Holy Spirit. Now, instead of striving, we are moving out of a place of internal rest, which allows us to pay attention to what God is showing and telling us to do next.

I am beginning to truly understand that it is the chaos of life that inhibits our ability to see God's hand in our own lives and others' as well, and when we connect to our Father through Christ Jesus, he eliminates the chaos and creates order in our hearts so our blinders can be removed.

There's nothing like a moment in life that you can simply

stand in awe and enjoy it knowing that it was God who got you there. It was the creator of energy, every micro molecule and the expanse of the universe that cared enough about little me to simply enjoy that moment that we couldn't have made happen on our own during this journey.

*   *   *   *   *

I love a great vacation. It's that vacation that you leave knowing you had just the right amount of time to do everything you wanted to and felt rested as well. Those are the best! That's how we felt upon leaving London.

We made new friends in London that we will never forget. Amazing meals were shared, we toured all around town, and we learned a lot about what the Lord was doing in the city. In fact, we had decided that we would return to London at the end of our time in the United Kingdom. We had an agenda, however, and this was to visit historical places of revival.

*   *   *   *   *

You know, I don't care for the term "revival." It, like many words today, are often used in improper contexts or used loosely. Some people make statements like, "We're having revival tonight at 8:00. Be there!" Others like to say, "We believe that tonight we are going to cry out to God, and there's going to be a massive revival here in this place." I tend to lean toward the more conservative side of the statement. Revival, in the context that I will use the term, is when God manifests in such a way that geographical regions are affected on a massive level.

In Acts 19:11 (NLT) it says, "God gave Paul the power to perform unusual miracles." I would sure love to know the difference between "unusual" and "usual" miracles. My view on revival is that it is when an overwhelming amount of unusual and usual miracles make their way into a general area, and also that the manifested power of God is very easily accessed and transferred. I simply can't compare one revival where people were literally falling over in the parking lot to another Wednesday night service. With all this said, we sought out to visit historical places of revival. These are the places that books were written about, filled with stories of God's radical power being displayed so much that cities were drastically changed.

The first place we scheduled was very special: Bristol.

*   *   *   *   *

I mentioned back in chapter five that one of the more important action steps we felt was vital in accomplishing a mission such as ours was through prayer, but I haven't walked through the thought process of how we decided prayer would be one of the most essential requirements of our journey. It looked similar to the time I came to my personal opinion on abortion:

When I was in high school, one of my mom's closest friends had adopted a baby from China named Charlotte, and she and her mom came over to hang out at our house one afternoon. I had never really interacted with toddlers before, and Charlotte was just beginning to really become confident in her walking skills. She was maybe 18 months old. Frankly, I had it somewhere in my adolescent mind that children didn't wake up until they were about the age of three, and until then, they were a burden on all civilizations. So, I didn't really have a pro-life opinion.

Then the moment came when Charlotte and I were climbing up a staircase together. We had stairs that went up halfway, did a U-turn and then continued to escalate. Charlotte made her way to the mid-level part of the staircase and was sitting down, standing up, and playing and laughing when she accidentally slipped, fell out of my grip, tumbled down the stairs, and bumped her head hard on the bottom stair which was hardwood. Wait three seconds. Then the crying began.

Thankfully her mom saw the whole event happen from a distance, and she ran over and picked her up to console her. During the crying process, Charlotte, who had hardly started speaking yet, was trying to communicate to her mom what had happened. She pointed to the top of the stairs, babbled a little, spun her fingers to signal she rolled down the stairs and babbled some more. Then she pointed to the bottom step, babbled and put her hand on the spot of her head that she bumped. It was the first time I had seen a child that young truly capable of communicating, and that was the moment I realized that all lives are valuable no matter what they can do.

We came to our conclusion about the importance of prayer through a similar aha-moment that both Jess and I had through reading an elementary-level biography on a man named George Müller. In a nutshell, George was a Prussian man who went to a Lutheran seminary because he heard that Lutheran clergy made great money. It was at his seminary that he gave his life to the Lord and became a radical leader during his time. By the end of his life, he had traveled the globe multiple times preaching the gospel, which was very rare for anyone to do during that era. After getting married and having a few children of his own, the Müllers found themselves in Bristol, England during a very difficult time economically.

Bristol was known at the time for its orphan population because poverty was extremely prevalent. George discussed with his wife the thought of taking in some of the street children, but they hardly had extra money of their own. George and his wife concluded that since they felt compelled to take in children, it wasn't necessarily because they wanted to, but because God wanted them to. As a result, George told the Lord that he would begin helping the street children, but God Himself was going to have to take care of the finances. George wasn't able or willing to take on more jobs or sacrifice more of his family's welfare, so either God was going to take care of it, or nothing would happen. He committed to a lifestyle of prayer, however, and the miraculous began to occur.

By the end of Müller's life, through prayer and having faith for the finances to show up, his ministry had facilities that were able to feed, clothe, house and educate 2,400 orphans. George would pray about anything and everything, and he expected each prayer to get answered. There was not one time a child went hungry in his care, even though at times the provision came down to the very last second. Many times, they would sit down to eat with no food on their plate, pray the blessing and thank God for the (invisible) food, and someone would knock on the door with a donation of food that was large enough to feed the entire group. George Müller knew what it was to live a life full of faith, and he is one of my historical heroes.

We read about Müller the summer before, right after we got back from our mission to Alaska. This was when we prayed that the finances for our flights to Bangkok would come in by Labor Day and that we would do so without ever asking for money except through prayer. All of the money we needed came in two weeks before Labor Day. It was this experience that shifted the approach of our journey from me running an internet marketing company to living completely in faith for our finances. It's not that we weren't willing to work (in fact quite the opposite), but it's that we wanted to see God come through.

*　　　*　　　*　　　*　　　*

Jess is a very connected woman. Usually if we need something somewhere outside of Florida, she'll know someone in some state or country whom we can at least connect with. She had a friend of hers that was connected to a family in Bristol that lived a very different lifestyle: communal living.

In fact, they lived in one of the homes that the Müllers housed orphans in years ago. This 10-bedroom, semi-detached home was beautiful, historic, and had many memories within its walls. The owners were a family with teenagers, and were fostering a five-year-old girl. Additionally, they had college students, young couples and other random people like us living with them – totaling to about 21 people. Everyone was open with each other, and "family" dinner was at 6pm every night. It was out of our comfort zones, but it was nice to have a sense of family. More than that, it was an honor to be in the same home that the orphans cared for by George's ministry had lived in.

The best part about this house and a gift straight from God Himself: it was across the street from George's home. Today, it is a museum with various artifacts from the time of his ministry, and in the back is a beautiful garden. In the museum was the very thing I wanted to see in all of Bristol: George's desk.

I love desks. My desk has always been a special place for me to do my work. I love desks so much that when I was 15, I spent my birthday money on a very large L-desk that took up a lot of square footage in my bedroom. George spent ample time at his desk, and history says that it is where he prayed many of the prayers that are still being answered today. Not only did I get to see his desk, but I got to sit in his chair and soak in it. This was by far one of the highlights of my life because without this man's faith that we could leverage off of, I'm not sure we would have had the faith to do what we have done today.

*   *   *   *   *

The same week came with very troubling news that Jess' beloved grandmother had died unexpectedly. Since this was Jess' first very personal death experience, she took the time to mourn while we were in Bristol. Waves of mourning hit her throughout the week, and it was during that time that we continued to plan out our road trip to some very specific spots throughout Wales, North England, and Scotland.

We learned that despite the ridiculous petrol prices in the United Kingdom, which came out to a little more than $8.70 a gallon, it was still relatively cheap to travel via a rental car. Upon leaving London before heading to Bristol, we were given £500 cash which was plenty for a week and a half of transportation. The thought of being given the equivalent of about $840 blew our minds, and it took a lot of the pressure off in terms of how the trip would be provided for.

*   *   *   *   *

Some couples road trip well together, and some just don't. Jess and I traveled perfectly fine in the states, and part of that is because I know the road systems fairly well, and we have always had GPS since we were together. Overseas, road trips were just a bit more difficult for us to get along. The main problem is that Jess can't read a map.

We have tried for many years to work this problem out. We started with a map of Disney World, to which I would ask her questions about how to get from Space Mountain to Thunder Mountain. Then we graduated to a Washington, D.C. tourist map, since we have spent some time there before, and she did great. When it comes to really being able to give great directions as a passenger in a vehicle, however, something just doesn't click for her. It made for some stressful times.

Since our iPads only had Wi-Fi capabilities, we had to get a little creative. I would look up directions whenever we could find Wi-Fi and screenshot different maps of the areas we would be traveling. While driving, I would switch through the different maps on my camera roll as if it was my own GPS. It got a little tricky at times, but Jess could keep up for the most part.

The first day of travel was very tiring. Not only did I have to adjust to driving on the left side of the road and the right side of the car, but I had to drive a stick shift as well. I hadn't driven a manual consistently for years, and I hadn't driven anything except for that motorbike in Chiang Mai since we had left the states. Add the squished roads, intermittent map reading, and trying to look at the scenery, a nice headache had settled in for the evening. Our little Fiat 500 took care of us well, however.

Since we had a car and we were semi-close, we thought that we'd try and go see Stonehenge. The only problem with it is that you can't legally stop on the side of the road to take your picture. You have to go to their specific parking lot and pay to get in and be transported to the actual location. Since that wasn't an option, we said that we would try and get a photo of it in the background from inside the car. After driving back and forth eight times, Jess got a picture of it in the background with my head in the photo, and it was only slightly blurry. The photo with Jess in it wasn't as successful since you can only see the front of a semi-truck behind her head. With how much gas money we spent going from the point we could make a U-turn to the other end, we probably could have just bought the passes.

Upon the completion of that joke of an event, we made our way to the Wales Bible College in Swansea, Wales, which was my favorite stop of our entire road trip. Frankly, we didn't know why we were going, but we were referred there by some friends who had connections, and it was well-recommended.

*   *   *   *   *

I need to go back and lay a little more foundation for how we got to this college in the first place:

Before we had left the states, I found out that Heidi Baker was going to be in Singapore for a conference in March (which you already know). I really felt like we were supposed to go, and the Lord made it happen.

The first day of the conference, we accidentally arrived early and ended up spending the majority of the day in a mall across the street until mid-afternoon (which you also know). We made our way towards the conference hall a little early. When we arrived, we heard the sound check going on inside the expo hall, so we went inside and listened.

Up on the stage were a man and a woman who were announcing each of the countries being represented in the audience by going back and forth while the flag and country name would show up behind them on the large screen. The woman for some reason kept making me laugh, and what I found out later is that I just think Singaporean accents are naturally funny. Well, we met that same girl over a month later when we flew to East Malaysia and stayed with our friend Rachel. It was our friend Sabrina.

Sabrina was starting a church with Rachel under the covering of Cornerstone Church in Singapore. Pastor Yang, the pastor of that church, through a series of events, actually bought the Wales Bible College and raised funds to restore it. As a result, there was a Singaporean representative from the church at the college who we got connected with to set up a visit.

*   *   *   *   *

The Wales Bible College hosts a significant amount of spiritual history. A lot of it is birthed out of the blue room which is a noted prayer room said to be responsible for changing some of the outcomes in World War II (no, really). Decades of fervent, nonstop prayer has taken place at the college (formerly known as Derwen Fawr), and it is still reflected today in an experience that I personally had while we were visiting.

It was suggested to us that we attend a Tuesday morning prayer and worship meeting on the campus, so we scheduled our trip specifically around the service. When we walked into the meeting room, I experienced the Holy Spirit in a way I never had before: through weightiness. It was like a heavy thickness so strong on me that it was difficult to focus while socializing. I just wanted to go to my seat and fall on my knees.

I've heard people talk about "how great God is" in terms of His magnitude or size, but I had never had an experience where that was the primary thing I noticed about Him. The best way I could explain the intensity of the Holy Spirit in the room that morning would be similar to trying to freely move around in a graviton at the county fair. It's not like I couldn't move, but there was a level of comfort in simply sitting still and taking it in. It was a very easy place to enter into worship.

It's moments like these that I look back and wonder how I could ever question the greatness of my God, let alone the mere existence of Him. I truly feel sorry for people around the world who have no grid or experiential history when it comes to the power of God. This is one of the main reasons we are to bring it to them. The moments in life that many seek to experience for their own benefit often miss the ultimate purpose behind them. These kinds of moments are to be spread globally.

Gary Chapman, author of *The 5 Love Languages* addresses the five ways people tend to receive and give love (acts of service, gifts, touch, quality time and words of affirmation). I believe the Lord also functions through each one of them, and when you get overwhelmed in one category (in this case, touch), then it is often that another category gets addressed soon after. The quality time got fulfilled in terms of the deep, deep worship that took place over a few hours, and then the words of affirmation came. If I've noticed anything about my walk with the Lord, it's that when I'm truly seeking Him first regularly, I tend to attract people who walk in the prophetic and have something to say regarding my life. It's also often that I'll have fulfilling conversations on matters close to my heart at the time when my eyes are set on the Lord's.

The meeting took a turn, and the leader of the meeting called us forward to pray over Jess and me, and it wasn't long before the congregation joined in. On a normal day, this would just be a session where people start praying, prophesying, and declaring various things, but on this day, it was different. Despite the many things said over us (which I'll again keep private for the sake of wanting to keep legitimacy when they come to pass), none of them were new items. They only confirmed the same things we had spoken over us from people all over the world. Words given to us have so much more meaning when someone in Thailand says the same thing to us from the Lord as someone in Sarasota and someone in Wales. The best part is that we were just worshipping and "minding our own business."

Mark Twain is famously quoted for saying, "Travel is fatal to prejudice, bigotry and narrow-mindedness, and many of our people need it sorely on these accounts. Broad, wholesome, charitable views of men and things cannot be acquired by vegetating in one little corner of the earth all one's lifetime." I couldn't find this to be more accurate, and our understanding of who we are, and what our personal destinies are, were developed, deepened, and solidified by visiting the Wales Bible College.

CHAPTER FOURTEEN

BROKE, HUNGRY, AND LOST

My Grandmom was loud, Northern and Italian. She showed her love by cooking you a meal and sharing a great conversation. One of my most memorable discussions with her was when she told me the Christmas present she would get when she was a child: a piece of fruit. I don't believe I've ever been given a piece of fruit for Christmas before.

Unfortunately, I have a memory that will probably never go away. It took place on the day Grandmom came to our new house for a visit when I was twelve. The house was over the top, even for today's standards. It was on a beautiful property, extremely large and in the nicest neighborhood in town. The house represented the epitome of accessing the fulfillment of the American Dream for my dad. I, frankly, was a bit embarrassed about it growing up, and it was because of what I heard my Grandmom say the day she came to the house to see it. I could hear her strong, raspy voice through the floor of my upstairs bedroom. I was finishing cleaning it in preparation for her to see it, and I heard her holler out, "These kids are spoiled brats!"

Now this was (honestly) very far from the truth, and she certainly didn't mean it that way. I was very thankful for the things my parents did for me within the understanding of my idea of what things cost as a child and a teenager. I was the kid that didn't play baseball because I felt bad for making my parents drive to multiple practices and games every week, so I stuck to soccer and basketball. What Grandmom meant was "Wow this house is unbelievable. Oh, to be a child and live in this kind of lifestyle…" Twelve-year-old Chris heard "you're a brat, and you'll never amount to anything without your parents' help. Nobody likes a rich kid."

I was instilled, in that very moment. with the drive to make sure that everything I did in life was accomplished by my hands only and not by the social and economic leverage of my upbringing. To this day I have a very difficult time receiving from my family, because the last thing I ever want is my integrity and identity to be falsely recognized. You could easily overanalyze me by saying, "Chris – it seems you went into the cleaning business to destroy every financial and educational access point created by the leverage of your parents' help to make you feel like 'you accomplished everything you did all by yourself.'" I'd say that wouldn't be an inaccurate analyzation.

If I were to plead the case that Jess and I were extremely out of our comfort zones to be financially reliant on God/other people only seeking provision through prayer, hopefully the above story paints a clear picture of how difficult it was for me. Even Jess, who grew up on the other side of the train tracks, worked for much of what she had besides her everyday needs. This style of living was completely outside our idea of living a respectable and responsible life, and there were more difficult days than others: like the one when we were in Edinburgh.

*　　　*　　　*　　　*　　　*

Our friend Heather from London told us we could stay with her parents who live outside of Edinburg, and we were honored to stay with them. I'll never forget the awful timing when we arrived: it was the last 10 minutes of the season finale of a cooking show Heather's mom had been watching religiously. When she answered the door, she sweetly and distractedly said hello and jostled us into the living room to watch the rest of the show. We immediately felt at home. There's nothing like a cozy couch after driving all day in a tiny car.

At dinner, like anyone would do, they told us about what to do in Scotland and in Edinburg when we visited the city. It was then they told us the price of the train tickets to get into town and back. I think they were like £20, which at the time was about $36 each. A $70 day just in transportation was daunting for us to afford on our quickly dwindling budget. It was in downtown Edinburg that I had a poverty meltdown.

We were walking around in the (yes, believe it) hot sun and were very hungry. Everything was expensive because we were in town, and we had spent $70 just on transportation. My mentality when budgeting throughout the year was to say, for example, "I have $300 this month; so that's $10 a day for us to do what we need to." That $10 figure would fluctuate depending upon how much money we had (obviously), but we weren't living a $2,000 a month lifestyle, so $75 was way over our daily budget. To compensate for the heavier days, we could compromise and eliminate expenses, but when you're on a road trip, it's just not always possible to do so unless it's with food and our lodging (which was free already). Food was what needed to cut back on.

We approached a corner grocery store, and there was no way we were going to walk around the city all day and enjoy it without eating something. Our minds were focused on our stomachs. After browsing the store twice, we walked out with a 6-pack of crumpets and two healthy juices for nutrients.

We were hungry.

*   *   *   *   *

Discovering and learning about cycles and patterns in groups and individuals is a passion of mine, and it helps point out the strategies of the enemy. For example, one of the patterns I was once told about was how a person knows when a thought that provokes action is from God or from the enemy.

When a thought all of a sudden pops up and says, "*I* should steal that pack of gum," it is not from the Lord. On the other hand, when a thought pops up that says, "*You* should go pray for that person," it is usually from the Lord. Stealing a pack of gum (for me) is completely out of *character* and does not represent the Chris that I am. Praying for someone is in my character. Pay attention to the pronouns. When "I" is used, it is usually a thought provoked by the enemy. When "you" is used, it is usually from the Lord. Pay attention to it sometime.

One of my main arguments for this is that Satan's top priority is for us to have a confused identity. It is always the first adjustment that we make after we sin or make a mistake. We say to ourselves, "I'm such an idiot" or "there's no way that God can forgive me for that." Guilt and shame follow, and our sights and thoughts are redirected to an unbiblical, insecure identification of who we are in Christ Jesus. By saying "I should steal the gum," Satan puts in our mind that we are the thief, and when we steal the gum, our identity is immediately challenged and accused.

But Jesus talks constantly about the things that *you* are to do and *you* can do *in Him*. When we have a strong and secure identity that reflects the fruits of the spirit, we can respond like Jesus confidently and see the same results He did and greater.

*   *   *   *   *

Yet, food was the focus in Edinburgh, not our identities in Christ. A few crumpets and a juice can only hold you over for a short time, and it was not long before we wanted to go home, to the home that didn't exist anymore. Was this trip still what God wanted us to do? What were we doing, throwing out the foundations we spent the first three years of marriage building in preparation for our family and professional experience? How long could we live off of other peoples' money?

Our identity was challenged that afternoon, and as a result, we broke out the credit card for something we felt we could not afford for the first time ever on the trip. Although we did actually have enough cash in our pockets, we would not have enough to last us much longer, so we pulled out the Visa out of the desire to get what we wanted. We swiped the plastic in exchange for two large Mexican burritos. Was it faith, or was it stupidity? Frankly, we didn't care.

*　　　　*　　　　*　　　　*　　　　*

It's amazing what great Mexican food did for the two of us. We left our little pity party and had a great rest of the day. Edinburgh became one of our favorite cities to visit.

Visiting northern Scotland was a bucket list item for myself, and we had planned in our agenda to do a day trip to Wick, Scotland which is just thirty minutes north of a small village called Latheron where the Clan Gunn Heritage Museum is located. It was worth the drive.

Not only were the Scottish Highlands one of the most beautiful places we visited next to Vietnam, but there was meaning behind it for me in particular. Located on the coast, the museum is inside an old white chapel surrounded by the town's deceased. We visited on a clear, warm day, and the sun shone magically on the green, sheep-covered hills that lead to a large cliff looking out to the deep blue waters of the North Sea. This place, a place dedicated to my family heritage, was the most beautiful place I had been on earth. I was honored to be the first member of my immediate family to have visited the area.

*　　　　*　　　　*　　　　*　　　　*

Like I said before, your identity is the very thing that the enemy wants to smear, and a moment we were very vulnerable was on the way back south to Edinburgh. There weren't many places to stay, and even if there was a place, it would have been too expensive for us. We decided it would be the first night we would sleep in the car.

Looking back, I don't know why it was such a big deal to us to sleep in the car, but it was easy for us to have a sense of failure attached to having to sleep in a vehicle. By not having had a place to stay, it challenged our American mentality of "it's not God if you're not secure." That evening, I was reminded of Luke 9:58 when Jesus said to a man who said he would follow Him wherever He went, "Foxes have dens and birds have nests, but the Son of Man has no place to lay his head." Today, I view sleeping in the car as modern day camping. I was never much of a camper, and I always end up sleeping in the car when I go camping anyways. So what was the big deal?

Despite our childish concerns of sleeping in the car, I did have a legal concern of sleeping in the car. The last time I had slept in my car was with my friend Brian from college when we took a spontaneous trip from Tampa to Ducktown, Tennessee because we had a bad week. While sleeping, a cop banged on the back window of my car with his flashlight (and about broke it) and told us we couldn't sleep where we were. I hate getting in trouble, so I didn't want to sleep in the wrong place in Scotland. We eventually learned the United Kingdom and Europe have pullover areas all over so people can freely sleep and use nature.

The peace came, however, when the end of our drive for the day was approaching, and I had a fuzzy station on the radio playing folk music that seemed fitting for the drive. We pulled our car into a pullover overlooking a picturesque area of Cromarty Firth (a river). As we parked the car, we prayed to see if we felt like it was an okay place for us to plant ourselves for the night, and as we prayed, a song came on the radio called "Rollin' Home on the River." Sometimes a song can be the very answer to a prayer that you need. We had a perfect night's sleep.

*   *   *   *   *

Looking back at the entire process leading up to Scotland, we had things relatively easy. We only ran out of money one time, and it wasn't long after until we were stable again. We had places to stay, people to talk to and plenty of people to encourage us along the way; many who fed us a meal. Neither of us had a job, yet we were seeing places even traveling retirees don't often visit, and only at the cost of not having a home and things to call our own. The hardest part, truly, had been the emotional rollercoaster that came with the changing of the way we viewed our lives, how we were to live and what was right for us that day.

We drove for two days, arriving back in Bristol to return our car only to catch a bus to return to London to rest at Zach's house. It is a comforting feeling to return to a place where you have a sense of family. Zach, Tim, Heather, and another flat mate, Carina, had quickly become family to us, and it was very special to return to our home away from home. Not only is London our favorite city in the world, but returning to familiar places on our journey was a bit like visiting family at Christmas time. We had stories to tell, dinners to share, and plans to make. Those plans involved Amsterdam.

Jessica had always wanted to see the red light district in Amsterdam with her own eyes. There was nothing particularly special that we sought to accomplish, other than to prayer-walk the streets, but we were open to settling for a long time. We didn't have any other particular plans at that point. Our problem was solely being able to secure a place to stay. None of our efforts to find any type of discounted place were working. It came time to board our pre-booked bus, and we were just going to have to work something out upon our arrival.

One contact did finally surface, and we met them for coffee in the downtown area at a quaint coffee shop on the water. As usual, we discussed our story and explained some of the desires to be a helping hand while being in Amsterdam. This particular person was clearly skeptical of our approach to ministry and was not interested in the level of help we had to offer.

"Working in the red light districts is not something you can do here unless you commit for a minimum of five years," they said. "The girls need to know they can trust you, and there is a team of people here working daily to gain that trust. The last thing we need is for short-termers to come and mess things up."

Although a hard pill to swallow in the moment, I realized how right they were after hearing some of their stories. After a few hours of a discussion, we were given a list of hotels in the area along with a fifty Euro note. We were grateful for the money, but it was such a shock to us that a person who was so highly connected in the city was completely unwilling to at least try to find us a bed or a floor to sleep on. It was a significant change from the level of hospitality we had received in Asia.

*　　*　　*　　*　　*

Sarah Lanier wrote a book called *Foreign to Familiar* discussing the differences between what she calls a "hot" culture and a "cold" culture. Hot cultures are warm and inviting, focus on the relational aspects of culture, often have no gage for time, and tend to not communicate clearly and definitively. Cold cultures are lonely and dissociative. They seek to focus inward on the individual need, are effective, efficient and communicate clearly and concisely. The coldest of cultures don't worry about offense and emotions, but rather, they focus on "getting the job done."

A great example she uses in her book of someone from a hot culture visiting a cold culture is when she received a bad haircut and asked someone from Northern Europe what they thought about the hair (looking for some reassurance). They, to her surprise, responded unfavorably, saying things probably similar to "Your bangs are uneven, and it is too short in the back." A Floridian like myself would have probably responded, "Oh, it's wonderful. It's totally the new you," while thinking to myself "her bangs look awful and it's too short in the back." Someone from a cold culture like Norway or Sweden would not respond in that manner because they would be giving "the wrong answer" which would be a disservice to the other person.

What we experienced in Amsterdam was this very type of culture. We asked for a place to stay, and this cold-cultured person we talked to is used to a society where everyone is on their own. They were being generous in their world by sharing with us a list of hotels and giving us a fifty Euro note. Our warm-cultured mentality got offended, however, and we felt that they could have kept the money and let us sleep on their floor. The fact was, however, that they didn't want people in their house, let alone two strange vagabonds like us. It was too invasive and dependence is not rewarded in their household.

*　　　　*　　　　*　　　　*　　　　*

Hot versus cold cultures aside, what were we to do? It was 3:00, we had about $250 in the bank account plus the note we were given. Cheap hotels were $80, so we could last about two days in Amsterdam before running out of money. Then I thought of it: The Marriott!

Our credit card at the time earned us Marriott rewards points, and we had saved them up. Additionally, we had a voucher for a hotel room for one night that I had forgotten about until Amsterdam. We found that the nearest hotel we could use the voucher at was a 30-minute train ride outside of town, and we could afford another night for free with our points. The train for two days cost us 40 Euro, but with the 50 Euro note we had just been given, it was, essentially, free. We decided to give Amsterdam a try for two more days and see what developed.

*   *   *   *   *

When Jess was 19, she went for a neighborhood bike ride with her brothers. It was a beautiful spring day in Sarasota, and all was well until she came to an intersection where she needed to stop, and the brakes went out on her bike. Just nearly avoiding a strike by a car, she crossed the road safely, but her trust of bikes was completely shattered.

Holland is a biking paradise. People bike everywhere, and the cities are built specifically to accommodate them. This meant bike mayhem surrounded us while walking the streets of Amsterdam, and Jess wasn't having it. Whenever we needed to cross the road, it started with our sidewalk, then the bike path, then the traffic lanes, then in the middle was the train path (some people refer to them as Sprinters), then the other traffic lanes, bike paths, and then the sidewalk. It was like a game of Frogger each time we wanted to cross the road. Europe also drives on the right side of the road which was a first for us since we left the states, and our brains didn't remember where to look first when crossing the street!

Despite Jess' anxious moments with bikes, we lived to tell the story, but it also means we lived to remember the faces of the women we passed in the windows of the red light district.

We both stopped at the side of a charming area: walls of tall brick buildings all different colors with thin windows and beautiful doors sitting next to a brick road with a canal passing through. As beautiful as it was, on the first and second floors were women standing in the glass, trying to earn their next sale. These women are paid to have sex over twenty times a day. I stood on the side of the road with my wife looking to see who the next person was that was going to solicit sex.

Sure enough, I saw a European man, old and bald begin talking to one of the ladies who opened her door to lure him in. They talked for a moment, and he walked away. A few minutes later he returned with a bag of Red Bulls. The woman gave one to her friend next door, and then he went into the unit with her. The blinds were closed, red light turned off, and that was that.

Our contact that we had coffee with in Amsterdam said something arguable that I'll never forget, "Prostitution is no different in Amsterdam than any other city in the world other than its legality, regulation, and open display to the public." In their opinion, the prostitution is just as prevalent in Amsterdam as it is in New York City. You just have to look a little harder in New York. I have personally found that once you know what a brothel tends to look like in a region, you'll be able to spot one just like it's another McDonald's.

*   *   *   *   *

Our stay in the Marriott was wonderful. It was nice to be alone and just enjoy our trip together, but we were still looking to get connected to someone in the region. Messages on Facebook asking for any info returned void, and we were unable to secure anything in The Netherlands. We made an ultimatum with our prayers and said by 9:30 am on checkout day, if we hadn't figured out what to do, we would return to London and figure out where to go from there. We knew Zach would let us stay for a few days until we could pray out a plan.

9:30 came and went. A bus back to London that evening was booked that arrived the next morning at Victoria Station. Just before lunchtime, we returned to Zach's house, knocked on the door, and when he answered, he could tell we were down. We returned like two puppies with our tails between our legs.

I stated very clearly in the preface of this book that our goal in recording our story is not to get you to sell everything and travel the world in faith. That was our journey. Our goal is to encourage you to get out of your boat; whatever that looks like. If God had sustained us thus far, there is no doubt that He will support you through the dreams He has put inside of you for you to develop. I hate to be superficial in saying, "If He did it for us, He'll do it for you," but if He did it for us, He'll do it for you.

As we prayed the next few days about what to do, I couldn't come to grips dogmatically about the style of trip we were leading. I couldn't develop it logically on a spreadsheet, so to speak, and I began to conclude that we were in fact crazy, over-spiritual sojourners, because I couldn't answer the question, "What's next, and what's the point of it?"

Frustration and anger began to settle because a few days had turned into a week of no developments about our next step. As a result, a routine had naturally developed in London. Thursday night church meetings. Friday night badminton. Saturday morning markets. It wasn't a bad lifestyle. London in the summer is an easy place to simply go to a park and think. So, that's what we did. Soon the winds changed from thinking about our next step to concluding we would be in London until the end of June when our only commitment for the year was approaching: our annual mission to Alaska that we lead.

Getting to Alaska and back to Europe wouldn't necessarily be considered a cheap itinerary, and it was a financial hurdle that we were going to have to trust for. Thankfully in some sense, our flights were already taken care of. Because my mom died when I was 18, her portion of my grandmother's inheritance was set to skip my father and be split between my brother and myself. We had received an initial check before we left the states (and it went to bills and gear for the trip since we didn't have jobs), but I knew at some point more funds would be released upon the sale of their house. The housing market wasn't favorable at the time, however, so I didn't count on seeing anything for a long time.

Then we found out in May that the funds were going to be dispersed, because the house was sold, but something went wrong judicially with the paperwork, and the funds would not be released until July 27th. That was a long way from mid-June, and we were absolutely determined in faith to stay 100% out of debt for our journey (minus two then-paid off burritos). We had to be in Alaska on June 24th, and our window to book flights at a reasonable price was closing quickly.

"God, I'm not going to use my plastic! You have to come through! You know we need to be there, and the price is right now. If I wait, we'll pay more. If I move now, we're in debt. I'm not doing it."

My faith was tired. I was spent between our experience in Amsterdam, the confusion about how to spend the month of June, and the lack of funds for our flights. A week before the trip, we decided that we would swipe the credit card knowing that the funds would come before we'd have to pay any interest on the card. I was not a happy camper, and I was quite bitter about it.

"God, you brought us here, and told us 'not to worry,' and here we are. We're homeless, $3,250 in debt, and for what?!"

Okay, so I was being a bit pessimistic. It's nice to be able to say that we traveled to such and such places, but it's hard to keep a good attitude when you are poor, even when you're ministering to people and affecting their lives. After moping and complaining that we used the credit card, I received an unexpected email two days after that said the paperwork needed in order to disperse the inheritance we were expecting was pushed through and the funds would be available within the week. We were told by the attorney that an earlier release date of funds was not possible because of the pre-set court date, yet at the end of the day, we boarded our flight to Alaska still debt free. The pressure had lessened a bit as a result.

By the time we had tithed the money, paid off the flights, bought a bus ticket to Frankfurt, Germany where we would fly out of and food along the way, we had about $15 leftover. Was this a coincidence?

*　　　*　　　*　　　*　　　*

A while after we returned to Florida from our journey, we had dinner with some friends of ours whom we had not met until we returned home from overseas but were connected to our journey. They told us a very interesting story we were not expecting.

As we had updated the home base via email about Alaska being the next part of our journey, they felt the urge to take care of our flights to Alaska with spare airline miles that they had. Unfortunately, time and everyday business got the best of them, and "before [they] got around to handling it [our] flights had been taken care of." They apologized for not following through more quickly on what they had felt like was God telling them to be obedient with.

This brought a lot of reassurance to my heart that we were not crazy. If anything, it has me believing that God miraculously pushed Grandmom's paperwork through faster because our friends didn't follow through in time. Either way, the provision came. It got me thinking: What is it that God has asked me to do that someone else is having to wait longer to see breakthrough for? Better yet, what is it that God has to have someone else step up to do because I didn't act?

What if we had never stepped out in faith for this journey? What if I only considered my long-term financial and professional goals, and reprogrammed myself to deal with my dreams by funding others to do theirs? How many people would not have stepped out in faith because they didn't hear how God showed up in our lives? How many people would not know the Lord today? Would God have found someone else to do what we were supposed to do? Would someone else have written this book?

CHAPTER FIFTEEN

TIME OUT. NOW, BACK IN THE GAME

What did we miss most about the United States? Not much. Southeast Asia had pretty much anything we wanted to eat and more. Europe provided most of the comforts of the West as well as beautiful weather and scenery. There were only four things that we missed more than anything: A good salad, Chipotle, Chick-fil-a, and stick deodorant.

In fact, the first thing I wanted when we touched American soil was my brand of deodorant which was impossible to find overseas. Asia offered us roll-on liquid deodorant with skin-whitening (because Asians want white skin) that made my skin stick to itself, and the only deodorant close to what I wanted in Europe was powder fresh Lady Speed Stick. When we landed, we went straight to Walmart and stocked up.

Unfortunately, Fairbanks, Alaska doesn't offer too much in terms of American chain foods. After eating a fairly fresh diet for close to six months, Denny's wasn't quite hitting the spot. Jess, however, didn't hesitate to jump back into her horrible American dietary ways.

Upon reaching our friends' house in Healy, Alaska, we were invited to a kid's birthday party, and Jess didn't hold back. Soda, coffee, baked beans, hot dogs, chips, and birthday cake "somehow" found its way into her mouth in a matter of an hour, and she paid for it the rest of the evening while hugging the toilet. If this doesn't indicate the high level of poisonous chemicals in our traditional cookout food, I'm not sure what else does. Needless to say, Jess eased her way back into the American food lifestyle a little more cautiously after that.

*　　　*　　　*　　　*　　　*

Healy, Alaska is a second home to us. We have ministry contacts whom are like family to us there, and we look forward to seeing them every summer. There was a concern, however, that our level of commitment would be changing. Either we were going to do something crazy like settle down in the area and work in ministry full time or we were going to phase out upon getting "real jobs" and growing up.

The desire to return home and develop my professional career further had begun to take precedence in my thoughts, and the discussion I had within myself internally changed with the direction of the wind. We had such an amazing journey so far that it was almost to the point where I was content to return home because I had felt a level of success. There was still a long journey ahead of us to complete, and I knew that, but the beginning of the end of the journey had started to settle.

One of the reasons Jess and I had a cleaning company in our first years of marriage was that it allowed us to free up our schedule and employ people to fill our jobs so we could travel to Alaska for the summer. It was tiring to work extra hard 10 months out of the year so we could take off two, but it was worth the sacrifice. Returning home and starting in an industry that only provided two weeks of work off a year would not allow us to be effective in Alaska in the way we had been previously, so it was our prayer that the right replacement for us would come if we were to step down from our annual commitment.

During our time in Alaska, we usually lead groups of teens from various organizations, and this year was going to be different because we would be leading a youth group. Youth groups are a bit intimidating to lead because some youth group leaders are very protective over their kids and how you handle them, so they can often be more difficult to work with than a random group of people. The opposite was true of this group.

The youth leader Danny and his team of kids were (as I call them) hungry, hungry hippos. They were excited, ready to work, and hungry to see God move through them and inside them. There could not have been a more perfectly hand-picked team for the village we work in, and we became very close to them. Throughout the time we were with them, it became obvious that each person individually was falling in love with the village we were working in, so much so that they decided to commit all of their attention to that specific region for future trips. They, to this day, visit multiple times a year and send their teens and older folks. There could not have been a more perfect group Jess and I felt comfortable passing our baton to.

*　　　*　　　*　　　*　　　*

Seven and a half months into our travels had brought a handful of learning experiences that we will never forget. A surprise to us was our increasing level of thankfulness for the basic necessities of life: a comfortable bed, food on the table, coffee in the morning, a mirror in the bathroom, hot water for a good shave, a cold drink. Any night we had a bed was an honor. Any meal that was provided was one more meal that the Lord blessed us with, and we were that much further into our journey than before. Any time we could take good care of our hygiene was that much less we would stink in the near future.

It's not overnight that your mind develops thankfulness for the things you never thought you took for granted. I wonder if I would have ever been thankful for a place to sleep if I hadn't given the Lord the ability to be my only provider. Would I have gone my entire life having never once been truly thankful for my bed? I'm sure that superficial "Lord, thank you for my home, my bed, etc." has and would have been produced at the result of some moving article I read online about someone who didn't have a bed, but would that moment have ever happened when I sank into a bed and truly said, "God, thank you, thank you, thank you for this mattress tonight. I'm so thankful to not have to sleep on the floor or on a bench or in the car or on another overnight bus or in the dirt tonight." I can tell you for sure that a refreshed mentality wouldn't have come without having been on the other end. It takes nights sleeping on floors, nasty mats, planes, buses, and benches, not knowing where your next coin or meal would come from, to truly become thankful for these "basics" we have all come to recognize as a standard of living.

The real test of our endurance would come when we arrived back in Europe and landed in Frankfurt. When we left Europe, we had made it clear to each other that we were not going to go back to Europe without having a plan set in stone and everything in order. We had seven weeks to get it planned out.

Towards the end of our time in Alaska, we had been contacting multiple people throughout Germany to connect with, but no one was available or returning messages. Once again, the deadline to lock down a place to stay was fast approaching, and things weren't looking favorable. Nothing produced.

There were no options for a second time during our trip, and this time, there was a sore wound that was pierced (and perhaps patched with a little entitlement). Entitlement is an emotion that would often manifest in our thoughts, feelings, and conversations, and it is a very deadly destiny-killer. If you want to eliminate the chances of fulfilling the destiny that God has laid out for your life, attach some entitlement, and you will have created a fatal recipe for it.

"Come on God, are you kidding me? I mean, we've sold everything. We've sacrificed our friends, our families, our financial security, the speed to which we have children of our own and buy a house, and you can't help us find one person in all of Germany that can host us? Really?" These were the kinds of statements that came out of our mouths upon returning to the Frankfurt airport.

"Chris?"

"What's up?" I wasn't really focused on Jess at the moment.

"What do you think we should do?" Jess nervously asked.

"We'll just deal with it in an hour when we land," I suggested.

That's what we did. Sometimes you just have to enjoy the fact that for the next hour on the plane, you don't have to think about anything except keeping your seatbelt fastened. I didn't have an answer, but I had one idea.

"Let's just get through immigration, and we'll pray and deal with it then," I suggested.

That was such a difficult moment for me as a husband: a moment when you can't provide the basic food, shelter, transportation, etc. without feeling guilty or responsible for setting our lives up for failure. Few people back home truly knew how deep we were into this trip, and many still don't to this day. I think many people thought we got some huge check and rode it out as long as we could.

*   *   *   *   *

Thankfully we had saved a decent amount of money while staying in Alaska through random gifts and some small monthly support: about $1,200. I knew how quickly it was going to fly out of our wallets, however, and I wasn't looking forward to it. We could do pretty much anything we wanted to, but that lurking thought of "how long do I have to make this $1,200 last" was always impeding my clarity.

After we landed in Frankfurt and exited immigration, we sat down near the exit of Terminal 2.

"Lord, what do we do?"

We prayed that we would meet the people we needed to connect with. We prayed that we would make the right choice. The only inkling of anything that I got was to rent a car and to enjoy the coming weeks ahead as a tourist. *To have fun.* A car would be shelter if needed, and the flexibility it provides is a much better option than trains.

The train system in Europe is great, but it comes at a steep price for multiple people. When you arrive where you need to go, you then have to take another local bus or train to the next place where your feet will finish the job. We may have packed backpacks instead of suitcases, but that didn't mean we wanted to carry them everywhere.

A two-and-a-half-week rental cost us $350 for a Peugeot 208. Gas ran about $8-10 a gallon in Europe at the time depending on where we were, but the tiny cars in Europe get such great gas mileage, so we were able to cover more ground at a cheaper cost. We are big believers in traveling via a rental car through Europe.

Right there in the terminal, we booked the car and walked downstairs to pick it up. That's when the notorious moment of truth comes when you decide how much you trust your own driving skills:

"Mr. Gunn, would you like to purchase insurance today?"
"Well, how much does it cost for minimal insurance?"

"It would be an additional 490 Euros for the 2.5 weeks you have the car. That would allow for a 1,000 Euro deductible in case of an accident."

(A moment of thoughtful silence)

"I think I'll just go without insurance," I replied.

"Okay, great! Well, in case of the occurrence of a situation, you need to bring the car back in the condition it was given to you, and if the car is totaled, you'll be responsible to pay the original cost of the car which is 25,000 Euros. Just sign here,

here, here, here, here...and here and here." (How is this woman so perky talking about such a potentially life-altering situation?)

I'm not usually one to fall for fear-developing insurance sales tactics, but in that very moment, I felt a frog jump in my throat. A lot could happen in 2.5 weeks. Being in a foreign country and not knowing the roads or the way people drive in that area of the world made me think about the decision a little longer than normal. At the end of the day, I trusted myself despite being a little hesitant to sign the lines. We simply just didn't have the $650 extra to throw away.

And we were off!

"Jess, do remember what side of the road Germans drive on?"

(Engine revving)

"Um...the left?"

(Car stalls out)

"Well, we'll just have to learn the hard way."

(Horn honking)

"Yep, they drive on the right."

*   *   *   *   *

I remember throughout my life and the time leading up to the trip when I would dream about "backpacking through Europe someday." That's usually when I pictured myself with a folded bandana across my forehead, a red backpack, and a walking stick, trekking up that hill in Austria used in The Sound of Music. Then we'd walk up to some farm with chickens and carrots in the garden, make a stew for an overweight Polish couple who so nicely allowed us to use one of their four spare guest rooms. The following day, we'd catch a local train into the city and snap a photo at the Eiffel Tower.

There was a dreamy excitement that came at the prospect of

being dropped in some town in Europe and just going wherever the wind blew. Although I have found life to be experienced entirely through perspective, the reality of this situation was nothing more than the reality of a fluffy romance novel. Frankly, we found that we preferred knowing where we were going to sleep and also preferred having a general idea of what we were going to be doing.

Our first stop was downtown Frankfurt. As we drove around, looking for "the places to go," we found very quickly that we were tired of traveling.

"What do you really want to do, Jess?"

"I really don't know. Frankly, I want to sleep. I mean, we just got off a 10-hour flight with screaming kids behind us."

"Well, it's 2pm, and we need to get onto the right time zone. Let's come up with something to do to stretch ourselves, and we'll go to sleep at like 9:30." Famous last words.

This day was one of those days where we began to learn something new about the line between faith and stupidity. It may have been daytime, and we may have felt slightly awake enough to conquer the next seven hours until bedtime, but we started to look like two ungrateful, bratty, sugar-crashing three-year olds.

3:30pm: "What are we doing with our lives? We're just driving around with no home! There's no place to eat in this town. Ugh!"

4:30pm: "Chris...I just can't do this anymore. I want to go home. I miss my family, and I have a headache."

5:15pm: "Where do we want to go? Jess, you want to 'see the world,' so where are we going?"

"I want to see Munich," Jess replied.

"Okay, I'll start driving to Munich."

"Fine, I'm going to sleep."

6:30pm: We were pulled over at a rest stop sleeping.

*   *   *   *   *

The thought of sleeping in the car another night simply bothered me. Frustration entered, because for the first time on this trip, I had felt like God didn't have our backs. We had absolutely no plan of attack other than simply traveling to a few spots, and it seemed clear to me that God was finished with us and this journey.

This was a moment we needed to go back to our last word and develop it further:

Every step would be laid out for us, and we were not to worry about any of the finances. We had to visit the YWAM base in Herrnhut, Germany. We were launched out like arrows into the mission field; God has us in his quiver, and He already has the next nation in sight as we land.

Although these are only a few words to recall, they were enough to prohibit us from booking a flight home and simply quitting. God may have seemed to be silent at the moment, but He wasn't done with us. It was frustrating, though, because we were homesick, tired of living out of financial control of our lives, baby fever had started to kick in, and we had no vision for the coming months. The idea of continuing was overwhelming, but we knew we had to finish the journey.

As usual, when God doesn't seem to be answering, it usually gets quieter before it gets louder. God was on vacation and off the grid at the time because when we got to Munich, the lack of vision and desire to travel set in even further.

"We're lost, aren't we?"

"Jess, our map isn't good, and I'm doing the best I can, but this country doesn't allow you to turn around anywhere!"

"Where are we going?"

"Downtown Munich; wherever that is. And when we get there, we can put our happy little faces on, take all the selfies together that we want and show the world how awesome it is to

205

not be back at home."

"Chris...get a grip."

"No. I don't want to. In fact, I don't even want to be here right now. I just want to go home, but we don't have one. We have no way of getting there without a load of debt!"

"I know. I want to as well."

"Fine then. Where's the line, Jess? I've given God the chance to work through our lives, and He has, but I feel like He's done with us. Maybe we weren't supposed to book a round trip ticket back to Frankfurt in the first place. I wonder if we're supposed to be here at all. We're just wondering around!"

"No Chris, we're seeing the world!"

"I don't want to see the world. It's all the same anyways. Grocery stores, H&Ms, and Burger Kings. Just different people."

"Then why did we even do all of this?!" Jess yelled.

"I don't know."

Silence sat with us in the car for 15 minutes.

"I'm done, Jess. I'm serious."

"But what was all this for then? We can't go home now. Everyone's watching. So many people will be let down."

"Who cares about everyone else? They're not the ones sleeping in a car in a foreign country, running around spending money we didn't earn!"

We got to downtown Munich both hard-hearted and in a bad mood. This was a city many people plan for years to vacation to, and we were ruining a potentially amazing experience for ourselves. At the end of the day, our desire for everything to make sense on paper inhibited our ability to have fun. I can look back at our Munich photos to this day and see the frustration deep in our eyes.

*   *   *   *   *

There was one place we did want to see, however, and didn't want to miss: Neuschwanstein Castle. As we awoke the following day to drive to the castle, rain and fog had settled in. We may have been in the car headed to the castle, but there was no guarantee that we were going to see it, because it was high up on a mountain. Neuschwanstein Castle is famous for its influence on the design of the Walt Disney World castle.

On the way, we stopped at a McDonald's to charge up our variety of batteries. I broke out the iPad and opened up a note. I sat there for about 30 minutes writing all of the pros and cons of going home and staying overseas. I tried so hard to keep my bias to a minimum. This was the result:

Pros of Staying	Cons of Staying
Get to see different parts of the world	Emotionally exhausted
God seems to keep coming through	Physically exhausted
"No regrets"	No financial or physical stability
Freedom of time	No home
Freedom of finances	No consistent bed
No bills or "debt" (so far…)	No consistent shower
People are watching to see if we succeed	Miss our family
Potential world connections	Miss our friends
Get the travel bug out of our system	Can't reason our style of trip dogmatically
Africa, Israel, Italy, Paris, Denmark?	High potential for failure
Write a best-seller	Possible debts we can't pay back to pop up
Find the line between faith & stupidity?	Longer wait to have children

Pros of Going Home	Cons of Going Home
Get settled down earlier	Hit the ground running
See family earlier	No startup money
See friends earlier	Instant debt from startup and flights back home
Establish routines	No freedom of time
Begin the road to self-sufficiency	No financial freedom
Start a family earlier	No car
USF football season	Can't stay with Steven & Kristen very long
Sense of home as a place	No quick source of cash. NO CLEANING
Consistent bed, shower, lodging	No more travel
Get plugged in with new ministries	No plans
Lead certain church programs	Disappointment from those watching us

This list brought a lot of relief. It's shocking how once you get all of your thoughts onto paper how it can clear your head and put things into the proper perspective. In fact, it helped us realize that we felt like we would return home around Thanksgiving. We were so confident in our decision that we booked one-way tickets home from London. Now we were definitely committed.

Although the cons of going home didn't look much different than the difficulties of returning home at the end of the year, we had to decide if the pros of staying out in the field were what we wanted as a couple. After a lot of discussion, it was clear that we needed to change our perspectives to be thankful for everything we could do. The realities of life could wait until November.

With this refreshed outlook and knowing that we'd be able to see our friends and family in a couple of months and live the lives everyone else does a few months later, we headed to Neuschwanstein Castle with a smile. The air in the car was a lot lighter on our drive to southwest Germany.

If there's any way that we felt like God was still servicing our lives, it was in the weather. Although we experienced quite a spell of wet weather during our time in Europe, whenever it was time to break out the camera, the weather would always clear.

"God, please let the rain stop and the sky be clear for when we get to the Disney World castle," Jess prayed earnestly. "Are you agreeing with me, Chris?"

"Yes, Jess, of course. It will be sunny in the name of Jesus!"

Sure enough, as we were getting closer to the castle, we could see the clouds clearing and the sun lightening up the general location of the castle. When we arrived at the entrance of the town, we fell in love. It had that beautiful traditional German look of pointy roofs, brick roads, wood-sided homes and multi-colored facades. It was difficult to recognize that it was actually real. Even better, we could see the bottom of the castle, and the clouds were lifting. For 30 minutes we got great shots of it; close ones and far ones. We were really thankful to be able to see it. After enjoying some time there, we parked the car so I could map out our day's journey. As we sat there, the fog crept back down, and as we left, the castle was nowhere to be seen.

A short drive got us to the Austria/Germany border. Jess and I high-fived as we entered our 16th country of the year. I could tell very quickly that we were going to fall in love with Austria. It is absolutely beautiful with its large peaks, beautiful forests and blue-green streams. The hills are green and yes, they have those pretty yellow flowers all over.

*   *   *   *   *

Jess and I are interesting characters, because if you were to ask us on the fly if we like to hike, we would confidently and boldly respond, "no." Yet, there is an aspect of us that enjoys it whenever we get conned into going. I love nature. I just don't want to get dirty. Jess likes the idea of the forest, but don't make her go up a large hill or mountain. We're Floridians, and we love our flatlands. Floridians like us stay indoors, away from the bugs, alligators, and ridiculous summer heat. There is nothing that attracts us about the outdoors in South Florida other than the pool and the beach in the winter.

An easy trail at the border allowed us beautiful views we would have never been able to see from the car, and we got to go inside the forest. Florida has woods, which we tend to avoid, but Germany and Austria have forests, which we want to go deep into. It's too beautiful and serene to not want to!

Then there it was: the greatest gift to man since Krispy Kreme Doughnuts. Instead of going down the mountain the normal, old-fashioned way, take a concoction no American insurance company would ever cover: a curvy, slippery, wet, steep, metal slide. It was tempting, and I stood debating for a few minutes if I would go down it.

This slide looked like a blast, and I wanted to go down it very badly. The risk? It was wet. I had my prized and only pair of jeans on, and the last thing I wanted to do was have a wet pair of pants for a road trip. I quickly decided to get over the idea and walk away, but then I hesitated.

"No regrets," I said to myself.

I took my windbreaker, wrapped it inside out around my waist and told Jess to pull out the video camera. Now, you would think someone who is of calculated risk would consider the level of friction on a wet metal slide against a smooth rain jacket, but I completely missed that. As I went down the slide, my speed picked up rapidly around each curve, and I went flying off the end of it, rolling out of control! I spent the next five minutes cleaning mud and dirt off of me in the creek while watching that video over and over with Jess and laughing hysterically. It was a great moment. That video now has thousands of views online.

*   *   *   *   *

We continued our way towards Switzerland. Our plan was to head to the capital of Bern, and we knew we were going to stop at some point in the Swiss Alps. Our goal was to wake up to an amazing view, so we headed west. Around 7:30, we decided to stop for dinner in a small town on the side of a mountain.

This restaurant was cheap, yet super-fancy, and Jess and I stood out amongst the crowd, for sure. We forgot that there aren't many people our age that get to travel like we were. It's mostly those who actually save money, retire, and follow through who visit many of the places we were.

"Do you feel awkward right now?"

"Yeah Jess, everyone's staring at us. I think they're wondering if we're on our honeymoon or something. They all speak different languages, so I can't tell. Either way, the salad bar is free, and we forgot the Tupperware." It was easy to make jokes about how little money we had.

That was our first "date night" in a while, and it felt great. We had a much better outlook, and more importantly, we were having fun. To celebrate, we got coffee to go with our dinner since we were going to drive a bit further anyways. Sometimes a great cappuccino can refresh your perspective on life immensely.

*   *   *   *   *

Once we crossed the border into Switzerland, we only got to see a little bit because the sun went down. For three hours, we curved up the Alps and would throw the car into neutral to ride down for miles. It was foggy, rainy, and pitch black. That kind of drive was not for someone like Jessica who does not like being behind the wheel of a car.

Because we had coffee, I saw the clock hit midnight, and I figured I could easily get to 12:30am without any problem. Looking at the map, we decided to go through the next large town and find a place to pull off the road and rest up for the night. We continued through the town of Disentis, up Route 19 and came to a construction site.

There was an overnight crew tearing up the road, and a man waved a flag at us to turn onto a different road and continue through a tunnel. We followed suit and climbed up another mountain through a neighborhood. Then we came to another one-lane road and stopped to double check that we were going the right way. There were arrow-shaped signs pointing us to the next town on our map, so we continued without any concern.

Then we came to a fork in the road. This time, the road went from pavement to dirt with a grass median. The signs still pointed in favor of the town we were headed toward, so we forked to the left. The road to the right had a large pile of gravel blocking travel, so we couldn't go that direction anyways. The area was pitch black, and the fog was very thick. The grass slowly started to come up higher, but we continued because the signs pointed in the right direction despite a little nervousness that we were getting lost.

Then we came to a second fork in the road. This time, the road continued upward to the left and the signs continued to point us in that direction. The right road turned fully into grass and had a bench on the side of the road prohibiting our little car from even getting through. At this point, we felt like we should have turned around, but we couldn't pull off a U-turn because the road was so tight. Our car would have fallen off of the mountain.

The right side of the road was a steep cliff which would have equaled us buying a ruined car if we couldn't turn it around correctly. The left side of the road was a wall of mountain, so there was no leeway on that side either. I tried turning the car around at the second fork, but I was too afraid to drive it off the cliff. After a few tries, I decided to continue a bit further until we could find a place to turn around a little more comfortably. If not, we'd have to take the very thin road backwards in the dark without any light. We continued further up the mountain looking for a place to pull off a maneuver. Nothing came.

"Let's just go over this next hill, and then we'll start going backwards if all else fails."

That was a bad idea. We climbed a bit higher to go over the hill. At the peak, it began to go down at a very steep angle. It was an angle that prohibited me from keeping control of the car because of the mud from all the rain. We couldn't see due to the fog in front of us, and the more I tried to slow up and reverse the vehicle, the deeper in the mud we would get stuck.

"Jess, it's time to start praying," I said.

I threw the parking brake on and got my flashlight keychain out of the trunk so I could get an idea of what was ahead. As I walked down the muddy grass trying to keep my feet from sticking to the ground, I saw a small house to the left and a large barn to the right. I looked back up at the car, and in a short distance there was easily a 50-foot decrease in altitude.

I saw that it flattened out at the bottom with enough space to turn around. It was our only hope at that point, so I figured we'd give it a shot. As we slowly went down the hill and got to the bottom, I tried to get a grip on some piece of land, but we just slid further down. When we reached the flatter area, it wasn't as flat as I had originally thought, and there was no way I could even turn the car. The car slipped and slid through that area as I tried to turn it, and we crept closer and closer, by default, to the house on the left.

I got out of the car again to see what was further up. Nothing. It was an enormous cliff, and we were only a few feet away from the edge of it now.

I knocked on the door of the house. Nobody was home.

"Figures. Who in God's name could get a vehicle out here

and back to civilization in the first place?"

I walked back to the car after looking around for some kind of solution and got in.

"Jess, you need to really, really be praying."

"I am. I really am, Chris."

"*Out loud* while I try and get us out of this."

She started praying loudly while I tried moving the car.

"JESUS!" We yelled. "JESUS! WE NEED YOUR HELP!"

The car just stayed put. After another round of praying and trying to get some grip on the mud, I decided to give up for the night, because no one was moving that car until at least sunrise.

*   *   *   *   *

It's moments like these that test your true level of faith. Do you crash and burn, or do you access the manifestation of the Kingdom of God that you cry out for during your prayers? I've heard too many crazy stories of people being in situations like these and an angel knocks on the window or after praying intensely, the people are transported to where they need to get. Sound crazy? You need to get around people who have experienced these things and see for yourself.

I've heard of many more stories where somebody "just so happened" to be in the area with the right tools and capabilities to get what needs to be done accomplished. I've heard stories that make things the apostle Paul went through just another everyday story! There was no reason why that couldn't happen for us. After all, God didn't call us overseas for us to drive off a cliff.

Jess to this day will say that she's never seen me pray in the way that I did throughout that night, which is sad if I may say. I screamed out to the Lord. I declared different things. I found tongues I never knew I had. I believed for the sign of transportation to occur on that night. I screamed out for the Lord to save us. We shook and trembled and prayed and prayed.

As we sat there in the dark on the mountainside, I was intently prepared to be lifted off of the ground, turned around in mid-air and planted back on the pavement. I was that confident in my God. I had seen him do too much in our lives and the lives of those around us. I stared into the darkness ahead, and I could tell that our car was actually moving…very slowly.

I kept staring as we prayed, and the angle that our car was facing was turning, but it was turning the wrong way. The front of our car was slowly but surely sliding towards the edge of the cliff we were just a few feet away from. We were not being transported. Gravity was simply doing its job. There was no sleeping or staying in that car. We had to get out.

CHAPTER SIXTEEN

WE'RE BACK UP! OH, MAYBE NOT

I remember a section in one of my college textbooks that says if a four-year-old skins his knee and begins to cry, it's hard for him to keep in mind that the pain will subside and heal. This is a profound idea that describes the cognitive understanding of how circumstances affect an individual based on their level of maturity. When little Jimmy falls off his bike and scrapes his knee, it can be traumatic that his body has gone through a physical alteration, and since his level of maturity hasn't been developed to understand the processes of scarring, healing, and pain, it wouldn't be unrealistic to see him overreact.

It's similar to times you're fooling around with superglue and get your fingers stuck together or you slide one of your legs between two columns on a balcony railing and get trapped. "I guess this is it. I'm stuck here forever," you conclusively decide. Eventually you tear your fingers apart or turn your leg so you can yank it out and experience freedom once again.

Many thoughts flashed through our minds as we were stuck on the side of that mountain in the Swiss Alps. My first thought was about our old apartment and our warm bed. I pictured us there, comfortable and relaxed, and for a split-second I completely regretted the decision to leave home. I thought of our friends and family back in warm, sunny Florida having no earthly clue where we were or what was happening. They were probably eating dinner on an average Monday night. Perhaps it was quiet; perhaps rushed. Who knows? Either way, we were screaming out to the Lord on the side of a mountain on the opposite end of the earth while slowly sliding off. Although thoughts reminding us that we were in the middle of nowhere in a pitch-black, foggy area wanted to seep in and destroy our sanity, we both tried our best to stay calm and have self-control.

"Hey Chris? Remember that time we got stuck on the side of a mountain in the Swiss Alps?"

"Um...yeah. Didn't that happen like an hour ago? Were we actually able to get the car off the mountain?"

"I think so. I can't remember. Oh, wait! I remember! It slid off and blew up! Too bad you didn't get insurance. We could have avoided a $600 per month car payment."

"Thanks Jess. That was probably a bit early. We haven't even gotten out of the car yet."

As the car began to slide to our three o'clock, we responded quickly by getting everything we had out of the back. Jess, shaking nervously, gently crept out of the car and took our items from the back seat and the trunk to the covered porch of the small house where everything could stay dry.

Once everything was removed and the car was lighter on the lower side, I explained to Jess that there was a flatter area a few feet ahead, and I wanted to get the car to it. This was an advanced maneuver because it was very clear that I had a 50/50 chance of getting the car there. If I missed, I would have to jump out of the car or go down with it.

I was drowning in emotion. The financial obligations, the responsibility for Jess, the reality of the moment; I went into problem-solving overload. The thought of driving a Peugeot off a mountain made me envious of the flat, well-paved roads back in Florida. I was angry at myself for going over the last hill. Did I miss a detour sign? More than anything, I was scared I wouldn't leap out of the car fast enough if I angled it wrong.

Before moving the car, I discussed all of our financials, passwords, and bank account information with Jess through the window and told her everything I felt she needed to know. I made sure to tell her to remarry, most of all. We kissed each other goodbye, just in case. I was nervous to make a mistake.

The car started up, and I had to run the engine hard to move the car to my eleven o'clock and angle it downward. I removed the emergency brake, started rolling, and caught the angle perfectly to land the car where it needed to be placed. Mission accomplished. I pulled the emergency brake handle back up as much as I could and was relieved to turn the car off and get out.

*　　　　*　　　　*　　　　*　　　　*

There are rare moments in life that our minds may be completely under emotional control, but we are physiologically responding counter to those emotions. Jess and I were both trembling, partly out of shock but also because of the cold rain. Jess paid homage to the phrase "being scared shitless" as she had to take a moment for herself on the side of the mountain. We weren't sure if bears roamed the area, but it's possible rumors are being spread among the locals that there has been a trace of one. The need to relieve ourselves developed every ten minutes.

A lighter bag was packed with an outfit for each of us, extra pairs of socks and underwear, our Bibles, books, memory cards, camera, and iPads. We also added Jess' makeup, our toothbrushes, and a few other light toiletries, along with a few bananas and apples we had, but everything else was left at the house. At least a five mile walk to the construction site that was four miles from town was ahead of us, and I wanted to stay light.

As we began walking, we had no clue what was lying ahead. The wildlife situation made us most nervous. We had just left Alaska where bears, wolves, and moose are just around the corner. Our guards were up extra high, and we kept the flashlight off to allow our eyes to adjust to the darkness. Once we settled into our walk, that's when we felt God's peace kick in.

We knew people were praying for us. Not only that, we knew that God had supplied angels to escort us back to civilization. How do we know? How do we really, really know that? You know that feeling you get when you feel like "you're not alone" or "you're being watched?" That's exactly what we felt. The hairs on our necks were sticking straight up, but there was confidence in our stride. It was a confidence displayed, not because we knew we would be okay at that point, but a confidence founded upon the feeling that we were walking next to friends, and that we were not alone. It was as if Jess and I each had a friend, and we just decided to hike the Alps in soaking wet shoes together.

*   *   *   *   *

What is protocol when everything around you seems to collapse? I have watched our world run to God in situations like the September 11th attacks at the World Trade Centers, and I have seen individuals blame God for attacks in their own lives. We respond emotionally and irrationally to situations in our lives even though the church has been called to transform how we think[1] and to forget the patterns of the physical world because, just how Jesus is not a part of that dimension,[2] we are not to be either. So many of us forget, or rather, never understand that, through Christ, we are no longer confined to the restrictions attached to fallen man. Our business as maturing members of an unseen kingdom is to express how the eternal and unseen world functions as we grow, because the fullness of life is experienced from the inheritance of eternal things.

There we were on that mountain with an opportunity to make a decision. Which world were we going to commit to? Were we going to call it quits and go home? Homesickness and tiredness seemed to overwhelm us. The journey of locating the path the Lord wanted us on was not something we enjoyed anymore, and the thought of a warm bed, hot shower, and good meal seemed out of reach.

The thought of returning to Florida and establishing predictable consistency, starting some kind of business, and developing a higher level of comfort again seemed satisfying. In fact, there was a part of us that was ready to immediately book a flight home, tell everyone we enjoyed ourselves and that God came through (for the most part), but we were ready to establish a foundation and a family. We were tired of trusting in the Lord.

If we really step back and look at the Christian body, how many of us truly believe what the Word says? How many of us are dedicated to the belief in the concept of Jesus but are completely ignorant of the purpose of Jesus' resurrection? How foolish we are! Our feet may be on the correct path, but how many of us are willing to keep them on it? It's often easier for us to walk in the waist-high grass on the side of a golden brick road! Doesn't Jesus bluntly say "Not everyone who says to me 'Lord, Lord,' will enter the kingdom of heaven, but only he who does the will of my Father who is in heaven?" (Matthew 7:21)

The church has focused so heavily on simply accepting Jesus as the way to the one true God, never realizing His purpose. Churches are filled with programs and media, which are all great tools, but if they are not helping activate us to walk in the identity God intended us to have, the church is nothing more than a motivational program backed with great speakers that guide people's hand to a doorknob that is never twisted.

I believe wholeheartedly that we are moving into a time in human history that the idea of "swimming against the current" will no longer be for the rebellious 2% of people. I pray, not that it would be popular to rebel against the typical patterns people live, but that the world would understand that the avoidance of conformity incites a mindset that God can transform more effectively and can help move us more toward our destiny. Isn't that what we all want? It takes risk! The "risk," however, became a guaranteed reward when Jesus said "I am with you to the very end of the age." (Matthew 28:20)

*   *   *   *   *

We were both surprised when we got to the construction site because it only took us 50 minutes, and we weren't tired at all. Our shoes were caked in mud, and our pants were soaked up to our knees, but we were at peace in our hearts even though we were still shuddering.

A bright light illuminated the entire work zone prohibiting the workers from seeing us waving them down from the edge of the site. Loud machinery wash out our calls from being heard. Since they were tearing up the road, we couldn't walk over to them either. We had to wait for them to take a break and walk towards us. After nearly an hour, we were finally able to get someone's attention.

Within a few minutes of using hand gestures to explain what had happened to us, a man who could speak minimal English was signaled over. He told us they were Italian workers, so I tried using some of my Spanish skills to better explain that we needed help. I quickly learned Spanish is nothing like Italian like I thought it was. Either way, they slowly figured out what was wrong. Within five minutes they had pulled up with a powerful forklift and another large construction truck to try and get the car. We jumped in the truck and headed back up the mountain.

I immediately explained to the driver the difference between the words "right" and "left" and told him that it was about eight kilometers up the mountain. Once we came to the dirt road we traveled down, his face began to shift from confidence that they could get the car to shock that we went up the road we had.

"I could not turn car around." I would speak to him in broken English to help communicate.

We showed him all the signs pointing toward the direction we had gone, and I could tell he could see why we went down the road we did, but he still shook his head with grave concern.

"I no can drive here. Is big for road." He started to slow his truck down out of fear the truck was too wide for the road.

He eventually stopped due to the thinning road, and we explained that it was only a ten minute walk up the hill. To help remember the direction we drove, I had put banana peels at various marking points. That was the extent of my skills in action regarding leaving tracks to be found in case we forgot where we came from or were murdered by Bigfoot.

"It's just a little further," we told the man with confidence. "Just up the hill."

We'd trek to the top of the hill, and there'd be another hill.

"Seriously, this is the last one. It's just over the next hill." We were now walking for over twenty minutes.

"What the heck?" Jess and I looked at each other with confusion. We knew we weren't lost.

"Ah, here it is. This is the last hill." I knew confidently that we had made it.

"You are very lucky," the man would keep repeating. "You are very, very lucky."

"It was the Lord." Jess kept responding.

This "it's the next hill" jabber continued for over forty minutes, but we had completed the walk to the construction site in fifty minutes. We had driven more than half of the way back up the mountain in the truck. How was this possible? We were even walking faster than the first time we walked the path! I stopped telling our help the next hill was the last hill, because we were more embarrassed each time it wasn't.

Have you ever had an experience where the Lord answers

your prayers, but just not in way that you wanted or expected Him to? I screamed out for God to transport us and our car back to the main road, but it never happened. I remember saying to the Lord back in the car, "God, I've heard too many crazy stories. There's no reason why you can't make this story one of those! I'm not asking you; I'm telling you to show up!"

Jess and I know without a shadow of doubt that we were transported that night. How could we have walked at a normal pace for 50 minutes and then driven half way and paced quickly back but taken twice the time? Even with inclines and declines, the path was similar going each way. None of it made sense, and it was the first time in our lives that we could say that the Lord moved in our lives in such a way that it was *embarrassing*. We felt bad for making our helper walk so far but were thankful that the Lord had showed up miraculously.

Although nothing bluntly physical or tangible displayed itself that night, we believe angels showed up and we were transported by the power God. This wouldn't be unlike an experience the apostles would have had, so we should expect no different in our lives. It should be normal for us to experience this world in ways that defy the design of the natural world.

*   *   *   *   *

Once we finally arrived at the spot of the incident, it was clear that there was no getting the car off the mountain. Neither of their vehicles could get to the car and properly turn around to get back up the mountain, especially in the rain that was forecasted to stay for the next week.

"You need wait for sun," we were told. "We cannot do."

We grabbed the remainder of our belongings from the site and spent the next few hours walking back to the truck and guiding it in reverse back to the main road very slowly. Once the truck could be turned around, we were escorted into town, but since it was after four in the morning, we could not get a hotel room for the night. Eventually, we just told the driver to drop us off at the main train station, and we would work everything out once businesses opened in the morning.

Upon arriving at our new home for the rest of the morning (a wooden park bench that reeked of urine), we took our soaking wet shoes off, changed our socks and bundled up in our blanket (which we had purchased at a Walmart in Alaska before returning to Europe....Thank God). Our shivering shifted from an adrenaline rush to simply being cold from the chill of the early morning. We were physically and emotionally exhausted but could only think about what had happened. The main question that needed to be answered was, "Could we even get the car off the mountain?"

Rain and fog were indefinitely forecasted. Our prayers were consumed with pleas for sunshine and dry ground. I pictured us hiring a helicopter to pick up the car with a lift and drop it back on the road. It would have been way cheaper than the 25,000 Euro price tag on the car. Sleeping was a difficult challenge, and only a few minutes had passed every time we woke up.

Finally, eight o'clock decided to arrive, and I took a walk in my flip flops up the steep streets of the town to find a hotel we could afford for the night while we worked out the details. I found a nice-looking hotel, went inside, and the owner was having an espresso in the side room. There was an awkward feeling that came over me while ringing the bell at the front desk to get the attention of a man only nine feet away, so I stood there for a moment until gaining the courage to ring it.

It was very clear after talking for a moment that I was being sized up. A rain jacket with shorts and flip flops with socks wasn't the attire representative of the clientele staying at the hotel, nor were people our age for that matter. Although it was conveniently booked-solid that evening, I was pointed down the street to a hostel that was much more fitting for the people group I was representing through my appearance at that moment.

Disentis was full of people who couldn't speak English, and I was very grateful to arrive at the hostel down the street to find that the manager at the front desk could speak it fluently. I explained our situation about the car, and she said she could call a close friend of hers that can tow vehicles.

"Can you take the tow truck driver up to mountain to show him where the car is in about 15 minutes?"

"Let me look at my schedule," I thought to myself.

"Absolutely," I replied.

Two men in a truck showed up, and I explained the situation to them. They were confident they would be able to do a quick job and be on their way until we started to drive up the dirt road that led us to the car.

"This is crazy. Why did you drive here?"

"The signs pointed this way, and we didn't see any other roads because of the fog. A lot of roads in Wales are like this, so I didn't think it was out of the ordinary when it turned to dirt."

I couldn't believe my eyes as I looked out the window. I, myself, was questioning why I had driven the road. The only thing making a drive down the road a step short of suicide was the darkness and the fog. The drop from the edge of the road was hundreds, if not over a thousand feet, and looking back, if I had seen this road in the daytime, I would have turned around and pleaded with the construction workers to let us through. I still don't know to this day what road we should have taken in lieu of the dirt road that led to a cliff.

Our little Peugeot clearly couldn't be towed by the truck we had, so another company was called that could possibly help. The only problem was they were based three hours away.

"You are a lucky man, Chris. The truck we need to tow your car is coming through town in one hour. He always takes many days to get here. No promises, but if no rain, we can try to get the car."

It didn't rain one drop that day although the air was dense with misty fog. There was no sun peering through the cloud cover but no wet weather either, and the ground dried just enough to get the car out of the mud. The second tow truck that came from out of town had a strong, long wire that could pull the car from the top of the hill that we slid down from, and it did the trick. Four men, two and a half hours of labor and $941 later, our car was safely planted on asphalt once again.

I would love to write a book that told some amazing story where the Lord came through and miraculously paid off everything that day. The truth is that we went into true debt for the first time since we had left home. We were forced to pay for an expensive hostel for one night (which we were thankful for the bed and good rest), and we had to buy new shoes as well because the washing machine at the hostel melted both of our shoes. Those weren't the most fulfilling days of our trip.

We must remember what really counts. The Lord may not have instantly provided the finances that day or made a tow truck appear out of thin air in the middle of the night on the side of the mountain, but He certainly held off the rain the entire day, transported us, provided us comfort during the night, provided angels to keep us company, sent us to a hostel that had a close relationship with the local tow company, and provided the right tow truck within the hour of it traveling through town. I'd say that all of this is amazing in itself and could be considered God-breathed. Who cares about the money? The money got paid eventually. We had put ourselves in a position where we weren't in control over our finances anymore, so what could we do through worrying about money to help our situation? Nothing. With that said, we kept moving forward.

*   *   *   *   *

After getting the car key back in exchange for a swipe of my plastic card the following day, I walked around and noticed the car's black paint was sparkly and shiny, even in the gloomy pouring-down rain. They had washed off all the mud and had given it a great coat of wax. Even the interior had been fully detailed. It was as if I was driving a brand new car off the lot.

While driving back to the hotel to pick up Jessica and give her the confidence that everything was okay once again, the reminder of God's nature had overwhelmed me. I have been cleansed. I was once stuck in a muddy hole unable to get out, and then picked up, given a bath, and polished. Now, even on a gloomy day, I am able to shine because of Jesus' life within me.

Our belongings were loaded back into the car once again, and we resumed our trip to Bern. As we drove out of the town and continued up the mountainside, we came to the very construction site we had to detour around originally, and drove right through it. Many emotions captured us in that moment.

Despite the slight trauma we had experienced, we were both brought to the point of a decision. We were still homesick, poor, incapable of making any dreams we had a reality, constantly fighting our desires within for an average life, and unsure of what the coming weeks held for us, yet we committed ourselves to finishing out the remainder of the year with assurance and delight. Our small internal victories were celebrated with some official Swiss chocolates when we arrived to beautiful Bern.

What now?

CHAPTER SEVENTEEN

BONJOUR. I MEAN, NEI HOU

It was a beautiful day in Luxembourg City, Luxembourg, and after taking an afternoon to visit (and also to buy a new pair of shoes), we found a donor kebab restaurant. Halal food (think kosher for Muslims) is yummy, filling, and cheap, so we didn't hesitate to eat at this particular restaurant. I scarfed down my food, and Jess took her time like a proper lady. It's a good thing she did.

As we drove out of town northward into the French countryside, "it hit me," and "it" wasn't going to give me much time. I began to search for a gas station or a rest stop, but Europe is notorious for having towns where everything is consolidated to one area rather than building a gas station or a restaurant every few miles. After another ten minutes of driving, "it hit Jess," and I knew we were going to have to move quickly.

There was a paper banner on the side of the road highlighting a petrol station one exit up, so we followed suit and continued past another sign that said it would be on the left. After circling the area a few times, there was no gas station in the area like the signs stated. Only a few warehouses were around, and we drove down a country road headed towards nowhere. Then we prayed.

As we followed around a curve, there was a lonely porta potty on the side of the road.

"Do you think it's unlocked," Jess asked?

"It's Europe, I'm doubtful," I replied.

I parked the car and walked up to try the door. It actually opened! The potty was pristine. Not only did it have thick toilet paper, but it had antibacterial soap and had hardly ever been used. Jess and I switched spots a few times, but sure enough, a crisis was averted! We have a picture of that porta potty (aka our miracle toilet) in our spare bathroom, today.

*   *   *   *   *

We had traveled through Germany, Austria, Switzerland, Luxembourg and a little of southern France for a solid week. We visited countless historical sites, snapped gobs of pictures, enjoyed people-watching, and visiting local stores.

I personally have two things I'm a sucker for other than desks: clocks and crystal. I love how a clock can be such a simple tool yet take so many different forms. My infatuation with crystal is more with flicking it and listening to the "ding" it expresses. A great ding from a crystal cup makes me warm and fuzzy inside. Switzerland is often known for its crystal, and when I found a combined coo-coo clock and crystal store, I simply stared at the beautiful art while struggling with the fact we had no extra luggage space, nor could we afford anything! Besides, even if we had enough money for anything, could you imagine a coo-coo clock sticking out of the top of my backpack?

A few places made our "if we ever return, we need to visit here" list, and one that is near the top of it is Spiez, Switzerland. Not only is it relatively close to the amazing mountains and hills of Austria and eastern Switzerland, which are guaranteed to take your breath away, but it is located on the two most beautiful turquoise lakes I have ever seen. It is a quaint town designed to show its beauty at every corner. Spiez was a pleasant surprise we were not expecting to drive through.

As much as we enjoyed the scenery and visiting some of Europe's highlights, we were still shaken up over nearly sliding our vehicle off of a mountain. Only a few hours would pass before we would talk about it again while replaying everything in our minds. Thankfully, a week after it occurred, a few people banded together and paid our bill for the tow. We felt honored, humbled, and relieved, so we began to focus again on more purposeful things. We were eager to get back on track with why we were in Europe in the first place, so we headed east to Herrnhut, Germany.

As we drove through the German countryside, we simply marveled at how far we had come and all God had done for us and through us. Lives were being affected both at home and our faith journey. We had been to 19 countries, and all we were doing was simply sharing our story, talking about what Jesus had done through us. Herrnhut wouldn't be any different because we would be amongst others who were on their own personal faith journeys as well.

Herrnhut is a quaint German town with a population of just over 3,500 people. A large percentage of Herrnhut's population reflects the YWAM base located there which is a hub for many other bases all around the world. What we didn't know until visiting is that Herrnhut is known for the development of the Moravian church, which was founded upon 100 years of nonstop prayer that lead to a true revival in the town in 1727.

As we prayed for the Lord to show us what we needed to know historically and spiritually about Herrnhut, we quickly realized there are similar traits between the area and the Wales Bible College we had visited. Both places have a rich history established in nonstop prayer and transformative revival. There are moments when you need to be extra alert of what may be around you, and this was a time we knew we needed to keep a cognizant look out for places we needed to see and understand about the area.

You know, when you commit your walk to the Lord, you often do things that you feel like you're supposed to do even though you don't necessarily have any reasoning behind it. Small, seemingly meaningless actions over time lead to breadcrumbs that form answers in an aha-moment that sparks awe and a more-developed perspective regarding the understanding of your destiny. I believe that this way of living life is an expression of what Paul discusses in Romans 1:17 when he says, "For in the gospel, the righteousness of God is revealed from faith to faith." Although we don't have complete answers about what connections we were to make in Herrnhut, we knew we were there for a greater reason, perhaps a long-term one.

*   *   *   *   *

Our world began to shrink as we connected to new individuals and discovered our mutual friends. Herrnhut provided us with a new friend who told us she was going to be moving to Sarasota, Florida to attend her YWAM Discipleship Training School. We could tell she was nervous, because she didn't know what Sarasota would be like, and we were able to get her excited about the move. After talking for just a few minutes, we knew we needed to connect her with a girlfriend of Jessica's named Jordyn. Nearly a year and a half later, we bumped into her at Jordyn's wedding, and she had a brand new engagement ring on her finger from a man she met through Jordyn. Perhaps we played a role in connecting the dots of her destiny!

Some people, however, maybe should have never crossed our path. One day, as we were getting into the car, an olive-skinned, brown-haired, young man came running out of the YWAM building and flagged Jessica down. He was bursting with excitement to see her.

"It is so good to see our people outside our country of Afghanistan!"

Jess was clearly caught off guard. She is very short with dark brown hair and olive skin, but she has a French-Canadian heritage and is far from middle-eastern. Sorry to let him down, she responded, "Oh, I'm from Florida."

Sadness and shock entered his eyes. His mouth dropped open and he took a step back. He began to argue, "No, you are from Afghanistan!"

"I am so sorry, but I'm not." Jess was sad to let him down.

I guess you'll never know who you'll run into in the world. Some people are looking for new experiences and many people are looking for just a taste of home and familiarity. Truth was, we were about to stay in a house full of people looking for familiarity in a foreign place - Paris.

Paris was one of those places Jess simply wanted to visit since we were in the region. Zach, from London, had connected us with a Malaysian friend of his who lives there named Yap. After connecting with him via Facebook, he told us that there just so happened to be an available room for the days we requested. It was the first vacancy he'd had in 13 years!

After making the eleven-hour drive from Herrnhut to Paris, we arrived at a large, gray house that was set along the river. A few knocks on the front door later, a Chinese girl answered and had a clear look of confusion on her face, wondering why two white people were standing there and speaking English. Hesitantly allowing us to enter the house, we set our bags to the side while waiting for Yap to arrive upstairs to greet us. Then we smelled it: Asian house. It is the glorious smell of last night's steamed noodles that saturates the walls of a home. We were experiencing something few people ever do - we had stepped out of Paris and into China. Yap explained to us that the house has thirty rooms, and he rents it out to Chinese foreign exchange students. His sole purpose is to minister the gospel to them hoping they would take it to their families and friends when they returned to China.

To say it was an honor to be a part of his ministry is a pure understatement. Yap's hunger for the Lord and desire to see his tenants come to Christ was clearly displayed through his passion and care for them. It is very difficult to break through the unforgiving Chinese mindset created by strict parental expectations and the spiritual bondages that eastern religions often develop in a person. Everyone who stays with Yap has various layers that need to be peeled back and addressed. Our evenings in Paris were spent with Yap and the students, praying with them and walking through their pasts by casting out evil things they were opened up to in their hearts and loosening peace and freedom to walk in the grace that's offered to them.

While we were there, we encouraged a young girl who had been tormented in her sleep for years to look for false gods she may have integrated somewhere in her room. After asking the Lord to reveal what it could be, she found a charm in her room that depicted some kind of eastern god and she removed it. Since then, she has not had any kind of torment. Sometimes, bondages can be dealt with by simply getting rid of ungodly items we have around the house.

There was another young girl who had an eye disorder that required her to receive a painful shot in each of her eyes on a monthly basis. We prayed that she would be healed, and the last time we had checked, she was only required by her doctor to receive the shot every three to four months, and he said that somehow the effects of the disease were reversing.

I'll never take for granted the excitement young believers express when they recognize for the first time that God truly wants to take them on a journey. The thought of seeing the hand of God manage impossible situations still seems just as far from reach as before, yet when they recognize they have the authority to speak life into the world through Christ, those who are hungry, and want to know the hows, whys, and the what to dos, ask eagerly. Our prayer, as we talk to people all over the world is that they begin to pray from the viewpoint of their destiny and not from their circumstances. Praying from a circumstantial position (such as the need for more money), allows for an insecure identity to arise and room for faithlessness and unbelief to settle upon that circumstance. Praying from a position of faith founded upon the belief that the impossible dreams and visions you have will come to pass allows you to have a heavenly viewpoint. This is a reflection of true repentance.

*   *   *   *   *

Paris ran our legs into the ground. We visited everywhere we possibly could in a short amount of time, and it amounted to us walking 19 miles the first day and 6 miles the second day. Something Jess and I are very thankful for is the fact that we tend to travel at the same vigorous level. Both of us walk fast while taking in everything that we can and enjoying the moment. Hundreds of pictures a day were taken, and we would do everything we possibly could that our bodies and wallets would allow us to. If you don't go to museums, you'd be surprised how much you can do for free in any place. Many times you can enjoy a city the most by simply having a seat outside a restaurant and ordering a latte. There are always people to talk to or watch, and there is always something to look at.

65 beds, 16 plane rides, 4 trains, 20 buses, 45 cities, 19 countries, and roughly 45,000 miles. The stats had developed, and we were getting ready to increase those numbers even more with a trip back east from Paris to Prague, where Jess has some family friends who pastor a church there. Our itinerary didn't make much sense to people since we traveled south and west of Germany then back up and directly through to east Germany, then back west through Germany again to France to turn right

around and travel back east through Germany to Prague, Czech Republic. Efficiency was not the goal, but rather knowing where God wanted us, and when.

It was a sad goodbye to our new friend Yap and the people we were able to connect with as a result of his ministry in Paris, but we were pressed to move forward. The only problem was that we didn't have any sort of agenda after Prague.

After returning our car back to the Frankfurt airport (in one piece), we had about 10 hours to relax in the airport before an overnight bus to Prague. The question kept tugging at us, however, "where were we to go after Prague?" The thought of showing up at Jess' friends' house in Prague and getting the dreaded question of "where are you headed next" wasn't ideal without having an answer. We had a place in mind, but I needed clear confirmation about it before heading that way. It was Copenhagen, Denmark.

The thought of going to Copenhagen wasn't exciting to me. I figured it was another expensive urban location for us, which always brought a wave of initial concerns, and I also didn't want to have another situation similar to Amsterdam. Copenhagen is cold-cultured like Amsterdam, and I wanted to make sure we had our ducks in a row before making any decisions to head that way. That's when I prayed boldly.

"God, we need a sign if we are supposed to go to Copenhagen or not, and frankly Lord, I'm asking that you do it…like…now. Please don't delay! We need an answer now, like, have someone walk up to us and tell us that we are supposed to go there."

Within thirty seconds of that prayer, over the intercom in the terminal a voice spoke, "Final boarding call for Flight 322 to Copenhagen." Our eyes looked up at the speaker in the ceiling.

"Jess, do you think that counts? Like, is that good enough?"

"Are you kidding me!? How much more clear can you get?"

"Well, I mean, we prayed for a sign for Copenhagen, and the person on the intercom just said Copenhagen. I guess that's what we were looking for. It's not like we're even inside security to where they would be saying those kinds of announcements."

After about twenty minutes it didn't matter, because we had a train booked from Prague to Copenhagen. Now we just needed to figure out the hard part: find a place to stay.

*   *   *   *   *

I sincerely enjoy encouraging people to develop their English. I have learned through talking with many people that language development is more about being confident when you speak than being worried about your translation skills when desiring to progress quickly. I can hardly speak but a bit of Spanish, so I get excited for people who can speak a second language.

I was asked to speak and teach at multiple churches in the Czech Republic, and each time, I had a different translator. It is extremely difficult to think about and time each talking point effectively when another language is blasting next to your ear from the speaker system, so it was much easier to communicate my message with a confident translator. Not only is there a level of teamwork that must take place when working with a translator, but it's also a bonding experience. Some people click with you, and others just don't.

While out with our friends touring Prague, we came to a large, busy square in the middle of town, and our friends pointed and said, "That's where we street-preach every Friday at 5:00." That was a convenient time for them to inform me that I was going to preach at that spot within a few days.

I'll be honest in saying that made me extremely uncomfortable. My mind pictured me getting spat on, tomatoes thrown at me, and even yelled at and punched by some random guy. Many "worst case scenarios" flashed through my mind throughout the following days.

Historically, I've been relatively against the idea of street preaching because I believed it to be a one-way ticket to have a fight break out or spark some emotional or philosophical debate that could easily turn nasty. I have also been concerned that the preacher has been diluting, destroying, or creating confusion about what the gospel actually says on a larger scale, because I (still to this day) had never heard the gospel presented on a street corner without a "fire and brimstone" approach. What's the point in street preaching unless you're truly doing it for another person to be touched by God? You can't have an ulterior motive.

The truth is, whether anyone I've seen preach on a street corner was truly "legit," I've honestly just been scared of the idea and didn't want to hold myself to the standard that the apostles did in the book of Acts. After all, yes, I do very much care about what others think of me, so I rationalized my belief systems into thinking that kind of evangelism was from "that time" when people were out doing stuff in the streets more.

The only thing that kept my cool was the fact that I was most likely never going to see any of these people ever again. It's a bit of a cop-out, but it helped me get past the thinking that I would become Prague's crazy corner preacher.

I purchased a Cherry Coke to chill me out a bit and deal with some of the dry mouth. The time had come, and when I picked up the microphone, the nervousness completely left me. In fact, I was more comfortable on that street corner than meeting a new person at a friend's Christmas party. I spoke for about fifteen minutes, and to my surprise, there were easily about 25 people stopped and gathered to listen to my spiel. I was relaxed, caring, graceful, and presented the gospel in a way that (hopefully) touched people's hearts and prompted them to action. At the same time, I made some uncomfortably bold statements about the power of God and guaranteed that whomever stepped out would be touched in that moment.

When the opportunity came for me to step away and pray for people, a woman in her early thirties named Barbara walked up to me and started crying.

"Why am I crying right now? I feel so soft inside."

"That's the power of the Holy Spirit," I said. "You're meeting Jesus right now."

"The knot in my gut…the stress…it's all gone. You didn't do anything." In fact, I specifically did not touch her except to shake her hand (and I made that point clear).

Barbara immediately understood her role as a new Christian: to share her experience and tell others about Jesus. A friend that was on her way to meet Barbara at the very location I preached was being ministered to within five minutes. I gave them some reading for homework (I like John, Romans, Colossians and Ephesians), and they were taught to fill up through prayer and worship daily so they could pour out what they were filled up with to others.

In the meantime, there was another lady who asked the famous question, "If God is so good, then why is there so much bad in the world?" After talking with us and working through the subject of our level of free will versus predestination, she gave her life to the Lord.

Frankly, I had spent 27 years of my life telling myself how ineffective this type of ministry is and how "scary" it would be. I didn't feel any differently than I would have in a church building talking to a bunch of sold-out believers. In fact, all I could think about was my excitement for Barbara because Jesus was just who she needed that day. He's whom everyone needs. God really gave me a grace on that day, because I really didn't care what people thought. It sure was a lot better than cleaning toilets.

*   *   *   *   *

Follow-through is often one of the hardest aspects to handle with a new Christian, because the enemy tries to come in quickly after to feed lies that the experience the person had didn't really happen and that it was all fake. Jess and I immediately went into intercession mode Friday night and Saturday because we wanted to make sure that Barbara got connected to the church body. We had invited her to the Sunday evening service I was speaking at, and she said she would come, but only time would tell.

Sunday evening came, and halfway through worship, Jess and I gave each other a glance that said, "I don't think she's going to come." Just seconds after, the door opened, and she walked in. While Jess and I worked our way out of our row to meet and greet her, so she knew she had somewhere to sit where she'd feel comfortable, she immediately locked eyes on someone sitting behind us and ran up to her. When we walked up to her, she greeted us with excitement and told us that the person behind us was a close friend from work.

I love how God works. In the entire city of Prague, with all of the people who could have been there, a good friend of Barbara's was there for her to connect, grow and stay grounded with. There is nothing more fulfilling in life than seeing people connect to the Father and receive just what they need. What an honor it was to be a part of her story. All I did was speak.

*   *   *   *   *

People often ask us what our favorite place we visited was and we always respond saying that the answer isn't that simple. We have to address the type of the favorite. Our favorite city in the

239

world? London, no doubt. The most beautiful places we visited? Vietnam, Switzerland, and the Scottish Highlands. Favorite people group? Definitely the Malaysian people. Favorite food? Without a doubt, Thailand (Sorry to our friends in Penang). There is no question whatsoever regarding architecture. Hands down, the winner was Prague.

Prague is a relatively cheap city to visit, which is always a plus. On one side of the river, Prague Castle stands tall above the surrounding buildings that are continuously interesting to look at. Then, as you enter the "newer part of town" on the other side of the river, the architecture gets even better. I remember asking our friends how old the new part of town was, and to my surprise the answer was about 650 years. I was shocked. Americans simply don't have a grid for a building that can stand that long.

Prague gave us another best, and that is one of the best meals that we had. Milos & Marcela, our connections in Prague, took care of us well by cooking us schnitzel to celebrate Jess' 25th birthday. Neither of us had eaten schnitzel before, but had always heard it is a great meal, so we were excited to try it. Paired with some freshly-soaked, sweet pickles from the garden, as we put the schnitzel in our mouths, our eyes rolled in the backs of our heads! It was Chick-fil-a!

Never had we put together that Chick-fil-a has made its billions by selling schnitzel sandwiches, but that is in fact what they are: pickle marinated fried chicken sandwiches served with pickles. After eight months of not having a Chick-fil-a sandwich, it was a wonderful birthday gift for Jess to receive, and we were thankful to celebrate with Milos, Marcela, and their family.

Milos & Marcela greatly encouraged us during the time we stayed with them, and their passion and hunger for the Lord ignited us for the future ahead. They are a hard-working family, and they have done tremendous work in the hearts of so many in Prague and the surrounding cities. Statistically, they are a minority as Christians in the Czech Republic, but they are pioneers to their region to see hearts transformed and renewed.

*   *   *   *   *

The concerns about our housing and connections in Copenhagen were still at the forefront of our minds while we were in Prague, and we tried many avenues to get connected with anyone who might be in active ministry there. It seemed to be a wise decision to go ahead and book the cheapest hotel we could find near town for two nights. At eighty dollars a night, we could afford a room for that long without going completely broke.

The depths of our pockets had been found once again. This result may have partially been because we decided to deviate from our everyday focus and tour a place millions of people once prayed to leave - The Auschwitz-Birkenau Death Camps in Auschwitz, Poland. Only a six-hour train ride away, we were too close to not make a special trip to tour it.

My family was, at one time, very close to a former prisoner of Auschwitz and other concentration camps existent during the Nazi regime. Having read and heard his story of survival, I had a personal interest to establish a visual for a place he will never forget. Many people we talked about the camps with said a variety of emotions would be felt during our tour - anger, sadness, shock, confusion. How could a nation get so out of hand? How could you persevere that long through the cold, hunger, and sickness? How could anyone carry a sense of hope? The people we talked to were right.

Bewilderment settled on us as we walked through the hallways of the processing facilities, viewed the countless shoes, stared at the mounds of hair, and we tried to wrap our minds around the number of people killed in the gas chambers and burned in the ovens. We stared at the photos into the faces of people just like us. Many were our age and confident in their God. Jess and I struggled to fully comprehend what had happened as two individuals whom the only "really bad event" that had ever taken place in our lives had been 9/11. There had to be intentionality to absorb what was in front of us and allow our imagination to explore what it may had felt like to live through such an atrocity.

The highlight of our tour of the facilities was (surprisingly) our tour guide. She expressed the emotions of each room beautifully, attaching her modus operandi to everything which was "never forget what happened so it never happens again." Many times she eluded to the thought that without the understanding and knowing of the history of how a nation spirals toward functioning in the way Nazi Germany did, future generations of genocide cannot be avoided.

Our guide was just about to celebrate her thirtieth year working at Auschwitz-Birkenau. She was only in her early fifties, and she told the story with passion as if it was her first day. When I told her about our family friend who had survived Auschwitz and how he got out, she was not only shocked but started to tear up. She was amazed to hear what he had done with his life since moving to the United States. I will never forget her.

*   *   *   *   *

When asked to talk about our journey overseas, many people inquire about the logistics and how we accomplished basic things. Laundry was a lot easier to handle than we had planned for prior to leaving. We had purchased a wash bag for our laundry called a Scrubba at the beginning of our trip along with a clothesline so we could always have clean laundry. Then we realized how cheap it was to do laundry in Asia, so we just fronted the $3. Not only would they wash our entire load of laundry, but they would press and fold it as well. It was a no-brainer.

As the year went on and we stayed at more homes, laundry was usually something our hosts would offer to let us take care of, but the drying part was always most difficult. We needed our clothes to last as long as possible, so if there was a dryer, we tried hard to avoid using it so they wouldn't shrink. As long as we stayed somewhere for a few days, we were able to have clean, dry clothes for the most part.

It wasn't until Prague, however, that two days on the clothesline outside wasn't long enough to dry our clothes in time to leave for Auschwitz, and we didn't have access to a dryer. An overcast day was followed by another, and we had cold, damp clothes that couldn't be packed properly. Thankfully our train to Auschwitz was purchased as a round trip ticket, and our host, Milos, met us at the train station two days later with our dry laundry. It was nice to not have to carry our bags on the tour.

We were glad that was the case, because the itinerary was brutal. Our train car was small with wooden benches on either side of a tight hallway. You could fit six people snugly inside, and we were paired with two girls traveling together for the summer. They were single and college-aged which meant that the time we were trying to fall asleep was the time their night was just getting started. Chatting continued into the early hours of the morning, and we arrived at our stop at 4:30am.

The camps didn't open until 8:30, and we weren't going to walk around a new city in the dark hours of the night, so we tried to catch some sleep on the concrete benches of the main hall of the train station. It was just what you would think Auschwitz would be like - hard and cold. Not only that, the guards prohibited us from laying down on the benches. We had to sit up or else we would be asked to leave. At one point, I had fallen asleep and leaned over on my bag, and the guard shook me awake. I woke up from such a deep sleep that I literally snarled at the guard. He knew I was not a happy camper!

It was a long day at the camps with that crusty feeling under your eyes and bad breath paired with too much useless coffee. Mix that with greasy hair, and we were very excited to get back on the train to return to Prague, but it wasn't set to leave until 10:30pm. Then, it showed up late. Waiting outside on a hard bench in the cold until after 11:15, we were reminded of the sleepless nights that many had experienced only a mile away from there. It was in the high forties and wet in the air. Sleep was not hard to dive into on the train's wooden benches that night.

After a long day of waiting in the charming Prague train station, we boarded our third overnight train to Copenhagen. Jess and I both had comfortable top bunk beds across from each other. Our train boarded at 6:30 in the evening. We were in bed by 8:00, and we both slept until an hour before arriving at 10:00am the following morning. It was a perfect night's sleep.

As we pulled in, there was only one thing on our minds: coffee. Thankfully, just outside of the station was a perfect coffee shop. When we checked out and used some of our newly exchanged Danish Crowns, something didn't click for me with the purchase. After doing some math, I realized we had just spent $9 on a cup of coffee! Then I remembered what part of the planet we were on.

Thankfully, financial pressure had been relieved through a love offering from two of the churches I had spoken at in the Czech Republic in the cities of Brno and Prague. We were shocked to open the envelope given to us with roughly $600. It was a sincere boost, but $9 coffee was not going to let us hold onto it for very long. We needed to know why God wanted us in Copenhagen in the first place. I felt that if I could resolve that issue, I could rationalize spending the money if necessary.

* * * * *

As we explored Copenhagen, we tried so hard to be interested in everything we visited. After nearly nine months of travel, the excitement of playing tourist had faded, the selfies all looked the same except for the area behind us, and we had to be intentional to care about the places that many people dream to visit. There was an underlying tone in our expressions, however, that displayed uneasiness regarding what the following eight days were going to shape up to be like.

We had booked a cheap flight back to London after staying nine days in Copenhagen. Zach's house was a safe place for us, but most importantly, we had special visitors vacationing to London: Steven & Kristen (who we lived with before leaving) and Steve's brother Jonathan and his wife Katie. It was without question that we were excited to see the four of them. We were desperate to connect with some familiar faces from back home, and they are some of our closest friends.

During the first night in our hotel room (which was about the size of a room on cruise ship), we asked an important question for the following day: "What church are we going to go to tomorrow?" It was a Saturday night, and I had found three churches on Google that seemed like a good fit.

"Jess, which one do you think we should go to?" I asked.

"I'm not sure."

"Well, I'm going to grab a shower. Let's both pray about it, and when I get out, we can decide on where to go." I already knew which I thought we should pick.

Sure enough, when I got out of the shower, Jess had picked

245

the one I had felt as well. The first one was too large, and it was easy to get missed. The second church started very early. The one we picked, although having a very poor website and appearing to be a much smaller-looking church, seemed to strike a chord with us. Sure enough, it fit the bill.

Have you ever had an experience with a church where it literally feels like "home?" The people there make it home. The smell of it makes it feel like home. Even some small details that no one except for you would care about could make you remember something from your teen years when you are in your seventies. This was the case with this church and our church at home in Sarasota. The teaching was meaty. The worship was deep. The people were caring, and most of all, the people were allowed to openly share about what the Lord was doing in their hearts during the service at the proper time. This particular church in Copenhagen felt like home.

The pastor was very friendly towards Jess and me when we showed up for the service. We both hate attending new churches and being "the visitors," and he made us very comfortable. He asked all about what the Lord was doing in our lives and was excited for us. He even called us up towards the end of the service and allowed me to give a quick nugget and pray over the congregation! This had never happened in nine months and 20 countries. In fact, I had been reprimanded for praying over someone in a church in Malaysia because I wasn't on the leadership team. To say I was honored to have the opportunity to speak into a congregation that was hungry for the Lord would be an understatement. I understand the complex struggles pastors and a congregation can have about handing a microphone to someone they don't know and them subsequently misrepresenting the church, but there is a great reward for those who can see integrity, truth, and power in an individual and trust that the Lord will humbly move through them if they give them the room to do so.

The end of the service had arrived, and it was a moment of truth. Either God would show up and prove His faithfulness regarding our adventure, or we would leave with more questions wondering if this entire journey was purely a long string of luck. Jess and I looked at each other, and we shrugged our shoulders. Nothing was happening. No connections were being made.

"I guess that's it?" I hesitantly asked.

"Yeah. What should we do?" Jess seemed a bit let down hoping God would intervene and a situation similar to what we experienced in Amsterdam would be avoided.

"I guess we should just walk around the city, get a good meal and a long night's sleep."

That's not what I wanted, but I knew that the next night we were going to be renting a car to sleep in on the side of the street, probably somewhere in Sweden. We couldn't afford a hotel for seven more nights in the city, or we'd be out of money.

Jess concurred, and we began to walk out of the main sanctuary into the lobby. That's when we were stopped by a Hispanic couple and their toddler. Chatter went on for a moment about the service, and they asked what we would be doing for the seven other days we would be in the city. We tried to portray that we had a confident plan of action, but we were far from winning an Oscar.

"Where are you staying?" The man asked.

Jess and I changed the subject to their little boy. We didn't want to come across as desperate. After talking for another brief moment, he stated the question for a second time:

"Where are you staying?"

CHAPTER EIGHTEEN

CALLING ALL ANGELS

Oftentimes I will think about the cost of items around the world and how they are different based on the supply and demand principles within the various regions. One of the things I would love to purchase more often, for example, would be a massage. At an average price of $1 a minute in the United States, I can't come to grips with spending that kind of money when you can purchase a massage for $5 an hour in Thailand.

An average pair of Levi Jeans that you could purchase at a department store costs roughly $40 in Florida. In Malaysia, someone purchased me a pair for $100. As I said, a cup of coffee in Copenhagen ran about $9, when in the states if I have to fork out $6, I start to gripe (and I'm a member of the $5 Latte Generation). Copenhagen also won our "most expensive fast food award" at $38 for a basic KFC dinner.

I think about the $13 bus ride from London to Bristol and the $45 taxi from the Hanoi airport to our hotel. We had a relatively nice hotel room in Laos for $14 a night, and $38 for our worst hotel room in rural Myanmar. There are so many times I look at the cost of items in the United States and am very thankful for the amount (like fuel prices), and there are other times when I get frustrated with US prices, such as the time I recall getting four antibiotics and a doctor's appointment in Malaysia for $22.

Copenhagen would have stretched us for every dollar we had left. Chances are, we would have probably spent $120 a day just to stay afloat and been broke by the end of the week, but it was that simple question from someone we had known for about two minutes that changed our world: *Where are you staying?*

*　　　　*　　　　*　　　　*　　　　*

There was a great Mexican joint just a few blocks away from the church, so we loaded up before our continued tour of Copenhagen that Sunday.

"I can't believe they offered us their home, Chris. They don't even know who we are. Do you even remember their names?"

"You know I never remember people's names. What's crazy is they are picking us up and making us dinner tonight. We didn't even need our room the second night. Are we sure this isn't a joke and they're going to change their minds?"

"We'll find out tonight, won't we?"

"I can't believe it was just that simple. We needed a place, and they just walked up and asked us where we were staying. I wonder if they're the reason we're here."

Sure enough, the husband showed up to our hotel that evening, and we loaded our bags into his car. Needless to say, it was a little awkward at first. We had talked for five minutes at church, didn't know where they lived or why they asked us to stay with them. In situations like that, I do what I do best: I ask questions to get the other person guiding the discussion so I don't have to think about what to talk about.

We arrived at their third story flat in a rural area of Copenhagen called Ballerup. It was cozy, and we could quickly tell that this was a family that had a different view on life than the average Danish person: they were hot-cultured. These were people who understood community and thrived on it, and it was in their nature to care for others. God had put us in the midst of people who were relationship-minded in the middle of a culture that thrives on individualism. This family didn't have plans in their calendars for the next three months like most people living in the region, but they were flexible, giving them the ability to share their lives with us for the next week.

As we joined around the table, the truth came out very quickly that we didn't remember their names, and they didn't remember ours! It was a great icebreaker, and we shared about our conversations wondering who these people were that would just ask us where we were staying and let us stay for a week. Their names were Eduardo and Sara.

"Frankly, I don't even know why I asked you to stay with us. It just came out. I looked at Sara, and she knew it wasn't like me. I just had to." Edwardo is calm and thoughtful, and Sara is outspoken and colorful. They are a perfectly balanced couple.

We shared our story with them and showed them on a world map they had next to their dining room table where we lived. One rabbit trail led to another, and I ended up talking about a school that a few of our friends had attended and highly recommended. That's when both Eduardo's and Sara's forks dropped on their plates. They looked at each other, started talking in Spanish and looked joyful yet teary-eyed.

Edwardo began to explain, "I felt like God was leading us to take a step of faith and move to the United States to attend that very school. I told him weeks ago that I wanted someone who knew something about it to tell me it was a good school, and that would be my confirmation to go."

He continued sharing some of the dreams he had, and was in complete shock that the conversation we were having was taking place.

"Hardly anyone in Copenhagen knows anything about the school." They just kept shaking their heads in thankfulness.

I often like to say to people "you just got used" when God uses them for a specific purpose. I found myself saying that to ourselves that evening. It's a good thing that God moved through us quickly as well because Eduardo told us that he had a business trip to South America and would be gone for almost the entire time we would be staying at the house. It was going to be just us, Sara and her son for the week.

What does it mean to be *in* ministry? What is protocol to be someone who ministers to another person? What must be the underlying purpose in order for someone to be in proper ministry? These are just a couple of the questions that burdened my thoughts regularly, and our week with Sara challenged my thinking. The church so often says to people, "God loves you just the way you are," and then they follow up by saying, "but you need to change this and this and that." Obviously there's a level of understanding, that in order to perceive the Kingdom of God at the level God intends for us to, we need to have certain things in order and be disciplined, but there is always an underlying tone that we need to act in a way that increases or keeps God's love for us. The church puts these demands and expectations on us as well, and they build the foundation for an identity developed upon the extent of the level of our moral fiber and good works. We must understand what covenant we are *currently* living under as Christians and believe in it fully.

Our week with Sara was simple. It was purely quality time. We read books, watched movies, went grocery shopping, bought frozen yogurt at the mall, and cooked meals together. It wasn't super-spiritual. It didn't involve us doing some service project around the house or hosting a VBS for all the neighborhood kids. All we did was live life and have plenty of conversations in between, and it was an answer to Sara's prayers.

The truth was that Sara was lonely. It was a difficult time in her life, and she asked for God to bring her someone to pour into her. She got us. To this day, Sara still thinks we are angels (with a home address and social media pages). We were just two people who needed a place to stay and hopefully had a purpose behind being in Copenhagen. At the end of the week, we left knowing we fulfilled our duty of simply being the conduits to which both Eduardo and Sara's prayers were answered. They did later end up moving to the United States to go to school and gave birth to a beautiful baby girl.

*   *   *   *   *

There it was again: the yellow-orange glow. Fall was beginning to make its way to the United Kingdom, and we were back at our safe house - Zach's. The weather was perfect in London for a light rain jacket as it randomly rains and then gets sunny and hot again. The relationships with all of our housemates were rekindling, and we slipped right back into our little routine we had prior to leaving for Alaska. Friday night badminton was what I looked forward to most. I actually got fairly proficient on a very amateur level and enjoyed some form of regular exercise other than walking. Afterward, all of us would go to the pub and connect. It was a temporary life that would be enjoyed for as long as we had it.

Ten weeks were still ahead until returning back to the United States. How were we supposed to spend them? That was the million-dollar question. There was only enough cash to sustain us for about a month let alone book flights and go to other places where we didn't know anyone.

Throughout our journey, we always asked each other about what we were feeling in terms of our mental travel itineraries. It was that same itinerary that put us in a position of wondering if Copenhagen was really where we should have gone. It just took an announcement on an airport intercom to confirm it. This time, however, there were two countries on our minds that required our faith to be in action yet again: Israel and Kenya.

Back in KL, we attended a meeting with one of our hosts about attending a conference in Jerusalem, and Jess had a desire to go. I never really felt right about it, but I trust Jessica's hearing, and since she felt like it was what we should do, I paid less-skeptical attention to the idea and adopted it as a good idea. There is also an orphanage in Kenya we are highly connected to, and we also have some friends there, so we thought it would be ideal to visit them. It made sense that in the beginning of October we would spend two weeks in Israel then fly to Kenya for three weeks. We would then return to London to fly home in mid-November. The prayers for the Lord to fulfill this opportunity began, and I told Him that I'd like to have the funds by September 15th.

Mid-September rolled around, and nothing financially substantial (like the $4,000 for the flights) had come through. So, like any faithful person, I thought that my expectations were just a bit arrogant, and I adjusted my deadline to October 1. It only made sense since our close friends Steven, Jonathan, Kristen and Katie were vacationing to London, and we were excited to spend time with them.

It had been a long nine months. It had been an emotional nine months. So much life had been lived. I think about how fast nine months goes sometimes and how much and how little can happen, but we had seen the world! God had shown up in our lives and in the people we were connecting with on a regular, if not daily, basis. Our story encouraged our new friends and helped push them to go after the dreams in their hearts. We were concerned, however, that our friends wouldn't "get us" anymore because we saw the world through a different lens and had an experience they couldn't relate to. Where do you start with your conversation?

Thankfully, we just picked up where we left off. We talked about some stories from the last few weeks, but we didn't want to just talk about our trip and all that had happened. We just cut up and laughed. It was an honor to experience our favorite place in the world with some of our favorite people.

*   *   *   *   *

Thursday nights became a ministry night for us after we were connected to a group of people who minister in some strip clubs in central London. Since we were "short-termers," we would prayer-walk the area and intercede around the corner of the club while another part of the group would deliver cupcakes to the bouncers and women. Although we weren't welcomed to be "in the action," we did get to hang with another girl who, at the time, was a hyena for *The Lion King* on Broadway. Her personality definitely fit the part. She had us belly-laughing a lot!

The process was short and simple: There would always be women coming out of the club to take a smoke break, so you had about five minutes to talk to them, share the gospel and try to set up any type of coffee date, English-training session (as many of the girls were from Eastern Europe and couldn't speak English) or have some type of impact. Then another group of girls would switch out for their smoke break.

The bouncers were certainly annoyed with our team at first, but after months and months of Thursday night outreaches having already occurred, they had opened up to the point of asking questions and receiving Bibles. Over time, the girls had opened up as well, and they knew who we were for the cupcakes. Little things had started to change, such as the removal of raunchy photos in the main hallway and the increased number of smiles on everyone's faces. It's easy to believe that a ministry is wasting its efforts if the girls aren't leaving their lifestyle and the bouncers aren't getting different jobs, but we are doing our part best by giving them a taste of the joy of the Lord, which is wonderful in itself. Additionally, the bouncers always joked saying that since the team had been delivering cupcakes, business was slower on Thursdays. I'm not sure they had put two and two together.

The really effective ministry happened after someone would agree to have contact outside of the club when they were not working. Most of that time was spent breaking down the false identities that they carried and the negative views they had of pastors, priests, and Christians who often visit their club. The goal was to show them the true love of Christ in the process.

Our hour bus ride home afterward was another ministry ground in itself. Since the Underground was closed in the middle of the night, we had joined the homeless, drunks, and broken who were headed home to sleep off whatever state they were in or those who just wanted a cheap, warm place to sleep. I could actually relate to the idea of resorting to sleep on the bus. It's not as far-fetched as many people may think it is. If you are ever looking for a great outreach, try the bus system. I guarantee you that everyone on that bus could use some level of uplifting.

*   *   *   *   *

October 1st had come and gone. I needed some time to myself, so I decided to skip church the following weekend, leave Jess at home and go to Hyde Park for the morning to pray, think, and organize some of my thoughts onto paper. It was a beautiful fall day, and nothing could help me enjoy it more than clear, blue skies, a nice breeze and soft grass under my feet.

As I arrived at Hyde Park Corner and crossed the road into the park, I heard a lot of commotion and remembered that "Speaker's Corner" was in session. Speakers Corner is thought by many to originally be a place designated where you are free from the law to speak whatever you want without consequence as long as you are on some kind of soapbox, but in truth, it was a common meeting place for strikes and revolts. Speakers Corner has now become famous for its Muslim, Jewish and Christian evangelists who are out to preach their religion.

I quickly realized few were receptive to anything being said, and most people were out for some level of interactive entertainment. Instead of going to some private area with a nice tree to lean against, I found myself on the side of a discussion between a Seventh Day Adventist and a Muslim man. It was obvious that it was not their first meeting. Their loud argument was engaging and the Muslim was really trying to understand a relatively sound Christian view until he got caught up on a few things that directly conflicted with the Quran. He would shut down and go in circles. It didn't look much different than a progressive debating a conservative.

After about thirty minutes of listening, I saw that a very young man, perhaps about 16, was standing next to me for a while, and I heard something that was said that was more direct to the heart rather than dogmatic (which is the kind of discussion I care about). I casually asked him, "What do you think about what that guy just said?"

It wasn't but a few sentences of discussion before he stated, "Let me get my teacher."

I stopped him, and tried to halt him by saying, "No, I don't want to know what your teacher thinks, I want to know what *you* think." You would have thought I had just told him he should steal someone's wallet by the shock on his face,

"No, I will call my teacher over, and we can discuss."

The next man I saw walking towards me was an Imam (Muslim priest) holding a Bible that was ripped to shreds. It had various colors of post-it notes marking tens of different areas, and when he opened it, it had different color highlights on nearly every page as well as items written all on the sides of the pages. This Imam had an agenda, and it was to shut me down.

Within five more minutes, the conversation had turned into what seemed like me trying to call a customer service hotline to get a refund for something, and I got transferred to the supervisor's supervisor's supervisor. I had three fully-dressed Muslims and the kid who I just asked a simple question to arguing with me about God's purpose in man. At the end of the day, I wasn't looking for a fight, but rather, I was trying my best to get them to let me pray for them so they could have an encounter with the Holy Spirit.

I had one precondition, and it was that they would let me pray for them to experience God through letting me hold their hands. Yes, God could move without me touching them (Barbara from Prague is a perfect example of this), but I asked for them to have an open heart, which is something that the Quran forbids them to do. After minutes of going in circles, I finally did something in front of these four men that I had never done and haven't done since. I lifted my hands and cried out to the Lord for the four of them to be touched by His love.

Within a quick moment, I had another older man standing next to me praying with me and a group had formed. It was uncomfortable, and I just wanted to find a tree and plant myself next to it, but I kept praying. Upon finishing, one of them asked me, "You done?"

I smiled. They were uncomfortable. One of them was looking at me with a deep stare. It wasn't a stare of hatred, but rather a staring that reflected a shift in a viewpoint. Something had happened. I'll never know what, but it did. I wanted out of that situation as quickly as possible. I never even wanted to get into it in the first place. When I started to walk away, I stopped and looked at the younger man (who got me into that mess) and said to him, "Your creator gave you the brain you have. Don't let these guys tell you what you believe. You search truth and find it." I could see the internal struggle from the cultural pressures being reflected in his face.

I did, in fact, finally make it to a nice tree in the park and began to work through some of the rebuttals that were said so I could be better prepared in the future; specifically ones dealing with the Trinity, which is a subject Muslims struggle the most with in terms of Christianity. To them, it reflects polytheism without the proper context and understanding. A large percentage of Muslims believe the Trinity is the Father, Son and Mary, and they miss the entire point of the purpose of Christ by not being introduced to the Holy Spirit.

I was shaking with nerves from the adrenaline of the moment especially since I prefer to not be the center of attention in political and religious debates. I like to go straight to the heart with a strong, unified context so understanding can be established in both parties that results in an outcome of change, further investigation, or consistency of opinion. The events that transpired at Speaker's Corner took precedence in the forefront of my mind, and I had forgotten that the main reason I went to the park was to ultimately work out our future travel itinerary with the Lord. It never got done.

*   *   *   *   *

October was a month of mental struggle. What were we doing with our lives? Had God given up on us? Why would we stay in London for a total of ten weeks?

Our money was almost gone, and were about to hit zero. We still had five weeks left until we would be home in Sarasota. How in the world were we going to make it this time? We hadn't hardly seen any money come through other than what we regularly expected. There was no way it would cover everything.

Then the unthinkable happened. While we were on our way to meet Zach for dinner one evening, we got stuck in traffic because of a problem on the Underground. We were already late, and Jess, who is traditionally a stickler to leaving early, was pushing us to hurry. The buses were slow as well, so we decided to hike quite a distance to where we were meeting Zach, and in the push to get there quickly, Jess tore her meniscus going up a staircase. The pain didn't really kick in until getting home later in the evening, and her left knee swelled up. Not only were we poor, but now I had a bed-ridden wife.

We then purchased the last bit of groceries we could afford. It would last us about a week until we would have to pull out the credit card. I had a shelf with £1.93 in coins stacked up. At the time, that was the equivalent of roughly $3.10 or a pack of gum or two. I struggled staring at that stack of coins but would rationalize, "well, we have more money than someone in debt at the end of the day."

Additionally, Jess had a friend who runs an orphanage in Uganda who needed to leave Africa due to some visa issues for a few days. Zach had a spare room for her to join us in London, and having never been to the city before, we were going to play tour guide. Since Jess' meniscus was torn and she was bed-ridden, I was on my own to show her friend a good time in London, but had no money to do any of the tours.

"Chris, you'll just have to pull out the card for this, and we'll make it up somehow." Jess has a knack for putting others' needs and desires before her own.

"Jess, I can't do it. We need to stick to what we said we were going to. It is not absolutely necessary for us to do this."

Our friend from Uganda had arrived on Friday, and we planned to tour London on Saturday. I went to bed with a sigh on Friday evening, ready to call it quits. I was ready to go home. One key problem: we were broke.

CHAPTER NINETEEN

RESOLUTION BREEDS MORE QUESTIONING

"Chris! Wake up!"

"What happened?" I'm half-blind until I grab my glasses, so I scrambled for them from the floor.

"Look at your email account!"

Sure enough, there it was. The day we were going to hit rock bottom, a $2,000 donation showed up in our account. We couldn't believe it. There is no feeling that can replace the relief and excitement that comes when you stand strong in your faith, even when you had the option not to, and victory arrives. That, right there, is George Müller stuff, and that's what we wanted to experience. Nobody said it would be easy or fun.

We took the next few minutes to praise God for his faithfulness and belief in us. The next thing we always follow up with is a discussion on who we are going to tithe to. Generosity flows out of a heart of gratitude, and we are so incredibly blessed to be able to give to people, especially in the times people sow into us. It is easy to rationalize your thinking to believe that since you are in ministry and living off of support that a "get out of tithing free card" is delivered into your hands. Generosity is required of all of us, and it is a way for us to sow seeds into the things that have the most meaning to us.

After my shower, I went downstairs to make Jess a cup of coffee and get her settled for the morning since she was still bedridden from her torn meniscus. That's when Zach walked into the kitchen and handed me a £100 bill ($163), and said to take our friend out for a good time. We were blown away. The following day we were given another £100 bill, giving us roughly $2,300 within 48 hours. That amount of money easily gave us the ability to ride a single wave all the way back to Sarasota.

Needless to say, our friend had a wonderful time in London and all of her desired sites to see were visited.

*   *   *   *   *

The next day, I was scheduled to speak at a church in Essex. I was told I was going to have 30 minutes to speak to this relatively new and small church of about 40 people, so I planned for that. I didn't like going without Jess, though. She's able to make up for my inability to catch the small details of people, places, and situations, and I count on her a lot of the time. She is also my prayer partner, so when I've got nothing, she's there with something to back me up. I had Zach with me, however, and he was there in case I needed any help.

What started off as a 30-minute talk, turned into 30 minutes of talking and over two hours of ministry. I prayed and prophesied over nearly every person in the congregation. The most exciting part, however, was when a sixteen-year-old girl limped her way to the front with crutches. She had a broken ankle and was wearing a soft cast, which was an ideal situation for me because she could test and verify her improvements. I prayed over her for a moment and asked her if she felt anything.

"It's tingly and hot." She remarked.

I prayed for a little while longer, and then I saw it. I saw her countenance change. Once again, I could see a healing took place because she wore it on her face. Some people start cursing out of shock. Some start to cry. She began smiling. That's when I knew that the Lord had touched her.

"On a scale of one to ten, how bad is the pain?"

"Well, it was an eight, and I couldn't move my ankle at all. Now I can move it all around."

"So you're telling me you couldn't do that before? What else could you not do or can you do now?"

"I couldn't bend my toes." She began bending them.

That's when I got excited, because I knew she was experiencing something she would never forget.

"The pain level is like a two now." She added.

I prayed in the name of Jesus for the pain to fully subside, and after one more minute of prayer, the girl was fully healed and she could walk without her crutch. She took the cast off and was perfectly fine. I got up off of my knees and looked up into her eyes. She was a very tall basketball player.

"How's your relationship with the Lord. Do you have one?"

"Well, I've been asking a lot of questions." She started to cry. "I'm pretty sure this seals the deal."

It is truly an honor to welcome someone into a new order of life; one that gives us joy, peace and authority. I am awful with names and bad with recalling events, but I remember every one of the faces of the people I have been able to help experience and accept the truth of God into their hearts.

Seeing that girl's ankle getting healed so she could get back to the basketball games she was missing, and seeing her light up when she got to personally experience God was the icing on the cake for that weekend. It helped remind me that although there are times God doesn't seem to be coming through like with Vlad's leg in Phuket, there are other times I get to see breakthrough, and there is no excuse for not trying! I don't know why some people get healed and others don't. Frankly, that is one of my largest personal struggles with God.

Why was my mom's kneecap healed in 1999 yet she died of cancer in 2005? Why was Jess still bed-ridden with a torn meniscus after hours of prayer, but a girl's ankle healed within five minutes of the same person praying on the same day? It doesn't make sense, and the inconsistency drives me nuts, but it is never an excuse to quit. It's never an excuse to let someone continue to struggle to limp their way down the street. Yet, I often continue to carry a lack of faith. Faith is hard. It takes personal sacrifice on many levels. We have to start asking, "What if this thing I want *does* happen" and stop concluding "it won't happen." The opportunity to impact someone who comes across our path may not follow the scientific method or have enough data and evidence to conclude success, but that should not be our indicator to quit as Christians. It sounds stupid, and perhaps it is. If we truly feel compelled to take a step of faith toward something, would God not reward us with His grace if we got it wrong?

Our story is nothing short of a miracle from start-to-finish. I often wonder what our lives would have looked like had we decided the risks were too great and just stayed home. It was an honor to trust in the Lord for the provision of absolutely everything, both physical and spiritual in the manner we choose to live by. I can't say if I would trust with confidence that He would provide for this specific type of journey all over again, but, what I do know, is that I can trust in Him to fulfill the dreams He puts into my heart for the future. That's easier said than done, however.

*   *   *   *   *

The last week of our adventure was filled with many emotions. We were scared to return to the states. I pictured ourselves jumping onto a treadmill running full speed and not being able to keep up. Where we were going to live? Where would we work? All of the questions about our future couldn't be held off anymore, and solutions had to emerge. We were excited and very nervous to get home. It felt like a never-ending layover.

We enjoyed every last part of London that we could. The relationships we had built had become so strong, and we were very sad to leave what felt like our second home. The time had come, however, and we had sought out what we were looking for. We wanted to see the world and see God move through our lives by living out a level of faith that was beyond our comfort level. We wanted to see if we could find the line between faith and stupidity. I have no answer for you to that loaded question other than this - it's wherever the peace is.

Peace was at the center of our hearts to sell our belongings, so we did. Peace resonated when discussing the idea of starting our journey in Thailand, so we went. Peace wasn't present when going to book a flight to Taiwan and South Korea (although we tried), but we definitely felt anguish about leaving Malaysia and found out I had misread our visa to be a 30-day instead of 60-day visa in actuality. We stayed in Malaysia as a result and felt peace. We had peace while driving up a mountain in Switzerland that we almost slid off of, but I'm still not sure why. Should we never drive up a mountain in the dark again?

What I can say is that it probably would have been stupid to book a flight to Israel and Kenya on the credit card. Perhaps the Lord would have come through. Perhaps we would have been $4,000 in debt for the flights. Perhaps a bomb would have blown us up in the airport. Who knows? What we did know is that we had peace about staying in London.

"So do not worry, saying, 'What shall we eat?' or 'What shall we drink?' or 'What shall we wear?' For the pagans run after all these things, and your heavenly Father knows that you need them. But seek first his kingdom and his righteousness, and all these things will be given to you as well." (Matthew 6:31-34 NIV)

All I know is that God knows the things that we need. It's my job to enter into His kingdom and change the way that I think so that I view life from His perspective and respond out of the overflow of that viewpoint. If I'm doing that, and if I have the peace that passes all understanding comforting me, I have to confidently take a large step forward even though I'm blindfolded. Who knows, you may just get to visit 21 countries and experience God in new ways in each of them.

*   *   *   *   *

We didn't openly announce we were actually returning home until a few weeks after. There was an adjustment period to eastern standard time we needed to work through, and we wanted to catch up with our families before our friends excitedly bombarded us. The constant traveling and questioning of our next steps had worn us out, and we felt rest and easing back into life in the USA was a smart approach.

Then the best gift that could have been given to a couple who had just traveled for ten and a half months was given. My brother and his wife gave us tickets for a 7-night Caribbean cruise, and two of my cousins joined the four of us for the trip at the beginning of December. What an amazing experience it was to sit out on the side of the boat and think about the future and remind myself of the grandeur of God's size. Our problems, needs, and destinies are literally in Him who created me, and it is just as much a part of His destiny to deal with our destiny because what is ours is His, and what is His is ours. If the ecclesia could truly make that notion as a part of their understood identity, imagine what we could accomplish!

We hope that our story encourages you to do that very thing that is inside of you. Take that leap of faith! Don't rush it, but don't prolong it either. Have faith. Don't be stupid.

"Trust in the Lord with all of your heart and lean not on your own understanding; in all your ways submit to Him, and He will make your paths straight." (Proverbs 3:4-5)

EPILOGUE

Yes, I did end the book without telling you what happened after we got home! Here are a couple of tidbits:

Upon returning, we didn't realize how long it would take for us to want to begin socializing again. Our bodies were tired, and we were socially spent. It wasn't until the first of the year that we began to get involved with our church body and friends and lead a relatively active life. Most of our time was spent at home with Steven and Kristen and with Jess' family.

By February, we had moved into a small duplex and traded the first month of rent for a remodeling of the unit. It was beautiful once we were done working on it, and it was perfectly aligned to our taste. The most exciting part of having a home again was to not feel guilty that we had to socialize with the people we were staying with and to cook in our own kitchen.

Jess ended up getting a job with a missions organization, and after six months of underemployment, I got a job working for a company focused on business as mission (BAM) projects around the globe. We both love what we do and intend on expanding our efforts further once we have more experience.

All of our friends bought houses and had kids before we did, while we returned home intending to build a strong foundation for our future family. All but one of our closest married friends had children while we chose wait. We didn't have a spoon to eat with when we returned, and it was as if we got married all over again. This was the hardest part of our adjustment back home, because we desperately wanted children.

We still live in Sarasota near Jess' family. All but the youngest of Jess' four adopted siblings remembered who we were when we surprised them upon returning home. The youngest,

Jasmine, cried because everyone knew who we were but her, and she felt like an outcast. Everyone is now close once again.

We have seen many of our new friends from overseas since returning home, as some of them have come to the states for various reasons. Hopefully, some of them will visit Florida and we can host them in our home someday, especially the ones who hosted us. Our birthdays are extra special on social media, because they start early and end late because of all the people around the world we are connected to. We do our best to keep regular connection with our international friends. Their generosity and care for us will never be forgotten.

Unfortunately, the man who was responsible for feeding us our first meal in faith in Penang, Malaysia passed away of sudden heart failure in 2016. He is survived by his wife and two young daughters.

*   *   *   *   *

The best is saved for last: A Chinese friend of ours in London was getting rid of some clothes and offered them to Jess before giving them away elsewhere. In the clothes pile, was an authentic burgundy Harvard hoodie, and hoodies were something we had sacrificed the majority of the year because of their weight. Jess fell in love with it and wore it every day for almost a month (and frankly she felt cool wearing a Harvard hoodie). The last day she wore it was the day we returned home.

While standing on the tarmac, boarding our flight from London to New York City, there was a good-looking, professional man in his thirties standing behind Jess who casually asked her:

"What year were you?"

To which Jess enthusiastically responded...

"Eight!"

The silence was strong. I no longer knew Jess at this point. I had never seen her in my life.

Then, what the man was asking kicked in, and Jess confidently responded, "Oh, I didn't go to Harvard."

Crickets.

She thought he asked, "What *row* were you?"

Notes

Chapter Six – *Here's Yer Sign*
1. Romans 10:10a
2. 2 Corinthians 5:17
3. 1 Corinthians 3:2-3a
4. John 14:12
5. Hebrews 11:6
6. Ephesians 4:22-24
7. Galatians 2:20
8. Romans 8:5
9. Galatians 5:22-25
10. Romans 8:17
11. John 5:19
12. Matthew 10:8
13. Matthew 7:23
14. John 11:25-26
15. Romans 6:5-11
16. Romans 8:2-4
17. Matthew 18:18-19
18. Matthew 28:19

Chapter Ten – *Fork in the Road*
1. Quran 4:88-91

Chapter Eleven – *The Glitch that Guided Us*
1. John 10:10b
2. John 14:6
3. Quran 51:56
4. Quran 4:48

Chapter Sixteen – *We're Back Up! Oh, Maybe Not*
1. Romans 12:2
2. John 17:14

Connect With
Chris & Jessica Gunn

www.hazinalife.com

Hazina Life exists to encourage and inspire people to take risks and go after their purpose in order to create effective and long-lasting change in the world.

Our vision is to see pockets of world-changers surfacing all over the planet passionately creating beneficial and sustainable change both locally and internationally. Follow our future journey on our blog.

Be sure, also, to learn about the Hazina Exchange, our integrated platform designed to connect those who want to do great things in the world and help them achieve their goals.

I want to take this page to sincerely thank those who were involved in the efforts of the creation of our story, the production of the book and the encouragement of our hearts throughout the process. There is no doubt in my mind that our story is nothing short of a miracle even though I often still wonder how much of our story was *us* and how much was because of the hand of *God*.

First of all, I want to thank our families (the Gunns and the Beaudoins) for putting up with the stress involved with having to watch a family member make decisions you were perhaps totally against; many to which were potentially life-threatening. We couldn't have asked for a better support system, even though you may not have understood the fullness of what we were hoping to accomplish. Jordan and Jacob, we hope our story inspires you to take more risks in your life. We love you.

I also want to thank those who came along side of us at the beginning and the end. To mention a few, Tyler, your support and curiosity throughout the process will never be forgotten. Steven and Kristen, thank you for having us into your home. We know it is always a sacrifice to have other folks into your space for a long period of time. We wouldn't have been successful without you. Dan – thank you for working in tandem with me as we seek to find the answers (and the questions) we are looking to find. Mark – I appreciate you helping us move, especially after the trunk door latch broke when we were ready to load the ridiculously heavy dresser and couldn't get it in. Vin & Laura – thank you for challenging us. Your family has impacted ours for generations to come.

Finally, thank you to *everyone* who crossed our paths during this time, fed us, clothed us, housed us, cried with us, counseled us; told us we weren't *completely* out of our minds. Without you, this wouldn't be a reality today.

About the Authors

Chris Gunn

Chris is an author, teacher, speaker, and businessman focused on one ultimate purpose: to see others' dreams that seem impossible come to fruition. The goal he wanted to accomplish by writing *The Line Between Faith & Stupidity* was to help readers "get out of their boat," whatever that looks like. By challenging dreamers who have worked their way from having a far-fetched idea to one that the focus of their heart, he hopes to provide the tools and guidance necessary to see them accomplish what they thought could never happen. More importantly, he wants to see God blow each person away through the process.

Since returning to the United States, Chris has been a social entrepreneur seeking to find sustainable solutions to global problems that deal with accessibility to food, water, shelter and education through developing profitable, yet generous business solutions. He and Jessica have been married since 2010. They currently reside in Sarasota, Florida.

Jessica Gunn

Jessica is a visionary with the passion to inspire everyone she encounters. She is well-traveled, and has been to over thirty countries spreading the love of Christ. Having worked in the not-for-profit sector for many years, she seeks to empower women and children to be able to live free and fulfilled lives.

As the main inspiration for the creation of the Hazina Life blog, she desires to impact people and organizations around the globe through inspiring others to step out, play their part and be challenged to maximize everything they were made to accomplish.

Jessica has a passion for foster care and adoption and has worked in the adoption field. You can often find her reading and drinking coffee in her free time.